Mexico

Mexico

WHY A FEW ARE RICH AND THE PEOPLE POOR

RAMÓN EDUARDO RUIZ

UNIVERSITY OF CALIFORNIA PRESS
Berkeley Los Angeles London

University of California Press, one of the most distinguished university presses in the United States, enriches lives around the world by advancing scholarship in the humanities, social sciences, and natural sciences. Its activities are supported by the UC Press Foundation and by philanthropic contributions from individuals and institutions. For more information, visit www.ucpress.edu.

University of California Press
Berkeley and Los Angeles, California

University of California Press, Ltd.
London, England

Library of Congress Cataloging-in-Publication Data
Ruiz, Ramón Eduardo.
Mexico : why a few are rich and the people poor / Ramón Eduardo Ruiz.
p. cm.
Includes bibliographical references and index.
ISBN 978-0-520-26235-5 (cloth : alk. paper)
ISBN 978-0-520-26236-2 (pbk. : alk. paper)
1. Mexico—Economic conditions. 2. Mexico—Economic policy. 3. Economic development—Mexico. 4. Poverty—Mexico. I. Title.
HC135.R777 2010
330.972—dc22

Manufactured in the United States of America
19 18 17 16 15 14 13 12 11 10
10 9 8 7 6 5 4 3 2 1

This book is printed on Cascades Enviro 100, a 100% post consumer waste, recycled, de-inked fiber. FSC recycled certified and processed chlorine free. It is acid free, Ecologo certified, and manufactured by BioGas energy.

A la memoria de Natalia, con quien compartí una vida

Juan era un candidato perfecto, tenía una promesa para cada gente y nunca lo oí repetirse . . . ni lo vi complir ninguna, por cierto.

Jorge Ibargüengoitia, *Los relámpagos de agosto*

Contents

Preface

This offbeat disquisition on Mexico's warped march from century to century opens with the sterling views of my father, a doting Mexican patriot who, when I was young, never tired of telling me stories from his country's past. As his own father had done, he had served in his country's military, but had abandoned that life shortly before the collapse of the Old Regime. Always in the grip of misplaced dreams and outright delusions, he would say Mexico someday would be "un gran país" (a great country). Well, my father died in Mazatlán, a port city on the Pacific Ocean, not far from where he first saw the light of day. He departed this earth in 1976 with unsettling echoes of the past in his troubled mind, never seeing his prediction come true, but never doubting that it would, as he swore when I last saw him. Nor do I doubt it, though I have devoted a lifetime to writing about Mexico, alert to any sign of an untrodden path, but until today my hopes have been dashed.

Still, it is possible, if one is so disposed, to argue that all is well in Mexico, particularly if one is pleased with what we are told by tourists enamored of the pyramids of Teotihuacán and the dance of the old men in

Uruapan, Michoacán, or seduced by tales of macroeconomic miracles told by mendacious courtiers of the oligarchy blind to the plight of the poor. But tourists are a notoriously poor judge of a country's social health, and official pedants are a rascally lot. Mexico may be picturesque, but for those of us who know the country, its glaring social maladies weigh upon our opinions. If truth be told, Mexico has been, and still is, a poverty-stricken, hungry nation and, to cite the opinion of some tortured Mexican souls, suffers the pains of a "distorted" economy, an idea I find sophistic.

Any interpretation of Mexican reality must bring to the table two truths, or else we will simply draw a lopsided picture. Not all is tragedy in Mexico: we must not blind ourselves to the triumphs of its people in the arts and literature and, from time to time, in the realm of social change. How these dramatic achievements came about, in the face of sundry ills, is a story I leave for others to explore. But surely it is multifarious: these triumphs were spurred largely by the "Revolution" of 1910, which achieved its ends only in fragments but was apotheosized by hypocritical Mexican politicos and an army of adoring historians on both sides of the border. Why did this conflagration ignite an artistic awakening and, after years of the arts lying dormant, open doors to a radical metastasis? And we also must acknowledge that Mexican history is the epic saga of a mestizo people, partly Indian and partly Spanish, trying to forge a nationality and a culture, an effort made all the more difficult by the omnipotent presence of the United States, the neighbor next door.

Despite this parade of triumphs, and they are mighty indeed, the history of Mexico, if the happiness and welfare of the underdogs are our barometer for judgment, is mostly a tragedy. From the Spanish Conquest on, when the cross and the sword of the Europeans bent ancient Anáhuac to their will, the poor, usually bronze of skin and racially more Indian than Spanish, have carried the burdens of Mexico, victims of man's inhumanity to man. Mark Twain said, "History doesn't repeat itself—at best it sometimes rhymes." Mexico's history certainly rhymes. Again and again, similar patterns of development, or, better put, underdevelopment, repeat themselves. But, then, to recall my father's steadfast faith in his country's destiny, does not hope spring eternally? A steady drop of water erodes even the hardest rock.

That is the topic of this book. Of the more than 100 million Mexicans, why do over half live in poverty, some 20 million of them enduring daily hunger, barely able to keep body and soul together? Whatever pundits might argue, whatever macroeconomic mumbo jumbo might say, Mexico is a peripheral country, part of the ubiquitous Third World, now more than ever at the beck and call of the mighty Uncle Sam and today failing to compete with China for a share of the American market, once Mexico's own hunting preserve.

"The one duty we owe to history," declared Oscar Wilde, "is to rewrite it."[1] That is what I have done, but not with a foolish academic pretense of disinterestedness. Nor can I claim expertise on any but small aspects of the huge subject of this study, and thus I am indebted to a multitude of scholars and writers, whose books and articles I list in the bibliography. They did the spadework for me. Their interpretations and theories opened my eyes to the nature and scope of underdevelopment. Some say that the subject is best left to economists, but when economists talk, they are really talking about money or, more precisely, about whatever it is that money is measuring. But Mexican underdevelopment is a supremely complex matter, its causes extending beyond simply money, or historical chance, or its fate of lying at the doorstep of a powerful, imperialistic neighbor (a favorite Mexican excuse), or the result of class, social, and racial bigotry, as I will endeavor to explain.

For reading my manuscript, and making helpful suggestions, I am indebted to Stanley Stein, John Hart, Peter Smith, and William Taylor. I also thank Lorenzo Meyer, equally troubled by his country's tortuous path, who looked at what I wrote with the critical eye of a Mexican scholar. I thank too Mexicans in all walks of life, including storekeepers, teachers, artists, and others who, over the years, have spoken openly about their country's legacy. I am equally indebted to the Rockefeller Foundation, which gave me the opportunity to spend six weeks at its Bellagio Center, where, with the encouragement of colleagues from around the world, this study took root.

Rancho Santa Fe, California

ONE Ramblings on Mexican Underdevelopment

I

Let me spell out why I believe Mexico is underdeveloped. But first, permit me to digress just a bit. Some pundits, fixated on the banal details of human idiosyncrasies, tend to think that we are the authors of our own fate, but life is surely more complicated. To that truism I can only say amen. I know that the millions of rich, and often arrogant, residents of this planet are the perfect historical refutation that the meek shall inherit the earth. Just the same, I do not believe that only the poor will pass through the eye of a needle on their way to salvation. So how to explain why inhabitants of certain countries, specifically the United States and Western Europe, and now Japan, are wealthy, while others, peripheral countries such as Mexico, are poor? I leave the first question to others far more knowledgeable; I can try to explain only Mexico's plight.

One apocryphal story portrays Mexico as a beggar sitting on a cornucopia of plenty. Mexico may be a beggar, but it is hardly well heeled, rich in neither rainfall nor land for the plow and harrow. Across the centuries, Mexicans have not lived high on the hog; instead poverty and sundry inequities have plagued Mexico, and not just because Mexicans wasted resources. Even presidents of the Republic, not always known for their candor, have conceded that their country is no Garden of Eden. José López Portillo, a leader prone to extravagant displays of emotions but at times speaking brutal truths, asserted time and time again in his gigantic autobiography, *Mis tiempos,* that Mexico "es un país subdesarrollado" (is an underdeveloped country).[1] True, that aphorism is complicated, and is as hotly debated in Mexico now as it was when López Portillo's tome was published. Underdevelopment—or, as some Mexicans, made skittish and fearful by what they refuse to acknowledge, claim is a "distorted economy"—has long been a controversial topic of study for economists, historians, poets, and writers. A popular descriptor favored by mainstream economists is "developing nation," which sounds more palatable, implying that it is only a question of time before Mexico will reach the promised land, that is, join the circle of the rich.

What exactly is underdevelopment, that pernicious malady I have ascribed to Mexico? Definitions abound, but what all of them have in common is that, more than anything else, an underdeveloped country is poor. Poverty is widespread and chronic, not some temporary misfortune. It has always been there. The lost, the damned, and the dispossessed live in poverty, and have always done so. That, unfortunately, describes Mexico to a T.

But underdevelopment is a complex illness. Underdevelopment means an extremely unequal distribution of wealth and income. A few are very rich; millions are very poor. Mexico, according to one United Nations report, ranks near the top of the list of countries with the most glaring inequalities of wealth and income. These inequalities take on territorial dimensions: the south is poorest, and the north, comparatively speaking, the richest. In the countryside, except for a favored few, Mexicans are poor, while Indians, constituting perhaps 12 percent of the Republic's inhabitants, are wretchedly poor. At the top of the list of the poorest regions stands Chiapas, where 76 percent of the inhabitants, largely Indian, are as poor as the proverbial church mouse. In Santiago del Pinar, one of its Indian communities, according to a United Nations report, lamentable conditions resemble those of villages in the Congo of Africa. Not far behind come the states of Guerrero, Oaxaca, Tabasco, and Veracruz, where, with Chiapas, nearly 19 million Mexicans live. In contrast, in Baja California, Nuevo León, Distrito Federal, Coahuila, and Chihuahua, only minorities struggle to obtain their *canasta alimentaria* (basic needs). In Baja California, to give an example, only 9.2 percent of the people are poor. But, before we jump to the conclusion that all is well there, bear in mind that 78 percent of urban dwellers across the country know poverty.[2]

At the other extreme one finds the wealthy. One Mexican, Carlos Slim, the telephone magnate, is one of the richest men in the world, and a dozen or so Mexicans lag not far behind him. Slim's bankroll totals almost 7 percent of the country's output of goods and services, one out of every fourteen dollars Mexicans earn. Every twenty-four hours of every month of every year, his income grows at the rate of 27 million dollars, yet one out of five Mexicans survives on just two dollars a day. Like the legendary King Midas, Slim turns everything he touches to gold. A fastidious collector of art, he takes special pleasure in two sculptures by Auguste Rodin he owns that grace the Museo Soumaya in Mexico City, which he helps fund. Slim also collects old editions, particularly those dealing with Mexican history.[3] Inequality, which Slim symbolizes, is found in many important areas, such as schooling, health care, housing, and child care. Equality of opportunity simply does not exist.

Narciso Bassols, a respected economist, insists that underdevelopment refers to a country that is not just poor but bereft of the technology required for economic growth.[4] As López Portillo pointed out, one distressing aspect of the malady, given the usually adverse commercial picture, is the inability to develop local resources for lack of funds.[5] One sure sign of underdevelopment is the flight of campesinos from the countryside to the city, a seemingly irreversible tide in Mexico.[6] Those who leave behind their small plots of land, when they have them, seldom, if ever, find the road back to the village.

But poverty implies more than simply the absence of material things. Poverty breeds alienation, an internalized feeling of deprivation and hopelessness, at times even feelings of inferiority, a belief that improving one's life lies beyond human capacity. One is born poor and will die poor.[7] It is psychological, as Fidel Castro, a flamboyant apostle of social change, acknowledged. People, he explained, who for centuries lived "without the hope and the resources and the education that make optimism possible, feel paralyzed by the challenges before them, the tasks required to build a nation."[8] The psychological aspects of poverty, he avowed, can be just as important as the material. It is the "filosofía de que no se puede," the belief that nothing can be done.

Underdevelopment is a historical phenomenon; it has deep roots in the past. Much time has gone by and much water has flowed under the bridge since underdevelopment first took root in Mexico. It is a logical result of a special historical circumstance not shared by the nations of the First World, the industrialized, technically advanced countries of Western Europe, the United States, and Japan. André Gunder Frank, the political economist, noted perceptively that neither the past nor the present of these countries resembles in any important aspect the past of the underdeveloped countries.[9] Underdevelopment rises out of a unique historical process; it is not simply backwardness in relation to the First World, writes Héctor Guillén Romo, but a structural characteristic that blocks economic growth.[10] For Alfonso Aguilar Monteverde, the factors that determine the "backwardness" of countries are not simply random. They did not just happen, nor are they merely skin deep; they are linchpins of the socioeconomic structure.[11] As the economist Paul Baran knew, the historical forces that shaped the "fate of the backward world still exercise a powerful impact" on today's conditions. Forms change, intensities differ, but "their origin and direction [remain] unaltered."[12] Given Mexico's colonial heritage, the results of a European conquest, and the failure of mother Spain to join the modern European world, the inevitable result was a Mexico on the periphery. But even had Spain not lagged behind, as the example of British India reminds us, the heart of the matter is the colonial relationship, not the nature of the mother country. It was a relationship of unequals, of dependency, with Mexico the tail of the dog.

II

How did this unequal relationship come about? History tells us that it evolved over centuries. It began, undoubtedly, with the Industrial Revolution, although some scholars argue that its foundations were laid earlier, between 1450 and 1640, when the European feudal mode of production transformed itself gradually into a capitalist economy.[13] No matter what the truth, by 1500, England, France, and the Low Countries had shed most of their serfs, their lands farmed largely by yeomen and free tenants. England's enclosure, the shift from the open fields of small farmers to the large fenced-in holdings of wealthy landlords, led to the commercialization of agriculture and abundant wool for textile mills. The use of the water wheel for power to grind corn, shape metal tools, and spin yards of woolen and cotton cloth began in England and spread to Western Europe, where nature had endowed the land with rivers and streams.[14] The English, nonetheless, cannot take credit for the water wheel, which came from the hill country of Mesopotamia, where its use languished for lack of water.[15] Meanwhile, the ocean harbors of England made water transport an inexpensive method for shipping textiles and iron goods to far-off lands, as well as obtaining raw materials.

Yet, before we jump to the conclusion that English ingenuity fueled the Industrial Revolution, it is well to keep in mind that Providence had a hand in the process. England led because of its bountiful deposits of coal, which eventually replaced water as the principal source of power.[16] British coal and the steam engine stood on the cutting edge of industrialization. Surely, without coal England's industrialization would not have occurred as it did and certainly not at that early time. The basic change occurred when machines replaced animal power. None of this happened overnight, but over a century or more, with England leading the way between 1770 and 1870.[17] During this era, James Watt invented an engine whose fuel efficiency was good enough to make the use of steam profitable; capital from the colonial trade, in turn, helped finance Watt's invention. New technology brought about a transformation in production methods, in the process cementing a growing asymmetry between England (and later France), the industrial core, and the laggards on the periphery.

But coal alone does not explain the giant strides of the English Industrial Revolution. History records that in 1492 Christopher Columbus, an Italian sea captain sailing under the royal Spanish flag, discovered what Europeans baptized the Americas. With their colonies, Spain and Portugal would eventually control much of the "New World." England, however, did not lag far behind, winning a colonial foothold in the Caribbean and on the North American continent. The chance discovery of the Americas proved a boon to England's nascent industry, for without the colonies, its own and those of Spain and Portugal, England faced an ecological hurdle with scant chance of an internal solution. To move beyond eighteenth-century levels of production and consumption, England, and Western Europe, needed a new trading partner, and the New World offered it. Its lands gave England a haven for its surplus populations, while its resources and markets helped England, as well as Europe, move beyond its ecological boundaries. Raw materials, markets for manufactured goods, and abundant cheap labor, whether Indians or their misbegotten offspring, stood at the beck and call of English farmers, merchants, and manufacturers.

The silver and, to a lesser extent, gold from the mines of New Spain and Peru, which because of the foolishness of Spaniards ended up in foreign coffers, opened the way for England to expand its imports of raw materials and food as well as fatten its share of New World markets. Cheap cotton from colonial Brazil and the southern English colonies transformed Manchester into a textile manufacturing giant. A goodly share of this prosperity came on the backs of African slaves, from the sweat and tears of the cotton and sugar plantations of the Caribbean colonies and the American South. The labor of these slaves, as well as that of the Indians of Mexico and their mestizo descendants, financed the capitalization of Western Europe's industrial empires. Later, the new republics of Hispanic America played a similar role for British merchants and manufacturers. These satellite economies were structured such that, instead of working for local needs, their systems of production and distribution mainly served their dominant metropolises. European control of markets, exports, and raw materials partly explains the underdevelopment of Mexico and the rest of Latin America, a relationship that Pierre Jaffee calls the "pillage of the Third World."[18]

We live in a capitalist world, as Immanuel M. Wallerstein, a world-systems theorist, reminds us, one that took shape as an expansionist European economy in the sixteenth century and three centuries later embraced the entire world.[19] Why then, if this is so, have some countries, such as Mexico, failed to enjoy development similar to that of other capitalist countries? Steps on the highway of capitalist modernization, as it is known, have been slow or absent. It is a good question, but there are good answers too. We must not forget that history never stands still; time changes nearly everything. What was possible in the past may no longer be possible today. The former colonies, now largely dependent economies, confront an entirely different situation than that faced by Western Europe in the age of discovery and colonization. The easy acquisition of capital is no longer possible. Dependent economies live in a world run by industrialized nations, owners of investment capital blessed with advanced technology and markets for the primary products of peripheral exporters. Capitalism has created a core of wealthy nations and, on their periphery, poor or moderately poor countries, among them Mexico, as Latin American economists under the tutelage of Raúl Prebisch, the Argentine political sage, have stated time and time again.

From its inception, according to Samir Amin, whose essays on Third World economies are legendary, capitalism has been a polarizing system of dominant cores and dominated peripheries, one developed, dominant, and independent, and the other subordinate, dependent, and underdeveloped, serving the needs of the other.[20] Economic development and underdevelopment, as Frank observed, are the opposite sides of the same coin. Or to cite Wallerstein, capitalism makes for a world of inequality: "In order to develop it needed the connivance of an international economy."[21] European plundering of the colonial world gave birth to the chasm that stands between core countries and peripheral ones, a relationship that endures. The incorporation of former colonies into expanding world capitalism reinforced their dependency, or, as some say, their underdevelopment. The nature of capitalism, after all, rests on the exploitation of resources, both national and international, and, to cite Fernand Braudel, opportunities.[22] Whatever its nationality, capitalism relies on legal or de facto monopolies, devised and controlled by powerful interests. Benefits seldom trickle down to the poorest of society. When searching for the roots of underdevelopment, we must understand the origins of capitalism: Europe's brigandage opened the chasm that separates core countries from peripheral ones.

Underdeveloped countries, furthermore, do not simply dwell at an earlier point on the road taken by modern industrial states, but remain entrapped in a subservient role in a world capitalist economy. At the dawn of capitalism, Westerners shaped and subordinated the economies of the peripheral world. Starting with the maritime discoveries of the fifteenth and sixteenth centuries, the mother of colonial commerce and the origin of early capital accumulation, the Europeans took it upon themselves, frequently in acts of piracy, to take what they coveted from primitive peoples unable to defend themselves. For colonials, there followed three centuries of living off exports and using the profits to buy manufactured goods, largely from English merchants.

Given these origins, Mexican society, as we shall see, found it virtually impossible to develop in an autonomous fashion. It is nonsensical to expect the historically exploited to march in tune with European phases of development. Today, the underdeveloped countries, or to use current jargon, the "developing nations," exist in a world dominated by rich nations, as well as subservient elites. As López Portillo wrote, the powerful seldom assume "responsibility for the ills of the economic system they have imposed on the world, let alone admit blame, but judge normal the negative results."[23] Yet the ills of the underdeveloped countries, he went on, are but different aspects of what is essentially a global problem.

Imperialism, wrote the Mexican poet Octavio Paz, has not allowed "us to achieve historical normality";[24] Mexican society displays abnormal contours. The ruling classes, he argued, had no other mission than to collaborate as associates of foreigners. Similarly, the local landed class, the most powerful, wanted an economy that maximized profits for their exports, opposed all restrictions on them, and demanded access to cheap goods from the industrial West. Foreign merchants posed no danger to them, whatever the damage to nascent industrialists, who might want duties levied on imports. Thus, the local *burguesía* (bourgeoisie) had disjointed goals. A national *burguesía* ready to battle for national interests did not exist, as Paz recognized.[25] The structure of world capitalism did not allow for the rise of a truly national *burguesía* leading the way out of dependency. Economic growth with social justice cannot be achieved without demolishing the "capitalist network of dominance and dependence."[26] Only when ties to the core countries are weakened—as they were for Mexico during World War II, when imports of goods from the United States were virtually cut off—can the dependent countries achieve a degree of autonomous development. Recently, only two countries, Taiwan and South Korea, have made the transition from agricultural societies to technologically advanced industrial ones, thanks partly to the Cold War and the American strategy of erecting barriers against China and the USSR.

III

How to fix this malaise of underdevelopment? Clearly, no one has come up with an easy answer. It is a baffling jawbreaker, as the literature on it amply bears out. An old theme, the study of the whys of economic growth, dates, at least, from Adam Smith's *The Wealth of Nations* (1776), a cornerstone of classical economics read avidly by early Mexican planners. Smith asked why some nations galloped ahead while others lagged behind. By serving their self-interest, he pontificated, individuals, as if led by an "invisible hand," bestowed benefits on the entire society." The interest of a country, in its commercial relations with foreign nations," he wrote, "is like that of a merchant with regards to the different people he deals with, to buy as cheap and to sell as dear as possible." Needed for this system to perform well was "perfect freedom of trade, . . . to sell dear, when . . . markets are thus fulfilled with the greatest number of buyers." He upheld three principles: "life, liberty and the pursuit of property."[27] Ironically, at no time did Smith use the term *laissez-faire*, and he supported some limitations on free trade. But his gospel of competition fosters selfishness and greed. Today his disciples belong to the neoliberal school of economics, which, with the exception of Cuba, dominated the last decades of the twentieth century in Latin America.

David Ricardo, another English classical economist, equally convinced that market forces—akin to the laws of gravity—regulated a capitalist economy, won public acclaim in Mexico with his doctrine of comparative advantage. In *Principles of Political Economy and Taxation* (1821), he argued that nations should specialize in what they did best. His example was the trade between England, a textile manufacturer, and Portugal, a producer of port wine. He based his theory on an international division of labor: each country producing the goods in which it had the greatest relative advantage. That logic would lead Portugal to concentrate on wine production and sale and England on cloth manufacture, with the resulting trade between them generating maximum benefits for both. An advocate of free trade, Ricardo impugned the mercantile practice of protecting home producers.[28] That made sense for the English because their country had become the world's major manufacturing center, able to outsell rivals and profit from free trade. By accepting this principle, countries on the periphery that lacked an industrial base doomed themselves to be suppliers of raw materials and grains. The lesson? Not everyone profits equally from comparative advantage, because some activities are more lucrative than others, as Portugal learned to its sorrow.

Other theorists of that age saw unchecked population growth as the roadblock, an interpretation known as the Malthusian theory, which postulates that a country can outrun its food supply and undermine its standard of living. Keep population in check; that was Malthus's tonic. Yet in most of the industrialized nations, mortality rates began to decline only late in the eighteenth century.[29] While high rates of population growth can hamper economic development, a truth Mexican leaders recognized tardily, low incomes, and not demographic explosions, are the primary reasons for poverty. All the same, balanced demographic growth will not, by itself, open the door to economic development, as the contemporary Mexican situation illustrates.[30] With a population growth rate of about 1 percent, Mexico is still underdeveloped, while poverty grows by leaps and bounds.

By the late Victorian Age, the subject of development had lost its appeal, revived briefly by the writings of Karl Marx, an acerbic critic of capitalism. Then, early in the twentieth century, the German Max Weber, with his monumental *The Protestant Ethic and the Spirit of Capitalism* (1904–5), injected new life into the subject. His interpretation, a deeply religious and ideological one, became the cultural explanation for economic development. For Weber, values and attitudes transcended everything else.[31] The Protestant ethic, which according to its apostles, enshrined hard work, thrift, and honesty in business practices, put the blame on supposedly anticapitalist Catholic dogmas that hampered business activity by condemning usury and glorifying the virtue of poverty. Weber held aloft Calvinist Puritans who preached the doctrine of predestination, by which only a select number of human beings were destined for heavenly salvation. To find proof of that salvation, Calvinists had to demonstrate it through visible signs of earthly prosperity; and woe to those who squandered profits on pleasure rather than reinvesting them in order to fully demonstrate their adherence to God's will. Earthly success led to heavenly success.[32] Weber placed the blame for the misfortunes of peripheral societies on their traditional beliefs and practices.

Weber's thesis has countless adherents, but questions abound; not all scholars embrace the German's views. First of all, how does one explain the industrial success of Japan and China, hardly Protestant societies, and that of several Catholic countries, Italy, for instance? A fundamental question dogs Weber's deceptive logic. Do ideas, practices, and values of a society emerge out of thin air? Does not history reveal that people had first to eat to survive, and that to do so they gathered berries and killed wild beasts and then justified what they did? Over the ages, men and women have rationalized their beliefs to square with what they must do. Religious attitudes most surely sprang from earthly reality, largely from fear of death and the hope for salvation in an afterlife. The Industrial Revolution brought about certain beliefs and attitudes, as the Englishman R. Harry Tawny asserted; capitalism arose when secular attitudes supplanted religious dogmas.[33] Weber, moreover, was a myopic historian. He forgot, as Fernand Braudel writes, that northern Europe had supplanted the place earlier occupied by the capitalist centers of the Mediterranean region, hardly a Protestant fortress. The sixteenth century simply witnessed the triumph of northern centers of power over older ones: Amsterdam copied Venice as London then copied Amsterdam, neither one coming up with much new technology or any fresh principles of business management.[34]

Weber, nonetheless, was not entirely wrong. Economic development, or the lack of it, may respond partly to attitudes, values, and ideas. Fatalistic views of life, not uncommon in poor Mexican communities, do not provide fertile soil for a belief that a better life can be achieved with political and economic change. For people who say that fate preordains who they are and how they live, it is difficult, if not impossible, to adopt new ways of doing things. I remember Manuel Gamio, the Mexican anthropologist, telling me how difficult it was to get the Otomí Indians of Hidalgo to make tortillas, their daily bread, out of soybeans and not corn, even though, in his opinion, it was a better crop for that desert region and a better food. Still, if men and women are to be motivated to change so as to better their way of life, they must know that the goal is attainable.

IV

In the 1950s, in the wake of the Marshall Plan for war-torn Europe, an outburst of interest in development took shape, mainly offspring of the talents of anthropologists, sociologists, and economists, disciples of "modernization" theories, scholars who wanted to patch up damage done previously to "backward" societies by "fixing" things. Modifying ways of life, so it was proclaimed, could open wide the doors to progress and a better life. It was simply necessary to transform a society's habits by introducing new techniques and ideas.[35] Panaceas abounded: one, a popular remedy, urged a change of religious practices (i.e., turn Protestant); others called for schools or roads or health clinics, or replacement of the wooden plow with a steel one, which digs deeper furrows and improves both irrigation and crops. People in traditional societies, it was alleged, placed less value on work, looking upon it as simply a means to survival, not something one did to get ahead. The men and women of these communities were often fatalistic, rarely motivated to adopt new attitudes and ways of doing things. Ancient habits were deeply embedded practices that persisted across generations.[36] The "experts" advised Mexico to welcome the salvation that came with the foreigners' know-how, including modern organizational and technological skills, ideas, and values, and, of course, foreign capital, all meant to rid countries, to cite the wisdom of Jorge Carrión, a Mexican psychiatrist, of their backwardness, poverty, hunger, and exploitation.[37]

Mexican scholars' response to these theorists came promptly. Patterns and ways of doing things adopted from Western nations could turn out to be obstacles to progress in a poor country. To be of benefit, education must fit local needs. That, too, could be said of modern technology. Its transfer carried hidden dangers: forms that replaced traditional ones in one sector of a society might just as likely produce stagnation in others.[38] While England built factories and found jobs for its rapidly growing population by relying on the appropriate technology, today's was much more capital-intensive and less dependent on human labor.[39] Mexico, however, like other poor countries, had an abundance of labor but a shortage of capital and skills. Reliance on foreign models resulted in distorted growth and unemployment. Countries that adopted the capital-intensive model risked concentrating available capital in a small modern sector, while leaving the rest of the economy lagging behind. As Jesús Silva Herzog warned, Mexican economists should not adopt exotic blueprints—theories elaborated by economists in New York, London, and Paris—without careful study, lest they cause irreparable harm.[40]

One critic of imitation, the philosopher Samuel Ramos, made headlines with his book *Perfil del hombre y la cultura en México,* a controversial study conducted in the 1930s, an age that sought to define the Mexican soul. "I limit myself," Ramos wrote, "to pointing out how readily ideas and theories imported from Europe are acted on in Mexico without any criticism whatsoever." So long as this continues, he went on, "we will be vulnerable to strange ideas which, having nothing to do with our needs, and deform eventually our national character" and, as a consequence, retard the "development of domestic potentialities." The Mexican fascination with foreign cultures signaled a "spiritual flight from their own land." Culture was a cloister in which men and women who disdained native realities took refuge so as to ignore them. From this erroneous attitude, he went on, Mexico's "self-denigration" arose, with devastating impact on its historical orientation.[41] Years later, Octavio Paz would add that "we have done very little thinking on our own account; most of our ideas have been borrowed from the United States or Europe."[42] An economist or sociologist from a peripheral country who accepted with *ufana pedantería* (overweening pompousness) word for word the wisdom of foreign tutors, wrote Jesús Silva Herzog, resembled the toady who grovels before his master.[43] When Mexicans endeavored to take on North American ways, explained the psychiatrist Jorge Carrión, they behaved as *pochos* (Mexican Americans), men and women who, having lost their psychological bearings, rush to imitate North Americans, to speak English, see American films and disparage Mexican ones, and scorn native ways and customs.[44]

Mexicans, so this argument went, must keep in mind the primary needs and aspirations of their people. The "models of development that the West offers us today," insisted Paz, "are compendiums of horror."[45] To cite Arturo Escobar, these models of development simply replicate the standards of Western nations, success or failure measured by their yardstick. In Western anthropological literature, Escobar charged, especially that of Americans, "there is an almost total absence of any reference to American imperial intervention as a factor affecting the theoretical discussion."[46] As Joan Robinson asserted, by detaching the economic aspects of human life from its political and social setting, Western teaching obfuscated rather than shed light on the nature of the problem.[47] Slavish imitation overlooked the historical experience of the underdeveloped country, and that of the world historical process, which helped make these countries underdeveloped, as Claudio Véliz, a Chilean economist, recognized.[48]

V

Psychiatrists tell us that history had a powerful hand in shaping the character of Mexicans, so it behooves us who want to understand them to carefully scrutinize their past, because it is seldom absent. As Paz admonished, "blood drips from all their [Mexican] wounds, even the most ancient."[49] Mexican traditionalism, though under attack, has been one constant of the national character, shaped by circumstances that prevailed early on. The controversial theme of the Mexican inferiority complex, at times vehemently denied, might be explained, added Paz, at least partly by the "reserve with which Mexicans face other people, and by the unpredictable violence with which their repressed emotions break through their mask of impassivity."[50] The Mexican is not inferior, argued Ramos, but "feels inferior," the result partly of measuring himself by the scale of Western European values, a malady as old as Independence.[51]

So how to explain the "underdevelopment" of Mexico? Well, I certainly cannot put that controversy to bed. The more I study the underdevelopment of Mexico, the more I am convinced that there is no solution, certainly not a simple one. It took five centuries for Mexico to become a distorted, dependent, dysfunctional society, and it will take a miracle to undo this legacy. The world we know today would have to change drastically, to return, if you will, to an earlier one, where the haves were less powerful, and the economic and social configurations that took five hundred years to evolve did not yet exist. That would be, to state again and again, a miracle. Mexico is condemned to be what it is unless the *burguesía,* ever the lap dog of the omnipotent Yankee, underwent a metamorphosis, akin to that of the rascally Scrooge of Dickens's *Christmas Carol.*

I am, after all, a historian, an expert, if I am permitted to use that term, only on one aspect of this baffling subject. I must rely on the research of others. I can only offer an interpretation, analyzing along the way Mexican racism and other social and psychological ills that exacerbate the all-powerful economic one. Not to do so strips the nuts and bolts from reality. Since colonial days, Mexico has had an economy built around the exports of metals and other primary goods. This activity, from the beginning, has been controlled largely by capital from abroad. Mexico has an export-oriented economy largely of primary goods, a semicolonial one. Underdevelopment afflicts a country that does not simply depend on the exports of what the land offers but also relies on a single market, the United States in the case of Mexico. That market decides the volume and character of the purchases and sets prices. In that manner, Americans dictate the nature of Mexico's subservient economy.

This formula spells economic domination. It is the legacy of colonialism, when the Western powers saw the peripheral world as a source of cheap raw materials and food as well as a market for their manufactures. Raúl Prebisch, who broke with the teachings of Adam Smith and David Ricardo, argued that core nations, in a regime of free international exchange, profited more than peripheral ones because the terms of trade favored them. Poor countries had to sell more of their primary products in order to buy the same value of finished goods. From this lopsided relationship arose balance-of-payment problems, since income received for exports either fluctuated or more usually fell, while the cost of imports stayed steady or rose.

Yet economics alone, overwhelming as they are, cannot fully explain Mexico's underdevelopment. So we come full circle: ideas and beliefs have roles to play in this tragic drama. The attitude of dependency, asserts the psychiatrist Carrión, "reveals itself in the Mexican's psyche," in an "emotional resignation towards future events, and so the Mexican adopts attitudes voiced not merely in words, not just in verbal expressions of dependency . . . but in the economic sphere."[52] Few Mexicans truly believe that their country will eventually join the industrial societies of the core nations. As Alan Riding noted perceptively in *Distant Neighbors,* "the disasters that befall Mexicans are not major disappointments, because they are considered unavoidable." Just "tough luck," or to cite a Mexican saying, "ni modo" (that's how it is).

Theories and interpretations aside, let us push on with the story of how Mexico became this underdeveloped country.

TWO El Mexicano

I

To comprehend from first to last how Mexican underdevelopment came to be, we must turn back the pages of time. By doing so, to cite F. Scott Fitzgerald, the American novelist, we will be borne back into the past. Only then can we begin to make out the raison d'être for the Mexican failure, not that Mexicans are solely responsible for their circumstance. Western Europe and, most assuredly, the United States have played leading roles in Mexico's story. That said, Mexican underdevelopment has two fathers, though one, the Spaniard, must bear the brunt of the responsibility. Most Mexicans are, racially speaking, descendents of pre-Columbians and Spaniards, referred to as mestizos. The Spaniards, say some anthropologists, had stumbled upon an "archaic" civilization, living in an earlier evolutionary stage. When they met, the two "races" represented totally dissimilar cultures and modes of interpreting human existence.[1] Nonetheless, they shared certain singularities, being autocratic societies, to cite one example, but Spanish individualism, which verged on anachronistic behavior, overwhelmed the pre-Columbians. *Mestizaje,* the blending of the two peoples, was the human material the nation builders had on hand, and sad to say, it never jelled as a coherent whole.[2]

Most of us have been taught that European cultures stood head and shoulders above the indigenous ones of pre-Hispanic America. That is an ethnocentric view that stems from our European heritage and cultural preferences. Europe had mechanical superiority, but in artistic sensibilities, in social and ethical values, as well as political organization, the amazing cultures of the New World stood on a par with that of Europe. As other writers have pointed out, millions of Indians, as the Europeans came to call them, were killed to "prove that Europeans were more civilized."

II

This story of Mexico begins to unfold long before Hernán Cortés and his intrepid band of Spaniards overwhelmed Tenochtitlán, the capital of the Aztecs. The Aztecs were only one of many diverse Indian groups—the Mayas, Tarascans, and Otomi among them—which the Spaniards encountered when they arrived in the "New World." Mexico was built on the ruins of the Aztec Empire, which, we are told, had under its wings a million and a half people in the Valley of Mexico and, probably, some 20 million more in provinces under its jurisdiction. This was a precapitalist society, one where a hierarchical, tribute-paying system held sway.[3] The Aztecs had made the transition from barbarism to a complex urban society at a time when that step had been taken only in the Middle East, and probably in China and Peru.[4] This ancient world was by no means homogeneous, but was torn apart by idiomatic, political, and military differences, where some societies prevailed over others and where cultures succeeded each other, the newer ones imposing themselves on the earlier ones.

These were old civilizations. During the Classic Era, the years from approximately 300 B.C. to about A.D. 900, labeled the golden age of the pre-Hispanic world by archeologists, the greatest of these civilizations was that of the Maya. The Maya had occupied the lands of Yucatán, Campeche, Tabasco, eastern Chiapas, and Quintana Roo, but their predominance had waned by the time the Spaniards arrived. These sites had lain abandoned for centuries until John L. Stephens's marvelous account, *Incidents of Travel in Central America, Chiapas, and Yucatan,* written in the 1840s, rescued them from oblivion. According to some scholars, Mayan glyphs are one of only three writing systems to have been invented independently, the other two being Sumerian cuneiform in ancient Mesopotamia and Chinese.[5] In the *Libros de Chilam Balam,* the Maya left for posterity their version of history. The heyday of Maya culture coincides with the fall of the Roman Empire.[6] Its demise can probably be laid at the foot of a society with a high population growth rate that had outrun its food supply. Its collapse made Thomas Malthus a prophet.[7]

III

The Aztec kingdom, which the Spaniards made the base of their colony, unlike that of the Maya, was very much alive when Cortés landed on the shores of Veracruz in 1519. The Central Plateau had sheltered vigorous civilizations, that of the Toltecs from Tula, dynamic builders and warriors, for one. Upon the heels of their collapse came the savage Chichimecas. The lords of these unruly people were the Aztecs, also referred to as Mexica. Over the course of time, these savages adopted more refined ways, putting down roots on the islands of Lake Texcoco. On these swampy lands, the Aztecs, in 1325, laid the cornerstones of Tenochtitlán, which became the capital of their empire. When the Spaniards arrived in 1519, Moctezuma II had under his sway lands extending from the Pacific Ocean to the Gulf of Mexico and from Guatemala north to Querétaro. Only a few states escaped the Aztecs' net, notably Tlaxcala and the Tarascans of Michoacán. In just over a century, the Aztecs had become the masters of a society exalting piety and religion while making killing and warfare common practices.

Some demographers estimate that, in 1521, as many as 25 million people inhabited central Mexico. Whatever the truth, the population of ancient Anáhuac was large. Dwelling in different towns and paying tribute to autocratic kings, the people of Anáhuac had a common language (Nahuatl), an oral tradition, civil codes, and religious beliefs. Tenochtitlán was a metropolis of vast stone pyramids and stucco walls of bright colors glistening in the sun. So magnificent were the temples of Huitzilopochtli and Tlaloc that upon seeing them Bernal Diaz del Castillo, one of the conquerors, thought he was dreaming.[8] Merchants, artisans, and farmers sold their wares at the *mercado* of Tlatelolco, the biggest and most famous of the marketplaces.

This was a hierarchical society. Individualism, a trait Western societies prize, was nowhere to be found. Society and the common welfare, not the rights of the individual, held sway.[9] As individuals, men and women counted for little. Individual rights mattered only marginally. Everyone had a place in society and duties to perform and obligations to fulfill. No one questioned the established order, "knowing perfectly" "his status in relation to his family, his clan, his community and his gods."

For Aztec society, the *calculi*, the clan united by blood and family ties, was the cornerstone; it conferred life on institutions and dictated property concepts. Each *calculi* (an *ejido*) owned lands of its own, divided among the heads of families, who tilled them and paid tribute. The farmer merely had the right to their use so long as he complied with his duties and obligations. There was also private property. Owned by a nobility, these lands, called *pillali*, were passed from father to son. *Mayeques*, usually conquered people bound to the soil like the serfs of medieval Europe, tilled the lands, bestowed as a reward for a meritorious deed—valor in war, for example—to a *tectecubtzin*, or lord. By the sixteenth century, the owners of these lands formed a powerful landed nobility.

Democracy, as Westerners know it, was nowhere to be found. A hierarchy of priests shaped politics, their presence felt even in military affairs. At the pinnacle of the theocracy stood the monarch, both priest and warrior, as well as chief priest, chief general, and chief judge. He ruled more and more as an absolute despot and presided over a larger and larger nobility. Once in a while, offices rotated, giving a select few an opportunity to share the responsibilities of public administration, in which the Aztecs excelled.[10]

The Aztecs, like most societies on this earth, glorified warfare. People, after all, will fight, writes one historian, for "any conceivable motive or combination of motives," including "for fun and profit, for . . . land, for glory and freedom, for honors and plunder." A bellicose people, the Aztecs believed aggression to be the best defense. Boys were taught how to fight, what their forebears had done since they had invaded the Valley of Mexico. Military victories added tribute to the empire and, concomitantly, made the Aztecs more parasitic, as they survived increasingly off the tribute of the vanquished.

Aztec women, like their male counterparts, lived in a two-tier society. The wives, mothers, and daughters of the nobility occupied the top of the hierarchy; the females of the *macehuales,* the great majority, occupied the base. Elite women, the *pilli,* though sheltered from childhood on and taught to weave, embroider, and sew, were excluded from political, military, and most clerical posts. Meanwhile, the *macehualtines,* the poor, not only did the cooking, cleaning, and caring for children of the home but, in addition, labored in the fields, made ceramic pots, wove cloth, and cooked tortillas and tamales for sale in the marketplace.

Like men the world over, Aztec males, whatever their status in society, employed a double standard. According to one anthropologist, they wanted their women "tied to her metate, the *comal,* and the preparation of the tortilla." It was the duty of women to bear children, to care for them, and, most important, to transmit Aztec culture and traditions to them. Men frowned upon talkative women, desiring, as one Spanish chronicler remarked, both their "ears and nose stopped up." Men of the elite prized virginity in their women, equating it with honor, but were themselves polygamists. Moctezuma II, for example, had two wives and a household of concubines, the daughters of nobles.

The Aztecs held valued schooling highly, declaring it obligatory. All children from the age of six had to attend, but the sexes were segregated. Social status determined what school boys attended, the sons of the nobility enrolling in the *calmecac* and those of plebeians in the *telpochcalli.* At the Calmecac, sons of nobles and priests learned to interpret codices and calendars, mastered the history of the tribe and its traditions, prepared themselves for high political office and military command; the sons of the common folk learned moral citizenship and prepared to be foot soldiers. The schools for girls, run by priestesses, taught the domestic arts and offered religious training.

A superstitious and fatalistic people, the Aztecs practiced a decayed and defunct theology, believing in a tempestuous and hostile universe presided over by capricious deities who had to be placated. Religion stressed the worship of natural objects and phenomena such as clouds, fire, earth, and forests and had a pantheon of gods, identified with special days, months, and years. The Aztecs identified Huitzilopochtli, their tribal god, with the sun. Quetzalcoatl, a god of fertility and learning, was revered, while Texcatlipoca, patron of the night, inspired fear. Tlaloc, the rain god, had a legion of admirers, as did Coatlicue, a goddess of fertility. One passed briefly through hell, and immortality awaited everyone. Aztecs confessed to priests and won forgiveness for their sins, a rite associated with the goddess Tlazolteótl, the Eater of Filth.

To learn what the gods wanted was the responsibility of priests. Living austere lives, they did the bidding of the gods, performing penance and teaching. As a reward for their selflessness, the state fed, clothed, and housed them, often in sumptuous palaces. Usually the sons of prominent families, the priests "wore a dark habit like a cassock and robes reaching to their feet," recalled a Spanish soldier. They never cut their hair, so it "was long, reaching to their belts," and, occasionally, to their feet. Men filled the ranks of the priesthood, but female priestesses catered to the whims of the goddess Cihuacuacuilli.

We come to the blood-curdling art of human sacrifice, which the Aztecs practiced zealously. The Spaniards, who witnessed this ritual firsthand, thought the Aztecs bloodthirsty. Why the ritual of human sacrifice, which scholars acknowledge the Aztecs had perfected to a frightful science? A commonly cited figure is twenty thousand sacrificial victims a year. Whatever the number, it was large.[11] How could these civilized people, masters of a sophisticated calendar, inventors of a script, impressive architects and builders, and master craftsmen, have engaged in such an abominable practice?

According to one interpretation, the Aztecs were a supremely superstitious people who feared the unknown and—in the belief that the source of life, the sun, would die unless fed human blood—sacrificed themselves so as to make certain that the sun rose, the seasons came and went, and the planted maize bore corn. The highest act of piety, according to this version, was the sacrifice of human life, for Huitzilopochtli, the all-powerful deity, relished human hearts wrenched from the living. The practice, interestingly, began during a prolonged drought in 1450, when the Aztecs, thinking that Huitzilopochtli was angry at them, set out to placate him. When the rains came and the corn flourished, the Aztecs, in gratitude, sacrificed more victims. As Huitzilopochtli helped the Aztecs to expand their empire, success led to wars in search of victims to sacrifice in order to expand more. No wonder, as the Spaniards discovered, that the walls and altars of the temples were "bloody with the hearts of victims."

Drought, therefore, may be partly responsible for the practice of human sacrifice, because as the population grew, food supplies became increasingly unreliable.[12] Droughts exacerbated the problem. The Aztecs depended also on wild game to supplement the diet; birds, turkeys, as well as deer, hunted until they became almost extinct. Wild game provided not merely meat but, equally important, proteins, so necessary for the preservation of human life. To complicate matters for the Aztecs, the absence of a suitable herbivore limited the production of domesticated animals. Most of the captives taken in war were eaten, human flesh rich in proteins being one of the objectives of armed conflicts. To add substance to this theory, it is only necessary to read *La historia verdadera de la conquista de la Nueva España* by Bernal Díaz del Castillo, who saw Aztecs feast on the bodies of his dead comrades, "eating their legs and arms" with "a sauce of pepper and tomatoes."[13] The result was, says one scholar, large-scale cannibalism disguised as sacrifice.[14]

In retrospect, the pre-Hispanic world appears both old and complex, strong and weak. Diverse cultures had their day in the sun. Tongues spoken by sundry tribes added linguistic spice to the mixture. The habit of obedience to priests and military lords, as well as religious orthodoxy and social distinctions, was deeply ingrained in this pre-Hispanic Mexico.

IV

The other mother, or perhaps better put, father of the modern-day Mexican is the Spaniard, because at first few Spanish women came to Tenochtitlán. The conquerors bedded native women in acts of sexual frenzy. From these encounters came the mestizos, those of mixed descent, the Mexicans of today, who inherited both the good and the bad of their Spanish ancestors.

Spain, to the despair of Mexico, had an intolerant, fanatical, and cruel underbelly, plus an economy harking back to the Dark Ages. The Spain of the Don Quixote of Miguel de Cervantes never became a modern state, as it was devastated by wars, hunger, and misery and condemned to an inexorable decadence. In the sixteenth and seventeenth centuries, Spain was filled with glaring maladies and injustices. Corruption flourished: everything had a price tag. Misery and shame were in ascendance. The Spain that discovered the New World and built one of the biggest empires of all time ended up being governed by a half-wit, King Charles IV, who spent much of his time hunting, and his wife, Queen María Luisa, an unscrupulous nymphomaniac. Charles turned over the business of running the state to a playboy named Manuel Godoy, the prime minister, who lavished his sexual prowess on the queen, with whom he sired royal offspring, as well as his own wife and Josefa, his mistress, with whom he had bastards. This motley band, depicted vividly by the art of Francisco Goya, a satirist of everything irrational and absurd in life, were the guardians of the "divine right of kings" while Napoleon was busy dethroning most of the monarchs of Europe. It was said that Napoleon had little respect for a country that allowed itself to be ruled by such a band of nitwits.[15] By 1800, Spain, once the master of an empire, had ended up, for all intents and purposes, a dependency of England.

Hernán Cortés and his band of plunderers brought a diverse cultural inheritance with them to the New World. Iberians and Celts had arrived early on the Iberian peninsula, and on their heels came the Phoenicians, the Greeks, and, in about 200 B.C., the Romans, who brought with them Latin, the mother of the Spanish language, Roman law, the essence of Spanish statutes, the Catholic faith, and a legacy of latifundia. After them, Visigoths and Moslems, or Moors, from North Africa came and stayed for seven centuries, causing science and mathematics to flourish and introducing an ornate architecture of mosques, cupolas, and richly colored *azulejos.* The Moors can be blamed for the culture of "machismo," the manly habit of putting women in their place: women were to be worshiped for their beauty, honor, and loyalty, not to mention their virginity at the moment of matrimony.

Quarrels among the Moslems opened the door to the Reconquista, the Christian crusade to purge Spain of the infidels, which went on until 1492, when Grenada, the last Moorish bastion, capitulated. The Reconquista left an ambivalent legacy. The long years of fighting the Moors and other infidels strengthened the prestige of the warrior class, as well its political and social clout. To oust the Moors, the Catholic kings, requiring popular backing for their effort, rewarded the nobility with huge grants of land, thus strengthening the latifundia system. The nobility, a tiny fraction of the population, had five thousand dukes, counts, barons, and the like, sixty thousand knights, and hordes of hidalgos, plus sixty thousand patricians, urban aristocrats who sat atop the social ladder.[16] Relying on the *mayorazgo,* which passed on the family holdings from father to eldest son, powerful landed family dynasties arose.[17] Hidalgos, nobles who never soiled their hands with business or any kind of manual occupation, robbed the Spanish economy of enormous human potential that ended up in unproductive professions, largely the military or the clergy. Men who risked their lives for God and glory in military adventures in Italy, Flanders, Germany or the Americas, willingly lived on a modest income from property rather than take on a profession or go into business.[18]

At the time when Christopher Columbus asked Ferdinand and Isabella to finance his sailing venture across the Atlantic Ocean, Castile, the most powerful of the Spanish provinces, was already a land of vast estates in the hands of a backward aristocracy, as was Andalucía, the land of birth of a majority of those who settled in Mexico were from. By the second half of the sixteenth century, peasants made up more than three-fourths of the population, many of them landless. Drifters, beggars, and the jobless wandered about the streets of every town, a reservoir of unemployed labor that kept wages at a starvation level.[19] At the close of the eighteenth century, persons spoke of a depopulated and technically backward countryside, ravaged by poverty and hunger.[20]

Isabella and Ferdinand, the Catholic rulers, left Spain to Charles I, who ruled for nearly forty years but spent less than sixteen at home. The Conquest of Mexico, and that of the entire New World, occurred during his lifetime. But Charles I of Spain was also Charles V, emperor of the Holy Roman Empire, which took in Germany and Austria. The first of the Hapsburgs, Charles was only partly Spanish. He wasted his time endeavoring to hold together the crumbling Hapsburg Empire and the *conquistadores* under his control. He faced outward, plotting a costly imperialism that put much of the Western world in Spanish hands, but siphoning off vast sums of money. Unable to promote his foreign policy on taxes culled from Spaniards, Charles ultimately had to borrow from foreign bankers. His reliance on credit bankrupted Spain.

Charles I and his son and successor, Philip II, converted the crown into a despotic master, its roots in the battle for supremacy between the landed nobility and the *burguesía* of the commercial cities of the late fifteenth century. Wanting national blueprints more to their liking, merchants, traders, and bankers asked the king for help. That invitation came back to haunt them because the monarch, once he had triumphed over the nobility, turned against the nascent *burguesía.* By becoming courtiers at the court of the king, the nobility saved for itself its economic and social advantages and kept its lands. But the *burguesía* lost its political independence.

In the process, too, local governments, once a powerful entity, relinquished their independence. More and more, the crown hand-picked members of the *ayuntamientos,* the city councils, which lost their power to levy taxes and lent themselves more readily to the abuse of authority, transforming public office into an opportunity for personal profit. These changes aborted the growth of municipal autonomy and, of dramatic significance for the future, the political importance of the *burguesía*, the voice of capitalist ideals. So was born the absolute monarchy of sixteenth-century Spain, mother of colonial Mexico.[21]

The patrons of the Reconquista had religious orthodoxy on their minds, to transform Spain into a haven for the Catholic faith and purge it of Moslems, Jews, and freethinkers. The goals of the Reconquista became dogma, a religious fanaticism transported to colonial Mexico by friars and conquistadores. For this endeavor, the Catholic monarchs employed the Catholic clergy, who fashioned a powerful *españolizada* (Hispanized) church. On the eve of the demise of the Spanish empire in the Americas, Spain had two thousand monasteries staffed by sixty thousand friars.[22] The church had acquired enormous power and wealth, huge estates, property held in mortmain and free of taxation. Not infrequently it was the biggest landlord in the region. Monks of the richest monasteries had social standing as well as political power akin to that of nobles over the people within their domains. The *fueros* (privileges), such as the right to hold property in mortmain, were granted to the clergy by the crown, eager to have allies in its battle with dukes, counts, and knights and the *burguesía*.

One generation after the Reconquista, Catholic Spain had to confront the Protestant Reformation, when Martin Luther, a dissident Catholic monk, nailed his ninety-five theses to the door of a church in Germany. Not long after, the Frenchman John Calvin broke with the Pope, giving Protestantism new recruits. A bit later, the opportunistic Henry VIII severed England's ties with Rome and established the Anglican Church, which became an ally of the Protestants on the continent. The Protestant Reformation had started. Under Charles I, Spain became the cradle of the Counter-Reformation, at times employing its military might to fight the infidels. To tightly close Spanish doors to heretical thoughts, Spain revived the Inquisition, employing it, especially under the notorious Fray Juan Tomás de Torquemada, not merely to homogenize Spanish thought and behavior, but to control a restless *burguesía* in the commercial cities, many of them Jews. Confronting the Inquisition, the so-called

Holy Office, meant risking horrors that included prison, torture, and death at the stake. By the close of the sixteenth century, Spain had become the champion of orthodoxy. The relative freedom to think for oneself was a historical anecdote. Heterodoxy, the spirit of the Renaissance, enjoyed a frigid reception in Spain, while Scholasticism, a discredited formula in much of Europe, reigned supreme.

Linked to the Jewish question was the ideal of purity of faith based on purity of race, or blood. The doctrine of *limpieza de sangre* (purity of race), which sank its fangs into the national spirit, helped drive out the Jews, the commercial and financial elite of Spain, as well as the Moors.[23] The expulsion of the Moors, like the earlier ban on Jews, hurt Spain, for the *Moriscos* were bastions of the wool industry of Toledo and Seville. *El valiente negro de Flanders,* a sixteenth-century Spanish play by Andrés de Claramonte, made clear that skin color also mattered. In describing the character of the Negro Juan de Mérida, the author writes that "only because of the color of his skin he could not be a man of gentle blood," and he laments the "disgrace" to be "black in this world." For "that outrage I will denounce fate, my times, heaven, and all those who made me black. O curse of color."[24] Color prejudice, part of the *pureza de sangre,* had old roots on the Iberian Peninsula.

For a while, the silver and gold from Mexico and Peru hid the ills of Spain from public scrutiny, but not for long. By 1600, signs of decay were manifest; at the close of the next century, the downfall of imperial Spain was public knowledge. Corruption and graft beset the regime of Charles I, who looked the other way when his sycophants robbed royal revenues; his chancellor, a rogue by the name of Juan de Sauvage, made a profit of 2 million ducats in just two months off royal rights to the African slave trade.[25] An inflated, incompetent, and graft-ridden bureaucracy had the upper hand in the circles of government.

The Catholic Church traveled down a similar path. To the delight of the rich and powerful, the church, rejecting the doctrine of secularism, preached a gospel that an earthly life was but a prelude to an eternity in heaven. The poor, it was said, would to go on to a better life if they followed Catholic teachings. Ritual and ceremony, rather than dedication and compassion, were its trademarks. Priests, like laymen, took concubines and fathered offspring. The high clergy, basking in wealth, enjoyed the life of the nobility, a reflection of a society where great wealth and dire poverty lived side by side. "Our condition," wrote a Spanish sage of that time, "is one in which we have the rich who loll at ease, or the poor who beg."

All the same, for two centuries Spain basked in the sunlight of an artistic and intellectual drama, a mirror of the values and beliefs of that time. Castile, where the spirit of the Reconquista, an outpouring of religious and nationalistic zeal, discovered a home, gave it birth. God, Spaniards were convinced, had designated them the children of destiny. The Golden Age, as the times are known, elevated Spanish authors to the pinnacle of European literature. Their forte was the novel, first with *La Celestina,* a moving portrayal of the human concept of life and the forerunner of the picaresque novel *Lazarillo de Tormes* in particular. But it remained for Cervantes, with his *Don Quixote,* a masterly study of the human psyche that succinctly portrayed the rise and fall of imperial Spain, to crown Spanish letters. Among the dramatists of the day, Lope de Vega earned fame as the father of the Spanish theater, which, in the opinion of one critic, "most perfectly, perhaps, reflected the Baroque Spirit," a signpost of the Golden Age.

Literacy, a hallmark of intellectual life, enjoyed no such renaissance. It is likely that during the Golden Age the urban elite read and wrote at the level of any literate person in England or France, but the run-of-the-mill Spaniard was largely illiterate. Publishing houses did not proliferate, nor did intellectuals fare well; some scholars believe that, between 1471 and 1781, Spain rid itself of many of them, executing some and jailing hundreds.[26]

Oddly, or perhaps logically, the Counter-Reformation, which enforced antihumanist thought and set in stone the belief, with injurious consequences for freedom of inquiry, that God controlled man's fate, spawned an artistic awakening. But before we wax euphoric over Spanish enterprise, we must remind ourselves that the seventeenth century was also the Golden Age of the Dutch, the age of Rembrandt, part and parcel of the larger European Baroque drama. Counter-Reformation painting promoted an exaggerated realism in the service of mysticism, a hothouse mentality that escalated into fantasy. Much of this art was propaganda offered on behalf of the church, home to clerical megalomaniacs who used art to control thought. Spanish painters, masters of a powerful art, labored alongside the writers. El Greco, a Greek by birth but Spanish by adoption and spirit, left behind monumental works, among them the *Burial of Count Orgaz,* which, with its aura of devoutness, mysticism, and mournful faces, enshrined religious dogma. Diego Velázquez, a devout Catholic artist at the court of Philip IV, who was at the beck and call of womanizing clowns masquerading as pious clerics, left to history portraits graphically depicting the mental decay of the Hapsburg monarchs. The curtain of history had descended on the Golden Age. Centuries earlier, *Don Quixote,* Cervantes's masterpiece, with its "parable of a nation which had set out on a crusade only to learn that it was tilting at windmills," had "aptly captured the gist of what was taking place." Why had this deterioration occurred?

V

Sundry Spaniards, economists, historians, novelists, and intellectuals have had their say. European and American scholars especially like to focus on the question of values, citing Max Weber's wisdom. Catholic Spain, with its dogma of life in the hereafter and its neglect of earthly endeavors, simply missed the boat. Church and state joined hands to stifle Judeo-Christian values that gave moral support to financial and commercial activities. Authorities banned unpopular books, among them Adam Smith's *Wealth of Nations,* while witch hunts scared off dissident intellectuals.[27] By erecting barriers to the introduction of the economic thought of capitalist Europe and discouraging foreigners from visiting Spain, the Inquisition helped sabotage development. Catholic teachings created a cultural *ambiente* hostile to change and capitalist progress. This was especially so from the seventeenth century onward. However, values do not just burst forth on their own; they are offshoots of a historical time, of a socioeconomic framework. Values may help shape a society, but they respond to the nature of that society. The reasons for Spain's failure to enter the modern world of capitalist economies are complex, rooted in economic and social factors.

The history of modern capitalism, from which Spain fled, began with the trade and markets of the sixteenth century, which set capitalism's perimeters. England and Western Europe stood at the core, and on the periphery people raising cash crops for export or, as in colonial Mexico, mining silver.[28] Labor was rarely free. By 1492, Spain was already an economic dependency of Europe, and despite its conquest and colonization of the New World, it remained so. It took Spain a century, from the union of Castile and Aragon in 1479 to 1580, to attain political prowess, and a century, from the death of Philip II in 1598 to that of Charles II in 1700, to fall into the ranks of second-rate power. One of the fundamental reasons for that disaster, starting in the seventeenth century, was that Spanish maritime trade had fallen into the hands of foreigners.[29]

Spain's economic backwardness had multiple causes, among them outdated technology, roads hardly passable by heavy transport, the absence of a dynamic entrepreneurial class, and especially a puny national market. Spanish manufacturing, what there was of it, could not compete with that of Holland, England, and France. By 1800, even Spain's wool industry, known for its scanty output and poor quality, had fallen by the wayside.[30] A bourgeoisie, the cornerstone of a capitalist economy, had taken root in only a few coastal cities, where ocean-going trade had a foothold. The decadent feudalism of Castile, meanwhile, smothered the nascent capitalism of Catalonia, home to a tiny but influential bourgeoisie. Add to this the monetary disorder of the seventeenth century, the alternating inflation and deflation that brought chaos in their wake, and you have one more reason for the frailty of the economy. With the expulsion of the *Moriscos,* a heavy blow befell Spain's agriculture, already suffering from centuries of sheepherding.

The influx of silver from Mexico and Peru, seen by the Spaniards as a godly gift, was in reality the devil's gift: its entrance into Spain's less-developed economy surely set back growth.[31] With their wealth, Spaniards did not need to manufacture goods; they could buy them from foreign merchants.[32] Instead, the silver bonanza was squandered on wars, gaudy cathedrals, convents, and luxury goods. By the 1750s Spain was deeply in debt, having gone bankrupt in 1557, 1575, and 1597. On the eve of Mexican independence, mother Spain was, for all intents and purposes, a dependent, peripheral country, the exporter, through its colonies in the New World, of silver to the core countries of Western Europe. Spain, itself a colony of the developing countries of Europe, set the stage for Mexican underdevelopment.

THREE The Legacy

I

Adam Smith, the classical economist, called the discovery of America one of the "most important events in the history of mankind." America's significance, he went on to say, lay not in its mines of silver and gold but in the new and inexhaustible market for European goods.[1] That surely came to be the accepted opinion in most of Western Europe, then on the threshold of the Industrial Revolution.

From that "discovery" emerged a New Spain, the ancestral mother of Mexico, a colony for three centuries, a hundred years longer than its independence. Those long centuries of Spanish hegemony set Mexico's contours. Those of us who seek to know its people, their singularity, the country's economic and political travails, no matter how modified by subsequent happenings, must start with a contemplative look at the colonial era, else we misinterpret and distort the warp and woof of Mexico.

Adam Smith's version of the fabled "discovery" of the New World was most certainly not shared by the inhabitants of ancient Anáhuac, who lived to bewail the heralded discovery of the New World. Whatever apologists for the Spanish Conquest may say, it spelled doomsday for the conquered, pitting Indians against meddlesome Europeans. As Guillermo Bonfil Batalla, author of *México profundo,* lamented, Spain set about the "destruction of the pre-Hispanic civilizations with no other goal than its own interests."[2] Of the once heavily populated Anáhuac of 14 to 25 million, now baptized Nueva España, by 1640 just 1.3 million survived, in one of the most catastrophic demographic disasters to befall humankind. The upshot of three centuries of diabolical colonial rule was the emergence of a dysfunctional society.

To start with, the conquerors put down Indian resistance with savage cruelty, raising, not for the first time, the question of who were the "savages" and who the "civilized." That disaster began when Christopher Columbus stepped ashore in the New World. Despite his much ballyhooed "discovery," Queen Isabella and King Ferdinand had the admiral returned to Spain in chains because of his cruelty on the islands of the Caribbean.[3] The Spaniards, who came upon a religious fiesta in the great temple of Tenochtitlán, cut off the arms of a drummer, then his head, watched it roll across the floor, then attacked the celebrants, stabbing and spearing them.[4] To justify their predatory behavior, the Europeans called up the blithering idiocy of white supremacy, nonsense that has plagued mankind ever since. The Spaniards rationalized the plunder of the ancients in terms of their race and religion that, supposedly, conferred on them a supremacy cast in stone. All of us, however, have a common origin. Our ancestors, whether white, yellow, black, or brown, came out of Africa thousands of years ago, and as they spread across the face of the earth they intermingled, creating a variety of genetic interrelationships. The myth of race is an insidious fiction concocted to justify exploitation and imperial adventures. European types, whether blonds or redheads, blue-eyed or not, gave birth to none of the early civilizations.[5]

The Aztecs had reason for worry. On the eve of the Conquest, terrible omens telling of dangers ahead had beset them: strange comets belching fire raced through the heavens, while a *macehual* from the shores of Veracruz reported seeing "towers or mountains floating on the sea, carrying strange beings, with long beards and hair hanging down to the ears." The Aztecs did not yet know it, but their universe was about to go up in smoke. From then on, Miguel de Cervantes would write, they could "expect nothing but labor for their pains." Or, to quote Bartolomé de las Casas, one of the few friars who chose to speak up for the conquered, the Spaniards "laid so heavy and grievous a yoke of servitude on them that the condition of beasts was much more tolerable."[6] For the conquerors, the New World opened doors not only to plunder, the enslavement of natives, and the rape of helpless females, but also to a hidalgo's way of life, but on a bigger and more lavish scale. If the rich of New Spain could have hired others to die for them, the poor could have made a wonderful living. As Cervantes said, "The New World became a refuge and haven for all the poor devils in Spain."[7]

A hunger for profits largely explains the Spanish Conquest. In the sixteenth century, Spain had neither a surplus population ready to emigrate nor any intention of colonizing the New World. Her purpose, Samuel Ramos the Mexican philosopher stressed, was exploitation.[8] From the start, the crown gave carte blanche to a horde of freebooters, asking only for a share of their plunder. The lust for gold and silver, whether pursued by soldiers of fortune or royal despots, laid the foundations of colonial Mexico. The lure of adventure and the crusade to Christianize pagans, of course, played a role; yet, when all is said and done, the dream of striking it rich drove the Spaniards to gamble their lives.

The spoils of war also meant women, the lighter their skin the better, thousands for the taking. Like Arab potentates, the conquistadores acquired harems. The Spaniards, reports a Mexican psychiatrist, used native women to satisfy their sexual appetites.[9] When Cortés died in 1547, he left a heterogeneous lot of offspring. Nor did his companions lag behind, freely sleeping with women who caught their eye; one, it was reported, had over thirty wives, though whether he married them is uncertain. Offspring of these Spaniards, mestizos by blood, were the first Mexicans, with all the psychological hang-ups of fatherless children.

When Tenochtitlán fell to Spanish arms, so the story goes, Cortés sent a detachment of his men to survey the damage. "We found the houses filled with the dead," wrote Bernal Díaz del Castillo, the chronicler of the Conquest. "The discharge from their bodies was the kind of filth evacuated by pigs that have nothing to eat but grass." The entire city "had been dug up for roots," which its defenders "had cooked and eaten." Defeat, say the Aztec accounts, produced a profound trauma. With their gods destroyed, their rule shattered, and their glory lost, writes a Mexican observer, the memory of the defeat embedded itself in the soul of the vanquished.[10]

II

The European conquest and colonization of New Spain brought Western culture, the Spanish language, Catholicism, and Roman law, as well as an economic and political system. That culture, alien to the indigenous ones, was superimposed and not integrated with them. Equally important, the conquest and later colony laid the basis for a capitalist economy, which began when Europeans, in search of much-needed raw materials and markets, organized their availability and sale.

The colonial economy became an integral part of the maturing capitalist world. Taking a page from David Ricardo's famous dictum, that one produced and sold what one did best, the economy of New Spain relied on exports and purchased abroad what was needed, thus primarily satisfying the interests of Spaniards. Like other colonial masters of that age, Spain discouraged the production of goods that would compete with its own. This unequal interchange helped introduce a semblance of a capitalist economy to New Spain, its activities intimately related with foreign commerce and mining.

With the discovery of New Spain's silver treasures, Spain sought to maximize their exploitation, a policy that placed scant importance on investments in infrastructure and the development of human capital. Aside from silver, the Rosetta stone of the economy, only the sale abroad of cochineal had maximum value. Spain, meanwhile, chose to close off local markets to outside suppliers, a policy that contraband trade rendered obsolete. The 1713 Treaty of Utrecht, imposed on Spain by England, opened the doors of New Spain to English merchants, thus relegating to the dustbin efforts to stamp out their contraband trade.[11] The outward orientation of New Spain blocked the development of an internal market.

Yes, the conquest bequeathed benefits: the dawn of the Iron Age, as well as the introduction of the wheel. The tools of sixteenth-century Europeans transformed the ways of the Indian, who took to the wheel and tools of iron like a duck to water. The Indian welcomed with open arms the arrival of beef cattle, sheep, chickens and barnyard fowl, the almighty horse, plows and carts, as well as wheat and vegetables unknown in the New World. But the conquest also brought with it small pox, measles, and diverse afflictions.

III

The hunt for gold and silver laid the cornerstone of New Spain's dependent economy. The Spaniards, reported an Aztec chronicle, "hungered like pigs for gold." When emissaries from Moctezuma gave them gold ensigns, "their eyes shone with pleasure." They "picked up the gold and fingered it like monkeys," seemingly "transported by joy, as if their hearts were lit up and made new."[12] Mining molded the export character of the economy. At the end of the colonial years, precious metals, largely silver, made up most exports. In September 1546, the Spaniards stumbled upon a windfall in Zacatecas, a mountain of silver. By 1600, shipments of silver ore and minted coins to Spain and the Far East totaled 80 percent of New Spain's exports. For Zacatecas, the brightest of the emporiums, silver symbolized halcyon days. With its advent, some Spaniards and criollos, their offspring in the New World, could wallow in wealth. Mining gave birth to cities, to Zacatecas and Guanajuato, bastions of elegant colonial architecture, and to Pachuca and Parral, less ostentatious settlements.

Mining also conferred on New Spain, the leading supplier of silver in the world, its initial centers of capitalist enterprise. Wage workers made their debut in the northern mining camps, which, exploding with people hungry for food, opened up vast hinterlands to the plow. The Bajío, the region between Mexico City and Guadalajara, and the province of Michoacán became the granaries for the miners of Zacatecas and Guanajuato, and as these areas developed, the haciendas, the latifundia of New Spain, made their debut. In the opinion of some scholars who wax enthusiastic over the benefits of mining, not only did it spur agricultural development but it promoted commerce and even industry.

But the economic benefits of mining seldom trickled down to the underdogs because mining gave jobs to just a small slice of the colonial labor force. And the emphasis on mining distorted the colonial economy. As the political economist Andre Gunder Frank observed, "the greater the wealth available for exploitation, the poorer and more undeveloped the region today"; conversely, "the poorer the colony, the richer and more developed it is today."[13] More than any other activity, mining cemented Mexico's export orientation. There was no market for silver or gold in New Spain; their value as bullion lay in Europe.[14] With precious metals the principal export, the colonial economy relied on external markets, a sure sign of what economists call dependency. The silver bullion ended up in Seville, used to settle the balance of trade with English, French, Dutch, and Italian merchants who supplied Spanish consumers with ironware, steel, nails, paper, and textiles. Warts and all, nevertheless, mining held the seeds of a commercial capitalism; by 1600, the technology of large-scale capitalist mining was firmly in place.[15] The patio process, the extraction of silver from ore with the use of mercury—a process invented by a Mexican in 1557—opened the way for the exploitation of low-grade ores and revolutionized the industry.[16]

Mining, in its monopolistic nature, had an Achilles heel: 95 percent of the mines produced only 10 percent of the total output, while the big ones, Pachuca, Real del Monte, Zacatecas, Guanajuato, and Catorce, produced 90 percent.[17] The mining industry grew unevenly, with growth spurts followed by years of stagnation, some because of the international scene, the depression of the late eighteenth century and the collapse of the price of silver, for example, but others had domestic roots: rising costs of production, the poor quality of ores mined, the need to dig deeper mine shafts, and flooded mines. For much of the late colonial period, the dynamic energy of earlier years spent, mining required royal subsidies to turn a profit; when those subsidies ended, mining fell on hard times.[18]

IV

Ultimately, agriculture came to hold center stage, yielding over half of the value of colonial production and employing a huge slice of the labor force. By the early 1600s, Spaniards owned two-thirds of the arable land in the Valley of Mexico, igniting an era of latifundia growth and the loss of Indian lands. Whatever the importance of Mexico City, Guadalajara, and other urban depots, New Spain was rural and dependent on an agrarian economy. More than mining, it was the hacienda, the rural estate, that controlled New Spain's development. Farming, nonetheless, had to thank mining for its rise to prominence, as Alexander von Humboldt, the peripatetic German engineer, noted in his *Essays on New Spain*. Without the workings of the mines, he asked, "how many places would have remained unpopulated, or how much land uncultivated?"[19] A city would usually spring up not long after the opening of a large mine, while nearby haciendas, raising food crops to sell, sprung up almost immediately to feed the miners and urban dwellers, as the history of Guanajuato, Zacatecas, San Luis Potosí, and Durango verifies. From this pattern of development arose the latifundia, which, as time went by, came to hold most of the fertile lands.

Despite the profit orientation of its owners, the hacienda was hardly on the cutting edge of new technology; instead, hacendados relied on cheap, easily exploited labor and early learned to multiply profits by keeping harvests of corn off the market in times of abundance, to be sold for high prices in times of scarcity. During the late colonial years, when droughts and diverse climatic maladies befell agriculture, the poor in such places as the Bajío were jobless and hungry, while hacendados reaped a bounty selling scarce grains at inflated prices.

Spaniards and criollos, Spaniards born in New Spain, hacendados by and large, most of them absentee owners who dwelled in nearby cities and towns, left the running of the hacienda to a majordomo.[20] At the center of the hacienda stood the master's house, a massive stone structure of sundry rooms and hallways built around patios and archways. Some haciendas had a private chapel, served by the local priest on Sundays and feast days at the behest of the hacendado.[21] A primary function of these mansions was to display their owners' wealth and grandeur, what Thorstein Veblen titled conspicuous consumption.

The eighteenth century was the golden age of the hacienda, but its heyday of growth had come a century earlier.[22] Not all was well on the haciendas; options were limited by Spain's restrictions on what could be cultivated.[23] Vineyards and olive trees, for instance, were forbidden—the making of olive oil and wines had no place in the colony. Most of the haciendas cultivated corn, wheat, vegetables, fruits of different sorts, and, in provinces such as Puebla, maguey for the making of pulque. Drought caused the "year of hunger," 1785–86, resulting in a severe shortage of corn in the Bajío and a reduction in the harvests of beans and wheat. Students of colonial history believe that the "year of hunger" permanently upset the relative parity between food prices and income. Droughts, especially that of 1809, devastated grain production.[24]

Only in the sugar belt of Morelos had hacendados made efforts to introduce modern technology. Elsewhere, most hacendados and rancheros, small independent farmers, relied on teams of oxen to pull plows, and they rarely fertilized the soil. Sugar, a large-scale capitalist enterprise, and the cochineal of Oaxaca, a source of red dyes produced from cactus insects, were the sole agricultural exports of any importance.[25] This was so because hacendados, with notable exceptions, had their sights set on local or regional markets, due largely to the absence of a large internal one. Because of the lack of a national system of roads, the hacienda had only a local or at best a regional outlet. Confronted with small markets, hacendados relied on cheap labor for their profits. What they feared most were years of overproduction, when competitors, rancheros usually, harvested more than the market could bear.[26]

Haciendas embodied a system of land monopoly; most of the fertile lands in the regions of reliable rainfall were controlled by them.[27] At the same time, haciendas became notorious for their idle lands.[28] With the expansion of the hacienda and the growth of the population, the situation in the countryside often turned ugly.[29] More country folks were landless, and more vagrants wandered about. Though most colonials, directly or not, tilled the soil for a living, only a minority did so on land of their own.

By 1800, many haciendas had undergone a transformation, becoming commercial enterprises of a more or less capitalist bent, but still half feudal. Their Spanish and criollo masters, along with wealthy merchants and mining barons, were the colonial *burguesía,* a class wedded to private property. Where subsistence farming held sway, this was the world of the *ejido,* or communal farm, of Indian pueblos. Wedged in between hacienda and *ejidos* was the rancho, usually belonging to a mestizo; the ranchero, its owner, tilled lands of modest size, marketed a part of his harvest, and raised a few horses, cows, pigs, and chickens.

Spain's political structure in the New World seldom left open doors for local input. At its top was the viceroy, who wore the robes of the royal monarch. The viceroy was a puppet ruler, a bureaucrat who served on bended knee. Since the king and his Council of the Indies, which oversaw affairs in the colonies, rarely trusted the viceroy or other bureaucrats, they established a system of check and balances, ordering authorities in New Spain to spy on each other. The checks and balances hardly encouraged bureaucrats to speak their minds.

Municipal government ranked at the bottom of the political edifice. The wealthy elected the *regidores,* who made up the *ayuntamiento,* or town council. An alcalde presided over the meetings of the *ayuntamiento,* which did what municipal bodies usually do: hire and pay police, keep garbage off the streets, bring water into town, and fill the granary. Spaniards and criollos had a monopoly on the political jobs, though little political authority. Mestizos were notable by their absence.

Whatever the intent, rot managed to seep into the design. Viceroys and other high colonial officials more often than not returned home wealthy men.[30] The best jobs were set aside for court favorites, hangers-on of the king and his clique, while a parasitical bureaucracy grew by leaps and bounds in response to the appetites of Spaniards and criollos for public jobs.[31] But royal appointments paid little, encouraging the view of public office as an avenue to private gain. From Antonio

Mendoza, the first of them, onward, viceroys stuffed their private coffers.[32] Judges of law courts, often with large families to support and wives with social pretensions, sold their favors. The Duque de Linares, viceroy of New Spain in the early seventeenth century, said that colonial justice was "sold like goods in a market place where he who has money in his pocket buys what he wants."[33] The worst and most corrupt of these officials were the *corregidores de indios.* Like the friars, they were supposed to aid the Christianization of the Indian, but most of them took advantage of the Indian.

The rot was not simply in the political sphere. It sapped the strength of agriculture and commerce. The crown's eagerness to intervene arbitrarily in colonial affairs compelled merchants and hacendados to operate with one ear attuned to politics. They used family relations, political influence, and family prestige to obtain loans and credit, to win lucrative contracts, to avoid paying import duties, and to defend fraudulent land claims. This was the inheritance bequeathed to Mexicans. To quote one scholar, "We know now that with rare exceptions ex-colonials . . . do not readily escape from the heritage of dependence."[34]

V

The black legend of a ruthless Spain is no myth, not that the English or other imperialists enjoyed saintly records. Apologists for conquest and empire may sing the praises of colonialism, citing the benefits of Western civilization, but all of the imbalances that afflict the economies, politics, and societies of the peripheral world, including Mexico, trace their origins to colonialism.

The Spaniard, after all, came to get rich, if not with silver and gold, then off the labor of Indians, a labor system that, in most ways, rested on the backs of the poorest of society, the wretched of colonial New Spain. Spaniards, it seemed, could do almost nothing for themselves. For the first decades of the Conquest, it was forced labor for the Indian, and then harsh paid labor *(repartimiento)* in the mines and in the planting and harvesting of crops. The Indians became the peons of the haciendas, indebted workers tied to the Spanish or criollo master, their stomachs at times bloated from hunger. So the Indians had to work, no matter how long the hours, how poor the pay, or how atrocious the conditions. The ravages of European diseases cannot be fully appreciated without taking into account the appalling conditions introduced by the Conquest.

By intent and by accident, Spaniards drastically altered the native cultures. Few, if any, made an effort to reach a cultural compromise. Before the Conquest, Indians ate raw food and vegetables in abundance and drank alcohol sparingly. The Europeans changed that. Alcoholism became a major vice, and the drinking of *aguardiente,* a raw white rum, commonplace. Women of the humbler families, accustomed to leaving their bosoms naked, were shamed into covering them with the *huipil,* before long their "traditional" blouse. The imposition of European culture, say scholars, even disturbed the sex life of the Indian, making men and women less active. Some Indian women, after their menfolk had fallen, slept with Spaniards, hoping to gain descendants of valor and strength equal to that of the father. Yet the archives also bear witness that some Indian women aborted such pregnancies or killed newborns sired by Spaniards.

Moreover, the Indians had to endure the theft of their lands, a devastating blow. When deprived of them, the Indians lost their means of production, for essentially they had lived off the land. Without it, they became wage workers, either tilling the land of the hacendado or wandering off to dig ores in mines. The ownership of land had bound together the Indian village and conferred meaning on family and individual. So long as it had lands, the village maintained its traditions and customs. Once the land was lost, life disintegrated. When Indians kept their lands, they cultivated infertile plots, often in isolated hamlets hidden in the mountains and far from markets. The expansion of the hacienda, the Indians knew, had come at the expense of their *ejidos.* For hacendados, nonetheless, the swelling rolls of landless Indians meant a plentiful supply of cheap labor.

Just the same, many Indian communities weathered the gale winds of change. Their resiliency astonished their exploiters. The Indian was hardly apathetic. While Spanish rule generated feelings of inferiority and worthlessness, it also spawned anger and hate. Indians took shelter behind their customs and traditions, relying on language and isolation to bar the enemy from their doorstep. Indian women emerged as pillars of strength, passing on to their offspring the language and beliefs of their people. And Indians proved adept at manipulating Spanish law. To escape their predators, they employed birth control, abortion, infanticide, and, when the need arose, mass suicide.[35] Riots broke out time and again over the price of corn. During the uprising of 1692, as Spaniards labeled it, mobs of Indians burned the viceregal palace, the office of the *ayuntamiento,* and the jail. The viceroy barely escaped with his life. Higher clerical fees for burials and marriages touched off uprisings against priests in Oaxaca and central Mexico. In Sonora, Apaches, Janos, and Jacomes, Father Eusebio Kino wrote, "robbed and killed" Spaniards. The rebellion of the Maya of Yucatán in 1761 sent shivers of fear through the hearts of Spaniards. What the intellectual José Vasconcelos labeled the "peace of the grave" did not imply that the Indian turned the other cheek.

Indians provided the back-breaking labor for mines and haciendas, though African slaves eventually replaced some of them in the mines, and mestizos replaced some on the haciendas. To use their labor, the Spaniard first relied on the *encomienda,* a royal grant of natives to a Spaniard; Indians were entrusted to the Spaniards but not their lands. The *encomienda* headed the list of Spanish institutions responsible for the fast decline of the Indian population of the sixteenth century. Its evils were endless. The *encomenderos* had their pick of Indian women, whether with or without their mate. They were used as concubines and servants, and when they were no longer alluring or were useless as servants, whether or not they were pregnant, they were driven away. This behavior led to much social displacement within Indian families; male elders, supposedly the guardians of family honor, lost their claim as protectors, their *huevos* (balls), to use a Mexican expression. The mestizo offspring, more Indian than Spanish, saw their mother sexually exploited by a Spanish father who judged himself superior, was seldom home, and left the care of his bastard children to the despised Indian mother.[36]

The tribute that Indians paid, originally in goods (corn, squash, and beans, to name three), put an awesome burden on them. The Crown barred Indians from bearing arms, owning a horse, or wearing European dress. They could acquire property only under certain conditions but could not sell their communal lands or abandon their communities. The Spaniards, meanwhile, undertook to manufacture a pliable native elite, to cite Frantz Fanon, the West Indian psychiatrist, stuffing "their mouths with high-sounding phrases, grand glutinous words that stuck to their teeth"; the natives were "whitewashed."[37] They attempted to forge a new ruling class from the remnants of the Indian elite of priests and nobles to control the exploited. These native caciques (bosses) did what they could to separate themselves from the Indian masses, adopting, writes one historian, "Spanish culture . . . and seeking to conform to the Spanish image of the gentleman hidalgo," indulging "in a taste for genealogy comparable to that of any Spanish hidalgo."[38] So was born the nefarious toady, a figure still common in Mexico today.

On the haciendas, Indians labored as peons, a role some scholars believe akin to that of a medieval serf, although without the legal security that theoretically made up for their loss of liberty.[39] Greedy for land, hacendados constantly encroached on the lands of the pueblos, not to raise more crops but to occupy them in order to compel their former owners to work for the hacendados.[40] To keep the Indians working for him, the hacendado relied on the *tienda de raya,* the company store, to advance them money and goods on credit. The Indians thereby gained a bit of security, but it came at a high cost: they lost their liberty, because, given their miserable wages, they could never repay what they borrowed. The system, known as debt peonage, gave the hacendado a guaranteed supply of cheap, docile labor and made him master of the peons' fate.

VI

Manufacturing was the orphan. At the end of the colonial centuries, not even an embryonic industrial *burguesía* had made an appearance. The crown prohibited manufacturing, seeking to protect its merchants and its textile mills, the weavers of silk cloth and producers of olive oil. To José de Gálvez, entrusted with enforcing crown dictates, "it behooved Spain not to permit colonials to live independently of it."[41] Local vested interests in New Spain, miners and hacendados, as well as merchants who profited from the purchase and sale of foreign goods, saw no advantage to them in a homegrown industry.

Yet here and there textile plants, called *obrajes*, appeared, sweatshops rarely employing advanced technology and depending on a small market, mostly in response to the high cost of imported cloth.[42] The European depression of the seventeenth century, which hurt trade between Spain and its colonies, helped the growth of the *obrajes*. Clustered in the Valley of Mexico, the Bajío, and the Puebla-Tlaxacala basin, they were quasi-capitalist institutions that held little in common with the mechanized textile mills of England. In a state of decline by the late colonial years, the *obrajes* employed, on the average, twenty workers, some of them debt peons and even African slaves. A few, however, had as many as a hundred, but they were the exception. As Alexander von Humboldt, the German visitor, described them, these sweatshops impressed visitors not just with their primitive technology but with their filth and the cruelty foisted on the workers. The *obrajes* wove cheap woolen or cotton cloth, to be sold to peasants and laborers with scant purchasing power. Had employers paid decent wages, they might have increased their sales and profits. In 1800, Humboldt put the annual value of industry output, which he referred to as retarded, at 7 or 8 million pesos, a sum less then that of a number of the crops cultivated.[43] Statistics spell out the economic unimportance of the *obrajes*, what masqueraded as industry in New Spain. Despite population growth, their output failed to register any increase between 1700 and 1800. A major factor in their lack of growth was the stagnant wages of urban workers, one sign of the absence of a vigorous internal market. The heralded free trade policies of Charles III at end of the eighteenth century nearly nailed shut the coffin of local industry.[44]

The Spanish failure to industrialize invited outsiders, mostly the English and Dutch, to plug the gap between colonial demand and the paltry supply of Spanish goods. The bonanza of Mexican and Peruvian silver, which filled royal coffers, inflated local prices and savaged fledgling industries.[45] Foreigners monopolized the commerce of New Spain; English merchants especially reaped a bountiful harvest. Spain's inability to supply its colonists and its unwillingness to permit local industry transformed New Spain's markets into virtual bordellos, with foreigners coming and going at their whim, the colonists, like ladies of ill repute, welcoming them with open arms.

That said, certain elements of New Spain's society profited from this dependency on outsiders for the manufactured goods consumed by the local elite. The Mexico City Consulado de Comerciantes, a chamber of commerce run by Spanish merchants, had grown rich collaborating with its cohorts in Spain, buying in quantity foreign articles shipped to the ports of Veracruz or Acapulco, then selling them either through their stores or occasionally to retailers in the provinces. What they failed to sell they stored in warehouses in Mexico City, to await the day when demand overtook supply.

These merchants became, in the course of events, the chief exporters; with their money, they bought hides, tobacco, cochineal, indigo, vanilla, cacao, sugar, and cotton for sale abroad. Allies of their associates in Spain, they saw no harm in obeying Spanish dictates, going so far as to actively block the expansion of *obrajes,* and they did their best to rig prices and keep local markets for themselves.[46] The Bourbon reforms of the late eighteenth century, which encouraged a kind of free trade within the Spanish Empire, broke the monopoly of the Mexico City Consulado, spurring an economic boom and the appearance of rival merchants in the provincial cities. The end of restrictions, however, failed to shatter the predominance of Spaniards in commerce.

VII

One other institution deserves careful scrutiny if we are to understand the background of what Mexicans refer to as *el atraso mexicano,* the backwardness of Mexico. That entity is the Catholic Church. When Cortés stepped ashore in Veracruz, Catholic friars, remembered as the first apostles of New Spain, accompanied him. The holy friars cut down the ancient gods and built churches venerating the Virgin and saints where temples honoring Huitzilopochtli had once stood. The cross and the sword came to symbolize the Conquest of Anáhuac. The friars arrived as conquerors, eager and ready to help subdue heathens, to rend asunder the ancient cultures and the pagan religions, and to instill loyalty to the Crown. A handful of friars spoke up for the Indians, but one should not forget that they came on a mission of conquest.[47]

The church was highly conservative, driven by a polemical ardor.[48] It came to the New World burdened by a bundle of retrograde views, among them the authority of a quasi-feudal lord over the land. It enjoyed a monopoly of the faith and came to be nearly the sole money lender and banker.[49] Usury was its calling. The clergy ran what there was of schools, usually, if not always, for children of the well off. Above all, it was asked to turn pagans into Christians and incorporate them into colonial culture.

These were the baroque centuries, with their overstuffed high-society salons, an era of ornate churches and majestic cathedrals, made possible by untold days of unpaid Indian labor, of religiously inspired art, scenes of angels, saints, and virgins, and of devout believers ascending to heaven, where God the Father, Christ, and the Holy Ghost awaited. The poor, perhaps in awe, looked to this baroque art entrapped in religious themes to compensate for their misery and suffering on earth. As one insightful scholar points out, Indians, in their own idiosyncratic manner, embraced this baroque art, "a style without strict rules, a style of excess, of lavish decoration and dramatic light and shadow that attempted to create an experience of the sacred, not merely to symbolize it."[50] Art, after all, speaks eloquently of the attitudes of a social class and of theological and philosophical convictions that reflect political reality. Given this interpretation, the whys and wherefores of baroque painting, which appeared just when medieval man's faith in God and his universe were shaken by unanticipated discoveries, become clear.

No other institution had more impact on the shaping of colonial society, because the church, to say it again and again, had the responsibility of converting the Indian into a good Christian and a loyal subject. The Pope, moreover, had placed the church under royal tutelage. In accordance with the Patronato Real, the Spanish monarchs, designated heads of the church, collected the *diezmo* (tithe) and appointed archbishops and bishops in the colonies. The crown assumed responsibility for the upkeep of the church, which in turn obeyed the state. Linked arm and arm, the church and state set about molding New Spain into a Spanish and very Catholic colony.

On the question of race, the clergy were no less blind than their lay counterparts. From lowly friars to the high echelons of bishops and archbishops, the clergy of New Spain were Spanish. They believed in the intellectual superiority of Spaniards and in the intellectual inferiority of Indians. Not until the seventeenth century did mestizos become parish priests. Conversion to Christianity proved fleeting, because Indian relapses were commonplace. Indians clung to their polytheistic universe, although they regarded themselves as Christian while never fully grasping the Christian abstractions of sin and virtue. One thing is certain: whether faithful or not, Indians drank pulque and got drunk. They were "very good Catholic[s] but very poor Christian[s]."[51]

If total success escaped the friars, it was not for lack of effort. Indoctrination of the Indian started early. Wherever they went, the Franciscans established schools to teach the rudiments of Spanish values, obedience to authority, and Christian doctrines, but they limited enrollment to the sons of the Indian nobility, earmarked, in the Spanish blueprint, to help rule their own people. To subjugate the natives, the church and crown tried mightily to eradicate their beliefs, customs, and traditions. Subjugation brought about a certain degree of Indian servility and reinforced old patterns of obedience, but it spurred rancor and mistrust of the Spaniard. In late eighteenth-century Oaxaca, Chiapas, and Yucatán, priests complained frequently of the Indians' "irreconcilable hatred for them."[52] Indian sweat and brawn gave life to solitary towers rising above the wilderness, to fortress churches, majestic yet simple, with walls topped by parapets. These monasteries, convents, and churches were designed to last ages. If the Indians failed to cooperate, they were made to do so with the lash if necessary. It was hard, back-breaking labor under the supervision of friars who were no less demanding of the Indians than were the lay masters. Indians, serving as servants, cooks, gardeners, and messengers, staffed every one of the Catholic shrines that were set aside for the use of friars and nuns.

VIII

Beneath the glitter of majestic cathedrals and the pomp and ceremony of the baroque years lay the ugly reality of colonialism. Foreign masters, the buyers of silver and other primary goods, wielded the baton. Inside the structure of dependency was a social pyramid determined by both class and caste. At the top was a pampered Spanish and criollo elite whose tastes were out of kilter with the rest of society, but not with the nature of New Spain, dubbed the "richest" country in the world by Humboldt. Only there was "a rich man truly a millionaire." Spaniards, the *peninsulares,* sat atop the pyramid, followed by the criollos. At the other extreme lay a sprawling lower class, almost a caste. Indians, the great majority of the population, stood at the bottom of this nefarious pyramid. The elite was fair of skin; the base, mostly the color of the earth. It was, to recall the judgment of Jean-Paul Sartre, a system that produced and profited from inequality, slavery, and racism.

Nowhere, wrote Humboldt, had he found such disparities in the "distribution of wealth . . . and levels of civilization." A tiny elite enjoyed the bounty of life, dwelling alongside the very poor. Race and skin pigmentation, not always one and the same, split society. *Blancos* (whites) were better off than *morenos,* the swarthy. The tragedy of New Spain's colonial heritage was a social structure stratified by color and physiognomy: an elite of whites and a mass of castes, the people of color, Indians, mestizos, Negroes, and mulattoes. The *blancos* used color to protect their place at the top of the hierarchy and keep the "colored" in their place. But, as time went by, more and more mestizos advanced socially, some as *blanco* as the Spaniards. More of them could pass, and wanting to be accepted by the elite, they tried by every means available to separate themselves from their mixed racial origins, ruthlessly exploiting those they looked down upon.[53]

Peninsulares, the Spaniards, stood over this society, aided by criollos, not infrequently merchants and landowners. Next came the *castas,* primarily mestizos. Indians sat at the bottom of the social scale. In the eighteenth century, Miguel Cabrera, a mestizo artist from Oaxaca, left for posterity with brush, paint, and canvas this world of *castas* and Indians, using skin pigmentation to depict differences. Still, since for three centuries racial miscegenation cut a wide swath, the dictators of social custom could not always adopt an inflexible attitude toward "race." Only recent immigrants from Spain, the *peninsulares,* had the certificate of *blanco.* Many criollos claiming to be *peninsulares* turned out to be mestizos, fair of skin and usually well off. Hypocrisy had a field day because money "whitened the skin" and confirmed one's *limpieza de sangre* (cleanliness of blood). It was a pigmentocracy, with status based, to a large extent, on appearance. To be light of skin was a mark of honor and prestige; to be swarthy, or *moreno,* condemned one to rot in hell. Of New Spain's 6.1 million inhabitants in 1810, just over 1 million were of the "white race." New Spain had between eleven thousand and fourteen thousand *peninsulares* and perhaps one million criollos, dwelling mostly in Mexico City, Guadalajara, Valladolid, and Puebla. The rich and snobbish liked to divide people into just two categories: *gente de razón* (persons of reason), the Spaniards and their kin, and *indios,* the poor and downtrodden. For the *gente de razón,* work had no redeeming qualities. No writer better documented this attitude than José Joaquín Fernández de Lizardi in his *Periquillo Sarniento,* a picaresque novel. In one of its scenes, a mother tells the father: "My son, a trade? God forbid! What would people say if they were to see the son of Don Manuel A. Sarniento apprenticed to be a tailor, a painter, a silversmith, or whatever."

Out of this relationship, Mexican psychiatrists write, were born the mestizos' behavioral characteristics: the absence of scruples, feelings of inferiority, servility, a willingness to sell oneself for private gain, as well as a gut resentment of those higher on the social and economic ladder. And with good reason, because Spaniards and criollos, the elite, closed off lucrative professions—careers in law, medicine, engineering, commerce, and, until later, the church—to many an ambitious mestizo. When occasionally successful, says one Mexican psychiatrist, mestizos aped the manners and values of the social class they longed to enter, denying their ancestral roots, ridiculing whatever the Indian potter or weaver turned out, admiring, along with the criollos, all that had a French label, adopting a French style of dress, wearing white wigs, and learning to dance the minuet.[54] If dark of skin, the mestizo felt shame.

This unequal and unjust social system had sundry repercussions. Given the inequality, the virtual impossibility for the downtrodden to climb the social ladder, and the rampant corruption, it is no wonder that a spirit of disbelief and cynicism flourished.[55] Government, it was widely perceived, could not be trusted, and contact with bureaucrats was to be avoided. People at all levels came to accept that everyone, public officials particularly, would lie, steal, and bribe to get ahead. Colonials were distrustful, suspicious of the motives of others, and always pessimistic. The submerged races, wrote Octavio Paz, always wore a mask, "whether smiling or sullen," daring to show themselves only when they were alone. "Our habit of dissimilating" (lying), Paz speculated, dated from colonial times, when Indians and mestizos had to "sing in a low voice . . . because words of rebellion cannot be heard from between clenched teeth . . . in a world of fear, mistrust, and suspicion."[56] In this dysfunctional society, national unity would come slowly.

FOUR Free Traders and Capitalists

I

The nineteenth century, celebrated as the glorious age of independence and the Reforma, and the bellwether of the Liberal Party, handed over the National Palace to exuberant disciples of José María Luis Mora, a dyed-in-the-wool free trader, and the English ideologues Adam Smith and David Ricardo. For the victors, talk of a national industry took a backseat to the prevailing doctrines of Western Europe. Capitalists and free traders, more and more of them mestizos, sat the helm of the ship of state. Their ascendancy set the stage for the thirty-year rule of Porfirio Díaz, an era of neocolonialism, social Darwinism, and pomposity. How did the glory of independence settle into this lamentable scene? The explanation starts with the character of independence, a triumph largely for the status quo.

II

In 1808, the French legions of Napoleon Bonaparte invaded Spain, forced King Ferdinand, contrite and cowardly, to abdicate, and put Joseph, the Frenchman's brother, known as Pepe Botella because of his insatiable fondness for wine, on the throne. Most criollos, having endured years under the tutelage of *peninsulares,* had no desire to grovel at Napoleon's feet. Before long, their clandestine societies honeycombed New Spain, debating what should be done. The club in Querétaro included influential criollos from as far away as Guanajuato. One was Miguel Hidalgo y Costilla, a criollo priest. History remembers him as the father of Mexican independence.

From Mexico City, it was a four-day ride by horseback to the Bajío, a fertile plain that stretched from Celaya to León and embraced Guanajuato. The Bajío was dotted with ranchos, homes of mestizos, but nearly half of its inhabitants were Indians, though rapidly losing their identity, many of the pueblos having lost their lands to rapacious hacendados. In this heartland, one of the most progressive of New Spain, Hidalgo unfurled the banner of rebellion in 1810.[1] As in much of the colony, population growth had outstripped the harvests of corn and beans, driving up the prices of the basic staples of the popular diet. At the same time, everywhere in New Spain the real wages of campesinos and urban laborers had stayed stagnant or had taken a precipitous drop, exacerbating the plight of the poor. Unemployment and rural flight to cities and towns had taken on a life of their own. Silver production, especially important in the Bajío, had its ups and downs, fluctuating between poor and terrible periods. Inequality of wealth and income had gone from bad to worse, an ill exacerbated by droughts, famines, inflationary spirals, and embargos on exports imposed by the British navy.[2] An economic downturn, dating from the last years of the eighteenth century, lingered on.[3] For New Spain, the last decades of the century were hardly memorable for their largesse; for the poor, whether Indian or not, it was a time of hunger. This sheds light on why so many of them joined the battle to usurp Spanish authority, even though it was led by criollo exploiters.

The prosperity of the criollos best explains why they severed the umbilical cord. A majority of them were well off, but they were denied a political voice at the higher echelons of power. Many of them, merchants especially, had chafed under tight restrictions on trade with Europe imposed by crown reforms. During the heyday of smuggling, they had stuffed their pockets with lucrative profits that came their way from trade with English, Dutch, and French merchants. They had outgrown the need for the crown; on things that mattered the criollos and the crown were at loggerheads. The criollos believed that trade with Europe, as well as domestic questions, could be better handled by them. Whatever doubts they had about their relationship with Spain were exacerbated during the interlude of European wars, when Spain joined France to fight England and then embraced John Bull to expel Napoleon. While the fighting lingered on, many criollos fared well despite the blockade of the colony by English frigates that relegated Spanish trade restrictions to the dustbin. Hacendados wanted the freedom to trade with the outside world, while merchants, earlier agents of Spanish houses, looked to transfer their allegiance to English firms. These criollo merchants and landowners who headed the independence struggle represented not new social forces but a prolongation of the old economic order.[4]

The Hidalgo insurrection, the unexpected harbinger of class warfare, unlocked for all to see the social and racist cancer of New Spain. In 1810, out of a population of just over 6 million, no more than 20 percent of New Spain's inhabitants were white, either Spaniards or criollos. When Hidalgo marched out of the town of Dolores, his motley mob of Indians and mestizos of the lower class doubled and then tripled. Wherever he went, lamented Lucas Alamán, a criollo intellectual, he picked up disciples; he had merely to appear to win them over.[5] After easily capturing San Miguel de Allende, Hidalgo's hordes pillaged and burned it. Celaya succumbed next and, like San Miguel, suffered the rage of the mob. By now, wrote a pale Alamán, Hidalgo had eighty thousand followers who resembled "savage tribal hordes." Guanajuato, the capital of the province, lay next on the line of march. When Hidalgo's men came upon its gates, the governor, Juan Antonio Riaño, gave the order to fire; his artillery killed hundreds. Infuriated, the attackers killed Riaño, and, braving the fire of the Spanish artillery, they set aflame the wooden gates of the *Alhóndiga,* the town's granary. When the gates collapsed, the army of the poor rushed in, slaying most of the Spaniards. For a day and half, pillaging took over as Hidalgo's allies sought revenge, not just against the *gachupines* (Spaniards) but against the criollos too. After that, fewer criollos thought independence a good idea.

These episodes in Guanajuato, particularly the massacre at the *Alhóndiga,* revealed the chasms that split a racist colonial society. Hidalgo had unleashed pent-up fury against Spaniards, *peninsulares,* criollos, and, not to forget, well-off mestizos, usually fair of skin. The swarthy, Indians almost always, their plight made worse by the hard times, hungered for revenge for centuries of humiliation and exploitation. As these conflicts amply documented, colonial society was split asunder by class, caste, and color. These social and racial chasms survived independence to plague the Republic of Mexico for years to come.

The triumph of the criollos in 1821 hardly altered the life of most inhabitants, especially of Indians and campesinos. The economy stood still, hampered by a drop in the volume of domestic and international trade. Foreign earnings, a pivotal source of federal funds, declined. Investors of every stripe took their money out of Mexico. Worse still, the exchequer was empty, plagued by a ballooning public debt.

Independence opened wide the door to provincial rivalries. Province after province began to assert itself against Mexico City, igniting the deadly sin of federalism, regional autonomy, which eventually divided the former colony into semifeudal states, each asserting its prerogatives. The result was the weakening of the economy and the emergence of a cast of military chieftains, the first being Agustín de Iturbide, a populist charlatan who was proclaimed Emperor of Mexico in 1821. A criollo, he was the son of Spaniards who, in the one year of his rule, managed to alienate nearly everyone in his kingdom. Once out of office, and a republic proclaimed, only one president, the tubercular Guadalupe Victoria, managed to stay in office for the years he was elected during this turbulent era of nearly four decades.

The criollo fathers of independence did not champion any substantial change, aside from replacing the Spaniards with themselves. As Mexicans say, "It was get out so that I can come in." The structure of the economy, however, was up for debate. The old model fitted nicely with domestic reality because its architects left the Republic in the hands of the property-owning class.[6] Spain had departed, and now the criollo elite, free to decide the shape of the future for itself, had taken over. The economy rested primarily on silver exports, which fattened the pockets of the merchant elite. Never ones to embrace duties on foreign imports, these merchants resold the imports at a handsome profit.

Though born in the New World, the new rulers were fixated on foreign ways.[7] What was good for Western Europe, or the United States, suited them fine. Economists call it "internal colonialism" when native rulers supplant European masters but keep intact the old system. The barons of mining, agriculture, and commerce stood ready to enjoy the fruits of free trade.[8] Others were provincial merchants, shut off from the lucrative commerce with European houses by their rivals in Mexico City. They were strong in the port city of Veracruz and in time would become part of the backbone of the Liberal Party, a voice for free trade.

This state of affairs was made possible by the nature of the European economy, then in the throes of the Industrial Revolution. English merchants and manufacturers hungered for raw materials and new markets. Mexico's underdevelopment and its neglect of industry did not arise just because of its isolation but, to the contrary, because its economy responded to outside forces, subordinate to the export-import trade controlled mostly by foreigners. The economic structure was not simply inherited from Spain but arose in response to the needs of the industrial powers. As Lord Canning supposedly said in 1824, "Spanish America is free, and if we do not mismanage our affairs, she is ours."[9] We can speak of Mexican capitalism, but one shaped by outside forces, not Western style.

The Spanish merchants were sent home and then replaced by the English and French, who were eager to keep alive the Republic's dependency. As Mariano Otero, an intellectual of that time, wrote, "Trade was merely the tool of foreign industry and commerce." Local merchants had little interest in altering Mexico's "present condition," Otero went on; the cabals in office "are completely committed to mercantile interests and deeply interested in keeping us in a state of wretched backwardness from which foreign commerce derives all the advantages."[10] Under this formula, economic growth depended on exports, and accepted implicitly was a two-tiered world, with Mexico a supplier of raw materials and the buyer of manufactured goods.[11]

III

Mexico was not yet a nation.[12] Nationhood awaited future years. In 1821, Mexico, as historical events testify, was a theater of the absurd and grotesque. Political incompetence had a field day, as egotistical and greedy generals and politicos clawed their way to the presidential chair. Colonial ills survived, exacerbated by the chaos and destruction of the wars for independence. The fighting that raged, especially between 1810 and 1815, savaged the economy and destroyed a good part of the physical infrastructure, ravaging mines and haciendas and shutting down *obrajes*. Not until 1870 did the production of silver and gold reach the levels of the late colonial years.[13]

For all intents and purposes, independent Mexico was bankrupt. No national market existed. According to George Ward, the English consul in Mexico, the absence of roads stifled commerce, making it cheaper to import wheat flour from Kentucky or Ohio than to transport it from Puebla.[14] Textiles from Puebla lost customers in the northern states because of the prohibitive cost of transportation. The Republic's fate continued to rest on exports of silver, which, in a catch-22 dilemma, determined the volume of imports and coincidentally the amount of duties collected at the ports, a chief source of revenue. On more than one occasion, Mexico simply declared a moratorium on the payment of debts—or repudiated them. The government was in hock to unscrupulous money lenders, usually greedy and wealthy merchants who extracted exorbitant rates of interest. Until the 1850s, some twenty to fifty commercial establishments controlled the country's financial market, their chief client being the government.[15] Lending by wealthy merchants became a common practice, in return for making their imports of foreign goods less costly. The ouster of Iturbide gave birth to a byzantine comedy. Presidents followed presidents, a few after just a month or two in office. The Constitution of 1824, a copy of the North American one, and at loggerheads with the centralized rule of three centuries, established a federal republic of nineteen states and four territories, a bicameral congress and a president. Provincial interests had emerged victorious, leaving the Republic more a confederation than a federal union.[16] Every state had a governor and a legislature, each bent on going it own way. The national Congress became the hobbyhorse of lawyers, journalists, and priests, the only ones whose schooling met the requirements for service. They, of course, shut their eyes and ears to the needs of the lower classes.[17]

Starting in 1823, politicos in Mexico City began the nefarious practice of borrowing abroad, convinced that once recovery came obligations would be paid off. Victoria's administration asserted that foreign capital was the panacea for Mexico's difficulties, since European capitalists would revive the moribund economy, either by lending money or investing in it. English speculators, thinking Mexico rich in minerals, were the first to invest. But, to cite Justo Sierra, a noted Mexican historian and politician, much of that money was wasted on "bad ships, bad guns, and war supplies."[18] So began Mexico's troubled journey down the road to indebtedness.

No better word than chaos describes this sorry picture. History, asserted Karl Marx, appears first as tragedy and then as farce. That aptly describes the newly independent Mexico. It was the theater of the *cuartelazo,* or military coup, a kind of comic opera graced by the silly uniforms of incompetent generals and servile and greedy political buffoons. *Cuartelazo* followed on the heels of the last *cuartelazo,* as general after general schemed to sit in the presidential chair. The public treasury was drained, because hiring soldiers to squelch the never-ending *cuartelazos,* whether successful or not, cost money.

The local *burguesía,* or what passed for it, hardly represented an authentic national one because foreigners controlled both commerce and mining, the mainstays of the economy. Mexico City, as described by José Joaquín Fernández de Lizardi in his famous *Periquillo Sarniento,* the abode of much of this nascent *burguesía,* only superficially resembled a

European metropolis. Its street were littered with rubbish and rank with the smell of feces, so much so that no one ventured out at night.[19] Santa Anna put it bluntly: Moneda, a cherished avenue of Mexico City, replete with horse-drawn carriages, had turned into "a manure pile and as I rode in my carriage I had to close my nose in order to endure the vile odors of the slop." But, he went on, "that has always been the grandeur of Mexico: the marriage of sumptuousness with shit." No wonder that *lambiscones,* sycophants, abounded. As soon as victory was proclaimed, confessed Santa Anna, the ambitious and servile groveled at your feet, while the poor, reported Otero, stood ready to carry politicos and generals on their backs in return for a jug of pulque or a loaf of bread.

The rush to copy Europeans enjoyed halcyon days as the criollos tripped over each other in their rush to adopt European ways, clothes particularly. Earlier, women had worn black dresses of similar cut and shape. Now, recalled an English traveler, London and Paris "do not exhibit more variety of color and shape in the dresses of both sexes."[20] But, Otero reminded his readers, we borrow the trappings of Europeans, but "we do not possess their substance."[21] Intellectuals, poets, and *licenciados,* anyone with literary pretensions, avidly read the French philosophes, on their lips the names of Voltaire, Mirabeau, Diderot, and Condorcet. Neglected were literary works faithful to the domestic scene, such as the novel *Astucia,* by Luis G. Inclán, which was replete with the sights and sounds of Michoacán—its hacendados, the peon, the smartly dressed—and told in colloquial language the story of rancheros who turned to smuggling to circumvent the tobacco monopolies of city merchants.[22]

Samuel Ramos, the philosopher, would later argue that the historical roots of the Mexican's sense of "inferiority," which he ascribed to the conquest and the colonial era, had burst forth with the advent of independence, as overnight the country sought to define "its own physiognomy." When Mexicans sought to emulate European culture, a conflict broke out between aspirations and reality. The "vice in the system," Ramos maintained, was none other than imitation, practiced assiduously for more than a century.[23] Many thought they had discovered the kingdom of God in the United States. One such devotee was Lorenzo

Zavala, a criollo politico from Yucatán. Having read the American constitution, "the most advanced in the world," he believed he had stumbled on the holy grail. After a visit to the United States, he recalled a system that was not just new but "brilliant," one that had cast aside ancient privileges and social distinctions, where people participated in their governance.[24]

As a Mexican psychiatrist would write, the "national *yo*" was conflicted, encouraging Mexicans to turn their backs on their roots.[25] In so doing, they turned their backs on the Indians, whether the dead of the past or the alive of today. Most criollos, and not a few mestizos, held indigenous ways in contempt. As the petulant Fernández de Lizardi had his Sarniento comment, "My latest calamities came about because of Indians and I said to myself . . . If it's true that there are birds of ill omen, the most baneful birds and the worst . . . are the Indians."[26] Or to quote Antonio López de Santa Anna, "We have failed because of our deplorable racial mixture, and the responsibility for this sad state of affairs lies with the Spanish missionaries who saved the Indian from extinction." The way out of this unholy mess, Santa Anna proclaimed, was "to bring Europeans to Mexico and so offset the ancestral laziness of the Indian."[27] The criollos tried to solve the "Indian problem" by stealing Indian lands and exploiting them. When that didn't work, they sought to annihilate the Indians, as in the morally bankrupt Caste Wars of Yucatán, pitting the Mexican army against the defenseless Maya Indians.

IV

Physical unity was but a dream. Mexicans were split apart by regional barriers. It took weeks, if not a month or two, to travel from one place to another. The Spaniards were not great road builders; not even from Mexico City to the port of Veracruz, New Spain's principal gate, did they build one, recalled José María Luis Mora, a criollo intellectual.[28] They left behind mostly trails passable by foot, horse, and, once in while, wagons pulled by oxen—if it did not rain. *Bandoleros* (bandits), often soldiers and officers of the army who deserted after each *cuartelazo,* infested the roads. As Otero recalled, one could not set out on a journey and not expect to be robbed.[29] The upshot was a country of autonomous localities and regions, each cut off from its neighbors by mountains, deserts, or tropical jungles. It was a world of isolated communities. A town might have a bountiful corn crop, and on the other side of a mountain neighbors faced famine. States and municipalities, strapped for cash, levied taxes *(alcabalas)* on merchandise that entered from outside their boundaries. Smuggling flourished at every port, especially at Veracruz, the exchequer of the Republic. The cities, particularly Mexico City, were worlds apart from the remote villages and towns of rural Mexico. Few dispute that geography, and the failure of Spaniards to deal with it, blocked change.

When Charles I asked, "What is the land like?" an envoy sent by Cortés picked up a sheet of paper and crumpled it into a ball. Then, opening his hand, he let the paper unfold in his palm, saying, "It's like this, Sire." That twisted and wrinkled land helped set the contours of independence. Though cast in the form of a cornucopia, it was more often than not an empty container. The Valley of Mexico sat atop the Mesa Central, or plateau. To the north lay arid expanses where cactus and thickets of mesquite thrived. Mountains occupied two-thirds of Mexico. Along both coasts rose gigantic mountain ranges, stretching to the Isthmus of Tehuantepec, where they disappeared to rise again in Chiapas. Nestled between the ranges was the Mesa Central, rising from four thousand feet at Ciudad Juárez to over eight thousand feet in the south. The volcanic peaks of Popocatepetl, Ixtacihuatl, and Orizaba towered dramatically over the coastal ranges and split the central plateau into dissimilar pieces, while giant ravines swept inland for hundreds of miles from both coasts.

From Ciudad Juárez to the Guatemalan border, Tlaloc, the ancient god of rain, ruled with a grim humor. He made most of the land arid or semiarid and compelled farmers to rely on low, seasonal, and variable rainfall. Droughts were common. The north was a desert and a novelty. On the southern and coastal lowlands of the Gulf of Mexico, Tlaloc annually dumped four to ten feet of water. The rain leached the land of its plant food and turned it into a green desert. Only from Aguascalientes to Mexico City did Tlaloc give his people the water they craved. These were the facts of the water supply. Some 85 percent of the land was arid or semiarid. Two-thirds of Mexico's arable land suffered from scarce, seasonal rainfall; crops thrived only during the rainy season. Navigable rivers were conspicuous by their absence, and only a handful of lakes dotted the landscape. Outside of the Mesa Central, generally speaking, this land was niggardly for human life.

Moreover, Mexican society had not jelled; Mexico had not yet come to know itself.[30] National unity was a pipe dream. Mexico inherited from Spain a society split by class and by caste. From top to bottom of the social scale, the color of one's skin influenced personal and class relations. Money and education "whitened" the skin but not entirely. How much this prejudice poisoned relationships between individuals and groups in society, no one really knows, but no one doubts that it did. By the 1840s, Mexico's society had approximately 8 million inhabitants, over half of them persons of dark skin, largely owing to Indian ancestry, the large majority of them woefully poor. A small population of mulattoes further darkened the country's complexion. Most persons of color inhabited the countryside; whites dwelt largely in the cities.[31] Although an oligarchy of whites, mostly criollos, ruled the roost, a mestizo universe toiled beneath it. The shaky pyramid rested on a bronze base, with mestizos exploiting Indians, and both criollos and light-skinned mestizos of the upper strata riding herd over everyone.

At the pinnacle, an oligarchy of criollos, increasingly infiltrated by mestizos, quarreled and split into factions; some became Federalists, and others joined the Conservative camp. The day when the well-off worried about the less fortunate had yet to dawn. By their "selfishness and cowardice," to quote Justo Sierra, the rich "were almost wholly withdrawn from public affairs, endlessly parroting in the drawing room their favorite maxim." Just below them, "bureaucrats served those who paid them . . . and plotted with deadly, unrelenting solidarity against those who failed to pay them."[32] One discovered the true Mexican character among the whites, proclaimed immodestly by José María Luis Mora.[33]

Independence, clearly, was not a blessing for the Indians, the overwhelming majority of the population. Their lot worsened. They lived out their lives in the isolated pueblo, attempting to defend themselves as best they could; their enemies were the *blancos*. Only a minority of them spoke Spanish. Mexico, the Republic, meant nothing to them. They rose before dawn, walked from the pueblo to the field, if they had a parcel of land, and came home at nightfall. They ate corn tortillas flavored with chile sauce and beans and drank *atole,* a liquid corn gruel. Once in a lifetime, they ate meat, but drank themselves into stupor with pulque or *aguardiente de caña,* a liquor distilled from sugarcane. For Otero, little had changed the Indians' way of life since the days of Moctezuma; so ignorant were they that three-fourths of them probably did not know that Mexico was an independent Republic. As before, the *tienda de raya,* the company store, kept many of them in bondage to the hacendado.[34]

But the outcasts of society were not just Indians. The poor were ubiquitous. Designated *léperos* by the snobbish, they filled Mexico City and the provincial capitals, where, hungry and destitute, they begged for alms. They squatted on their knees or lay down, "dirty and half naked," to quote Guillermo Prieto, a contemporary intellectual. For them, home was a miserable barrio, squalid and stinking, where rats, lice, and flies infested every niche and cranny; one such barrio was Santiago Tlaltelolco, site of the famous Aztec marketplace. The squalor they lived in consisted of jacales with crumbling adobe walls, "mangy dogs, ulcerated sores, misshapen human beings, the humpbacked," and pulque, its manufacture a source of profits for many of the wealthiest families of Mexico City. For the urban poor and the Indians, politics, the unending national charters and vows by generals to change this or that, lacked rhyme or reason.

Sandwiched between the poor and the rich was a tiny, parasitical, mostly urban "middle class," its members largely *licenciados,* or lawyers, and bureaucrats, nearly all of them feeding at the public trough. These *señoritos* aped the well-off, despised the poor, and feared that an unfortunate accident might jeopardize their standing on the social ladder. Initially criollo, mestizos were infiltrating their ranks. A mere six thousand attended school beyond the primary grades. This ill-defined "class" dwelled in the Republic's capital and the provincial cities. Public jobs were their staff of life; few could survive outside of the public bureaucracy, that "superb normal school for idleness and graft," Sierra lamented, "that educated our middle class." Mexico City was the fountain of public jobs and favors, a metropolis of 250,000 inhabitants dotted with churches and convents and graced by streets lined with poplars and elms, where the weather was lovely, the air fresh and clear, and the sky one expanse of blue. Given the nature of the economy, they could not survive outside of the public bureaucracy. Entrance into government, the key employer, kept alive hopes for a better life for self and family. Peace and order on the national scale meant that officials in Mexico City had the money to pay bureaucrats' salaries. An aphorism held in Mexican politics: "When salaries are paid, revolutions fade." Mora labeled it *emplomanía,* a hunger for public jobs.[35]

Corruption in public life, the bane of the early Republic, was linked intimately to this struggle to get at the national treasury. A bankrupt Mexico could rarely pay decent salaries, emboldening office holders to sell their services, magistrates among them, to the highest bidder. They did this with impunity, knowing that higher-ups behaved in an identical manner and, if honest, would not linger in office long enough to punish malfeasance. The bribe, the famous *mordida,* was an accepted fact of life. So widespread was the evil, believed Mora, that only an exceptional public servant rose above it. The most corrupt of the corrupt, reported the American ambassador of that day, may have been Antonio López de Santa Anna, a man who knew his people well. "Some who accuse me of corruption now," he once lamented, "at one time or another came to me to ask for *chichi* [breast milk]." One-half of Mexicans, he proclaimed cynically, were born to rob the other half, and when that half comes to its senses, it sets about robbing the half that robbed it. These maladies made a mockery of public office. The *cuartelazo,* the visible sore of the military cancer, was linked to the aspirations of lawyers and their ilk, who, lacking firepower, could not enforce their will and so looked upon soldiers for support, a gang with similar designs on the national exchequer.

Then there was the army, its officers among the most illiterate and ignorant, according to Otero. Most of the generals and colonels were no more than bunglers and thieves. No general could be counted on to command an army, since few possessed even the most rudimentary military training. Generals became presidents, and virtually every state in the Republic had them, whether as governor or as military watchdog. The army ate up 80 percent of the Republic's budget, money for ninety thousand men by 1855. Without firm political convictions, though more conservative than liberal, the officers of the army allowed ambition to determine their behavior, placing matters of pay and promotion over everything else. For army officers, the government was no more than "a bank for its employers, a bank guarded by armed employees called the army." It was an army composed of *leva* soldiers, Indian conscripts drafted against their will, brave in battle and long-suffering. The favorite occupation of the military was the making of revolutions, with each administration brought to power by them obligated to reward the soldiers.

The worst of the lot was José Antonio López de Santa Anna, unbelievably president of Mexico eleven times, who boasted that Spanish blood ran in his veins. A lover of women and fighting cocks, he had a favorite saying: "A quien madruga, Dios lo ayuda" (God helps those who get there first). When he lost a leg in battle, he jested that the size of his penis shrank, so from that time on he could only have sex with the patria. He boasted that he had never read a big book and delegated the writing of letters, the composition of speeches, and the fashioning of public manifestos to underlings. What mattered was power. When confronted with some challenge, he left the presidential chair to a subordinate and retired to await a better day at his hacienda de Manga de Clavo, lands he acquired from neighboring Indian pueblos, and devoted his time to his cocks and cockfighting.

No less troublesome was the role of the church, now free of crown oversight. The church, paradoxically, was rich and powerful, but also weak. Bishops and canons lived handsomely off tithes and money collected on religious holidays. The archbishop of Mexico spent his days in a palatial house, but most priests fared less well. The wealth of the clergy varied. The nunneries were richer than the monasteries, being havens for the daughters of the wealthy, who brought with them large dowries. The church was the biggest property owner and the Republic's chief banker. Virtually every hacendado had a church mortgage to pay off. Though willing to lend money, the church had no intention of divesting itself of either its wealth or its influence, dabbling in politics and wooing soldiers for support. A political as well as a religious entity, the church was no better and no worse than its times, its monopoly of education enabling it to parrot conservative doctrines no longer at the forefront of Western thought. Its clergy ranged from the saintly to the rascally, as Fernández de Lizardi testified: "I witnessed this whole scene, as well as the crooked schemes our priests came with for keeping his money box stuffed."[36]

V

On the economic front, two schools of thought held forth: that of the Liberal José María Luis Mora, and that of the Conservative Lucas Alamán. A criollo priest, theologian, and ideologue, Mora looked to Western Europe. For him, this was an age that attributed magical powers to liberty of thought, of the individual, of the individual's right to work, of religion, and of course, of commerce. Rigid of mind and enamored of the rugged individual, Mora wrote for the educated minority, worshiping the wisdom of Adam Smith's *Wealth of Nations.* The "right to property," he affirmed in *México y sus revoluciones,* "is the foundation of political association." He was a dyed-in-the-wool free trader who welcomed foreign investment and opposed protective tariffs, ascertaining that trade with the Western world was the answer to Mexico's ills. He was an advocate of a "free economy," believing that competition, the panacea of classical thought, kept prices in check, though willing to accept revenue tariffs to shore up government coffers, but not so high as to hurt trade between nations. He ridiculed the idea of industrializing Mexico: national self-sufficiency was a myth.[37] Accepting the wisdom of David Ricardo, free traders such as Mora coined a phrase: "The tailor does not make his shoes, nor the shoemaker his shorts, and both buy their hats from the hat maker who relies on them for his clothes and his shoes."[38]

For Mora, as with his Liberal cohorts, a capitalist Mexico required a healthy mining industry, with silver at the top of the list, as well as a commercialized agriculture for export. At that time, aside from silver, Mexico exported only small quantities of vanilla, cochineal, and tobacco, while the mining industry lay in shambles. Silver remained the Republic's chief export. The recovery of silver mining, crippled by the wars for independence, would take time. Mora believed that the products of Mexican industry could not compete with foreign goods, because Mexican workers were neither technically prepared nor sufficiently intelligent.[39]

This was no time for paternalistic formulas; the Indian had to be set free, no longer the pampered child of paternalistic legislation. All Mexicans were just Mexicans, free of racial distinctions and equal before the law. Nevertheless, Mora held Indians in low esteem, implying that they were unambitious if not lazy. He asserted that, even when somewhat educated, Indians lacked imagination. Not even the dead Indians of history won his admiration; he ridiculed the myth of the grandeur and enlightenment of the Maya and Aztecs and groveled before the legend of the conquistador.[40] He took for granted the superiority of some races. Mora spoke for wealthy property owners and merchants who purchased goods for home consumption and resale.[41] His disciples were the founders of the Liberal Party.

On the other side of the ideological aisle stood Alamán, a patron of industry, who helped give form and substance to the Conservative Party. An architect, Alamán was the son of Spanish merchants who struck it rich in mining; his mother traced her ancestry to the sixteenth century. A fervent Catholic, he asked a priest to bless each meal, and at bedtime he recited the rosary. Alamán, who longed for the irretrievable colonial empire, was a complex man of ideas, more and more conservative ones. His *Historia de México* copied much from Edmund Burke, with whom he liked to compare himself. He saw property as the basis of society; without security for its owners, society could not exist.[42] Religion would help extirpate the terrible habits of the poor, the unwillingness to save for a rainy day, the drunkenness, and the filth. He warned against educating Indians, because once able to read and write, they might read subversive literature and awaken their latent spirit of rebellion. Once an advocate of independence, Alamán came to see it as a tragedy. Still, judged by contemporary economic criteria, Alamán was man ahead of his times, asserting that free trade, the panacea of Mora and his Liberals, stifled development.

To spur industry, Alamán, as minister of the economy, got Congress to establish a *banco de avío,* a state development bank, but it was attacked almost immediately by Federalist party naysayers, among them merchants, as a sure waste of public monies. Its loans to buy looms and spindles, as well as machinery, opened doors to a new class of *empresarios* (entrepreneurs). The development bank was financed by customs duties and, for additional capital, by national and foreign investors. It lasted until the 1830s, when it was abolished by Santa Anna, then president, this time as a Federalist, on the grounds that funds were no longer available. But the reasons given had only partial veracity. When Santa Anna, in his latest *cuartelazo,* toppled the government, he had the backing of Mexican and English merchants who wanted Alamán, then the minister of industry, dismissed. English merchants looked to profit from the Mexican market for textiles, then endangered by Alamán's tariff policies. The British had transformed Latin America into a veritable colony, first through the contraband trade and then by opposing local manufacturing.[43]

English exports, some two-thirds of what Mexicans purchased abroad, rapidly crushed local industry, which was technically backward and unable to compete. English manufacturers, merchants, bankers, and shippers consolidated their victory at the expense of native ones. As Henry Ward, the English minister declared, Mexico would never industrialize, then or in the future.[44] It was this policy, anathema to local industry, that helped drive Mexico to look for exports to pay for imports, the trademark of dependency. This was, of course, what the import-export–oriented merchants who made their fortunes off English manufactures, along with their mining and hacendado allies, wanted; tariff protection, the panacea of Alamán, would have cost them dearly.[45]

Alamán and a handful of farsighted men laid the foundations for Mexican industry, confined largely to textile plants, their output cheap cotton cloth, but a first step on the road to a relatively autonomous development. The textile industry relied on water power; only two mills used steam. Machinery was imported. Even much raw cotton had to be purchased abroad, usually shipped by boat from the United States, which raised the cost of the finished product. The cloth produced was sold to urban workers and the rural poor. There were fifty-five cotton textile mills located in Puebla and Veracruz that employed some two hundred families. Not all turned a profit, and as Otero pointed out, some of their owners used their mills as fronts for the importation of foreign cloth.

From the start, the shortage of capital hampered industry.[46] The local wealthy, what passed for financiers, preferred to work with foreign investors, ties that discouraged investments in risky enterprises. Most damaging to the textile industry was the size of the market. There were too few consumers, owing largely to low urban wages and, in the countryside, where 80 percent of the people lived, peonage. In his writings, Otero spoke of the abject poverty of the masses, while Fernández Lizardi recalled "crowds of vagrants who wander around meeting each other in the streets or lying drunk or . . . hanging out in pool halls, pulque stands and taverns." Decades earlier, Alexander von Humboldt had written of the hunger of the poor. Unemployment had a foothold in city and countryside, not to mention the mining industry, then in decline. In 1845, according to official statistics, average per capita yearly income stood at about 56 pesos; in the United States it was 274 pesos, and in Great Britain 323 pesos.[47] The country clearly could not count on the buying power of its inhabitants to support industry.

Tariff wars erupted with the drive for industry. No sooner was independence won, than a battle broke out between free traders and protectionists. The issue was muddled because the main source of funds for the government in Mexico City came from port duties on imports. Both free traders and protectionists, therefore, supported "revenue tariffs," not necessarily protectionist measures but ad hoc levies on specific items. In the beginning, tariffs on behalf of woolen and cotton cloth woven by *artesanos* and the old *obrajes* had the upper hand. Smuggling drastically reduced revenue from tariffs collected at the ports, which was required to keep the ship of state afloat. Veracruz, where powerful merchants ran affairs, played a key role: most imports entered through the port, while its duties amounted to three-fourths of the income of the national exchequer. The financial stability of the government, whether Liberal or Conservative, depended on duties collected on imports and exports. Mexicans went back and forth on the matter of tariffs, adjusting tariff levels in 1829, 1837, and 1842, theoretically on behalf of a variety of articles but largely cotton cloth. As Alamán noted, absent cheap cotton and wool, capital to invest, and modern machinery, the textile industry, unless protected, could not hold its own. It was a catch-22 situation, because tariffs on behalf of the textile industry spurred the smuggling of cheaper English cloth and reduced revenue at the ports; conversely, the absence of tariffs (free trade) made industrialization, the one road to a relative independence, difficult if not impossible.

The bickering criollos, at the same time, had to confront the United States, which to gratify territorial dreams invaded Mexico "in one of the most unjust wars in the history of imperialism," declared Octavio Paz.[48] That war, which came on the heels of the earlier loss of the province of Texas to American rebels, cost Mexico half of its territory and dealt a psychological blow from which it never recovered fully. For Americans, who bask in the joys of the paradigms of success and progress, grasping the psychological dimensions of defeat at the hands of foreigners is impossible. But the Mexican collective memory is infused with such themes. The cost of the war left Mexico more bankrupt than ever and exposed the rot of the Republic: the myth of national unity; the farce of a conscript army led by bunglers; the callousness of state caudillos, who stood by as the enemy invaded the country; and the perfidy of a clergy that, only on the threat of military force, lent money to the country's defenders. Yet, when the enemy captured Mexico City, the Catholic bishop had a Te Deum sung to celebrate its victory. Many of the wealthy, meanwhile, stood by, applauding the invaders, and some welcomed the idea of annexation to the United States. When the Americans opened Mexican ports to foreign goods, they reversed strides that had been made in establishing a national textile industry.[49] The Treaty of Guadalupe of 1848 put to rest Mexican dreams of a glorious future.

Still, by the early 1860s the winds of an economic revival had begun to blow, particularly in silver mining, which had climbed again to the pinnacle of the better colonial years. A decade later, of the total value of exports, nearly three-fourths came from silver and gold.[50] But this was also an era of global capitalist expansion, a time of cutthroat competition and inflationary spirals.[51] Prices of raw materials—cotton, sugar, tobacco, and rice—tumbled, the result of an abrupt decline in European demand, which coincided with a worldwide increase in their production. In Mexico, only henequen, a new export crop from Yucatán, and coffee held their own.[52] Prolonged droughts occurred again and again, hitting central Mexico especially hard.

To complicate life, the French, monarchists and capitalists who wanted to enlarge their empire and obtain cheap cotton for their textile mills, set out to conquer Mexico. The opening for the French was provided by traitorous Mexican conservatives smarting over their defeat in the War of the Reforma (1858–60), the culmination of the Liberal triumph. In that bloody conflict the church had lost its holdings and its conservative allies saw their dreams of regaining the national palace evaporate. They looked for allies in Europe and convinced Napoleon III, a mediocre interloper who needed little encouragement, that Mexicans awaited a European savior with open arms. The French Intervention and the ephemeral monarchy of Maximilian, an Austrian archduke, cost Mexico dearly. Speaking of this thwarted imperial enterprise, Marx would label it, with abundant justification, "one of the most monstrous in the annals of history."[53] To make matters worse, the United States intervened officiously in Mexican affairs, barely concealing its designs for more territorial conquests and demanding transit rights over the Isthmus of Tehuantepec, while Antonio López de Santa Anna, again president, had to sell the Gadsden territory, a large slice that eventually became parts of the states of Arizona and New Mexico, under threat of forcible annexation by the United States.

VI

The Reforma and its aftermath, considered the triumph of capitalist ideas, have gone down in the annals of history as Mexico's "bourgeois revolution." These momentous happenings are unfailingly associated with the name of Benito Juárez, a president born of a Zapotec Indian family in a village of Oaxaca. The Liberal Party, the voice of capitalism and free trade, owes its life to this man. Much ado has been made of Benito's Indian ancestry, although at that moment in history genetics and privilege most likely adjudicated one's fate. Justo Sierra, one of the many adulators, wrote rhapsodies to "that Indian of porphyry and bronze," dedicating his biography of Juárez to "the great Indian."[54]

It behooves us, however, to see what Juárez stood for, else hero worship cloud our judgment. No one can deny Juárez's indomitability, his ferocity in the face of a powerful European foe bent on subjugating Mexico. As Carl von Clausewitz wrote, he saw through the "fog of war," to marshal his forces at precisely the time and place and in precisely the right manner to prevail over the enemy. Against huge odds, he held the Republic together, standing for a nationalism conspicuously absent when the Americans invaded Mexico. Just the same, Juárez had another side, one very much in step with the capitalist dogmas of Western Europe and the United States, most of them antithetical to the welfare of the poor. He was a man of his times. Like José María Luis Mora, he put the blame for the Republic's maladies on the shoulders of the Spanish past, but he failed to see that free trade ideas, adherence to the doctrine of an export economy of primary goods, harked back to the dependency of New Spain.

Born poor, Juárez did not learn to speak Spanish until he was twelve years of age. He went on to become a lawyer, beginning his political climb as a *regidor* of an *ayuntamiento* and rising to become governor of his state. But, as Emilio Rabasa, a writer and politico from neighboring Chiapas, recognized, Juárez was hardly an Indian, even though he was born one and was swarthy and short of stature, with the profile of an Aztec deity.[55] Juárez never took pride in his indigenous roots; he had little good to say about Indians, seeing his ancestors through the eyes of Westerners and holding village customs and traditions in contempt.

Rarely did he refer to his Zapotec ancestry. If he ever had the Indians' salvation on his mind, he thought of education, the formula of the conservative who hates to unduly rock the boat, and urged the colonization of Mexico's empty lands by Europeans. By schooling and values and by his behavior, he was a middle-class Mexican. Speaking and writing in Spanish, and as a lawyer thinking in Spanish, he did not see himself as an "Indian." No one recalls that he also spoke Zapotec, his ancestral tongue. When Juárez married, he chose the daughter of a family of Italian origin, one of the wealthiest of the City of Oaxaca, for whom Juárez's sister had once served as a maid. She was, Sierra recalled, "white of skin." The absence of a racially homogeneous ruling class had opened doors to Juárez, an ambitious, pragmatic political man.[56]

Not until his exile in New Orleans in the 1850s, where he met Melchor Ocampo, a Liberal Party firebrand, did Juárez fully embrace liberal ideas. He learned much from Ocampo. Known as the *filósofo de la Reforma,* Ocampo, who uncritically admired "European civilization," personified the spread of Western capitalist ideology among Mexican reformers.[57] Three times governor of Michoacán, he owned the biggest hacienda of the Valley of Maravatío, home to 787 inhabitants, among them family members, employees, "*capataces*" (field bosses), and peons, whom he reputedly treated fairly.[58] He thought ill of the hacendado who employed the *tienda de raya* to lend money to his workers, making them *peones acasillados,* and he tried to persuade the hacendado to pay wages instead. This was the capitalist formula: the hacendado would get more work out of his peons, who, having money of their own, would work harder to keep their jobs.[59] Ocampo was an advocate of small, private property, calling again and again for the subdivision of church lands into small farms. Not entirely free of the racial nonsense of those days, the mestizo Ocampo wanted Europeans and North Americans to settle in Mexico. He considered these to be colonists who "by mating with our races would better our habits and customs, introduce new techniques to our industry and agriculture and spur our economy."[60] He longed for "the enterprise and energy of the Anglo Saxon race" and worshiped the spirit of the economy "predicated by that good man [David] Ricardo."[61] It was "an axiom of political economy," Ocampo asserted, "that one must not tax capital but income [*renta*] instead." In 1847, he tenaciously fought the signing of the Treaty of Guadalupe Hidalgo, so costly to Mexico, asking Mexicans to fight on.[62] He believed his country a cornucopia of plenty, one of the richest in the world: "God gave us everything" but, he lamented, "we have squandered nearly all of it."[63]

Like José María Luis Mora, Juárez belittled the Spanish past, labeling it backward and unenlightened.[64] His economic views were derived from Adam Smith and John Stuart Mill, his political faith from Jean-Jacques Rousseau and François Quesnay. In theory, laissez-faire was his credo, reserving for the state only a passive role, chiefly as a safeguard for the basic rights of the individual. He believed private property to be sacrosanct.[65] He rejected high tariffs on behalf of industry, holding aloft the ideal of a free market, a key to it being a high level of international trade, the spur for national prosperity.[66] Still, the number of the textile mills grew slightly under his watch, some powered not just by water but by steam. Here and there one encountered soap and candle factories.

The generation of Juárez was the first to openly break with colonial traditions, transforming a struggle to rid the country of old beliefs into a search for a national identity, albeit one based on Western values.[67] For the victors, Liberalism, the visible face of capitalism, was not a system but a state of nature, thus the need to convince doubtful cohorts to embrace this apothegm. The invisible market conferred benefits on all Mexicans, or would eventually if they just believed. English and French Liberalism, it was claimed, would shower favors on Mexicans until the angel Gabriel blew his horn on Judgment Day. With Liberalism came the doctrine of secularism, by which the state would employ its resources to limit the role of Catholic clergy and religion in the public sphere.

At one *tertulia* (literary club) after another, poets, writers, and intellectuals met to talk and debate Western ideas, the influence of French thinkers permeating the atmosphere.[68] One of them was Guillermo Prieto, later, on four occasions, head of the ministry of hacienda. A fervent apostle of Western culture, he never questioned the truth of Adam Smith's assertions and never doubted the efficacy of the laws of supply and demand. Above all, he was an enthusiastic free trader. "The faith I have in free trade," so goes a famous quote of his, "is the faith I have in all sublime manifestations of liberty."[69] No less important was Ignacio Ramírez, also a member of Juárez's cabinet and, like Prieto, a disciple of Smith who had also read Malthus's treatise on population. A free trader, Ramírez looked askance at protective tariffs and, as a delegate to the constitutional convention of 1857, he had much to say on matters dealing with international commerce.[70] Another delegate, Ignacio Vallarta, a provincial lawyer, worshiped the virtues of competition, saying that they had amply validated the ineffectiveness of protective measures. For Miguel Lerdo de Tejada, successor to Juárez in the presidency, the foreign commerce of a nation was no more than the interchange of surplus merchandise. This was, of course, the old Ricardian law of comparative advantage. Lerdo justified tariffs only if they did not unduly disrupt international trade.[71]

Oddly, out of this mélange of free traders and mimics of the European and North American capitalist model there emerged an anomalous figure: Ignacio Manuel Altamirano, a pure-blooded Indian from Tixtla, a village in Guerrero. Altamirano was small of stature, with deeply bronze skin "the color of the Aztecs"; he had a wide, flat nose and was proud of his Mexican heritage. But he was also a free trader. He recalled in *La Navidad en las montañas* that he was happiest when visiting a rural hamlet, where he "forgot his troubles." Simple virtues, he concluded, were rarely part of life in the "opulent cities," places of a society "tormented by terrible passions."[72] But Altamirano was the upholder of European concepts of female beauty: "tall, white and thin," as he wrote in *Atenea,* a novel set in Venice with scenes of Roman palaces, gorgeous Italian women, and gondolas on canals.[73] Versed in the classics, Altamirano had an exalted faith in the ideals of the French Revolution. Yet he glorified his Mexican soul, chastising authors for neglecting Mexican themes, asserting that the structure of the French novel, which he found "unsuitable for our customs and manner of thinking," had led to mediocrity. He told writers that it was not enough to want to entertain: the novel had to inculcate moral, ideological, and patriotic values, using typically Mexican themes taken from the pre-Hispanic past, three centuries of colonial rule, and the wars for independence. This free trader went on to become the father of Mexico's national literature.[74]

The Republica Restaurada (1867–75), the years of Juárez's rule, inherited an empty pantry that invited foreign meddling in Mexico's affairs.[75] Lucas Alamán, in one of his less lucid moments, had naively proclaimed that it was sound policy to borrow from Europeans, especially the English, in order to identify their economic interests with Mexico. In that manner, he explained, they would rush to Mexico's defense if it was threatened by the United States, a country he distrusted. English bankers stood ready to oblige. In 1824, Mexico had borrowed 16 million pesos from Goldshmitt & Company, a London firm, and a few moths afterward, additional money from Barclay & Company. From these loans, the Republic received, by all accounts, only about 12 million pesos.[76] Those loans, on top of the debt inherited from the wars for independence, marked the beginning of the national burden. That debt over time planted in the Mexican mind the nagging fear of national insolvency.

VII

The Ley Lerdo of 1856, the cement and steel of the Reforma, enshrined the cardinal principle that property must be owned by private individuals.[77] To achieve that goal, the Liberals legislated the *desamortización* (disentailment) of corporate property, which barred ecclesiastical corporations from owning it. The objective was a mishmash of liberal dogmas, resting on the wild assumption that disentailment would create yeoman farmers, a cornerstone of a healthy capitalist society. To the sorrow of apologists for the Reforma, the Ley Lerdo also took in the *ejido,* the communal lands of the Indian pueblos, which had to subdivide their communal lands among those who tilled them. The Indians, either because they misunderstood the intent of the legislation or, more likely, because they knew that it guaranteed the breakup of their community, did not comply. When the Indians failed to comply, rancheros and hacendados denounced the lands in order to buy them for piddling sums. True, if the Indians did not take the disentailment lying down, the Liberals backtracked a bit and declared that thenceforth *ejido* parcels would be given only to their tillers. That, nonetheless, failed to halt the acquisition of communal lands by greedy outsiders, who colluded with local, state, and federal authorities to circumvent the law, at times, the record shows, by giving Indians mescal. The Caste War in Yucatán, the uprising of Manuel Lozada in Nayarit, and the burning of cane fields by campesinos in Morelos persuaded the Liberals to plunge ahead with their plans to destroy the Indian community, which, they rightly assumed, was the citadel of Indian resistance.[78]

The soul of the Reforma was the Constitution of 1857, which included the Ley Lerdo as Article 27. No Indian, campesino, or urban worker darkened the halls of the convention that drew it up. The delegates were arch-typically representatives of the tiny, provincial "middle class," over half of them *licenciados,* who found guidance in the Rights of Man of the French Revolution and, for the political organization of the Republic, in the Constitution of the United States. According to the Mexican charter, imbued with the logic of Rousseau, "man is born free" and "nature created all men equal." With the stroke of a pen, social classes and differences of race vanished. The truth was that the charter had little meaning for a people unprepared for Western-style democracy.[79] Equally certain, as Ponciano Arriaga, another influential writer and politician, noted, nothing was done to improve the lot of society, where a tiny minority monopolized the land and the country's wealth.

The framers of the document of 1857 had simply affirmed the rights of the nascent *burguesía.* Nothing in the charter called for a social transformation of society. So doctrinaire were the framers of the Constitution that even Ignacio Ramírez, the radical among them, and a man troubled by social inequalities, felt no qualms, because "Mexican capitalists were not enemies of the working man."[80] The charter's framers had not hesitated to write in guarantees for capitalists, as Ramírez explained, pointing out that nothing in the charter obligated the state to provide jobs, a principle enshrined only in Communist societies. The sole right of labor recognized by the Constitution was the "freedom of the worker to look for a job." Articles in the Constitution called for Europeans to colonize the land, set aside lands for them, and specified that colonists be exempt from paying taxes for five to ten years. Barred was state intervention to achieve a more equitable distribution of wealth and income. The framers may as well have erected an altar to the principle of laissez-faire.[81]

The intent of the Constitution of 1857 was to enshrine capitalist doctrine. On one issue the framers were adamant: the principle of free trade, to cite Francisco Zarco's passionate argument. In Western Europe, the industrial bourgeois, patrons of the liberal philosophy, had espoused protectionism, but in Mexico, the reverse held true; liberalism became free trade as the ideology of hacendados and merchants. Although not necessarily averse to industrialization, Liberals never hailed it as a panacea for Mexico's ills. With the Liberal victory, hacendados and the commercial *burguesía* emerged as masters of the economic life of the Republic.[82]

It was believed, with almost religious fervor, that Mexico could not industrialize because it lacked risk-taking entrepreneurs, and though over time they might appear, they would never be able to stand up to their English and French rivals. Mexican capitalists, it was claimed, were few and timid, willing to gamble their money only on agricultural or urban real estate ventures.[83] The ability to compete, however, was the heart and soul of the liberal formula. Nations unable to do so fell behind the vigorous and daring. Along with the need to privatize church and pueblo lands came a belief in the miracles of foreign investment, the need to court outside money to alter the face of Mexico. Spokesmen for producers of primary goods and powerful merchants, usually from Mexico City, slowly began to integrate the country into the world capitalist system.[84] Mexico had gone from a Spanish colony to a semicolony of the Western nations. At this juncture, it was England, needing raw materials for its industry and markets for its manufactures, that Mexicans courted.

Given this logic, advocates of industry never had a chance, for one because of the state of manufacturing. Textiles, the one national industry, survived but did not thrive. Only textiles and one or two industries of lesser note (paper making, for one) represented industry. Manufacturing, including *artesanos,* employed just over two hundred thousand men and women; those in agriculture dwarfed this figure.[85] The centers of industry, basically textiles, were Puebla, Guanajuato, and Veracruz, replete with antiquated machinery. Prieto even talked of the "paralysis" of industry.[86] Imports of fine cotton cloth and clothes, much of them contraband goods purchased by the wealthy, had risen despite a tariff hike in 1872. Some textile magnates, moreover, had damaged their cause. In Puebla, site of the largest concentration of mills, their owners had bet on the wrong horse during the War of the Reforma and later sided with the French invaders, while church propaganda, unbelievably, equated industrialization with Communism. When the Republic enjoyed economic growth, it was thanks to the sale of silver.[87]

VIII

Committed to an export economy of primary goods, the Liberals did little to stimulate the growth of a consumer class.[88] Nothing better documents this than their willingness to sit by and watch the growing concentration of land. Whether campesinos, the majority of Mexicans, had any purchasing power or not apparently troubled few of them. They helped fortify the latifundia of yore, and debt peonage too. Both Juárez and Lerdo de Tejada, acolytes of private property, regarded corporate ownership as the devil incarnate of economic development, a nefarious colonial vestige. So in 1863 the Liberals approved legislation declaring the *terrenos baldíos,* so-called unoccupied lands, open for sale. To no one's surprise, these lands included pueblo holdings.[89] Unless the Indians could prove title to them, which required documentation, anyone could lay claim to them. The result was a wild speculation in rural real estate at the expense of the pueblos. Voracious hacendados, and *empresarios* eager to share country life, took advantage of the legislation to enhance their holdings, blaming, incredibly as it may sound, the poverty of the disposed. For doctrinaire Liberals, privately held land, no matter what its size, led to economic development. Mexico now had a bigger gang of landowners, as well as a bigger mass of landless campesinos unable to buy much of anything.

Defenders of Juárez—and they are legion—believe that the goal had been the Jeffersonian ideal of small private property. But this grand scheme, if it truly existed, came to life only here and there, in the Bajío, for example, where some church lands were subdivided. Nor were the Liberals blind to what was going on. One had to close one's eyes not see the thousands of landless rural families and the jobless masses in the countryside. The agrarian question, moreover, had come before the delegates at the Constitutional Convention of 1857, but they did nothing. It is impossible to believe that the Liberals did not know what was the condition of rural Mexico. Some even brought it to the attention of their companions. One of them, Ponciano Arriaga, decried how a few had "huge expanses of land lying fallow that could provide a living for millions of men," while others dwelled in abject poverty, "without land, a place to call home, and a job." How, he asked, can a people be free, regardless of what theories, constitutions, and laws proclaim, given society's "heartless economic system"?[90] To quote a popular Mexican saying, "The rich got richer, but no poor man became less poor."

Nothing tells you more about the Liberal mentality than how it dealt with the ostracized Indians. At midcentury, the Indians—to state again, the poorest of the poor—made up more than half of the Republic's inhabitants. If Mexico were to jettison the much-maligned colonial heritage, the Indian had to come along, else he be the anchor keeping the past alive. Yet, when it came to implementing their cherished capitalism, the Liberals behaved ruthlessly. Some of these Liberal gentlemen displayed outright fear and loathing toward the Indians. Guillermo Prieto, to cite one, voiced repugnance for the idolatrous religions, the "accursed offerings to the gods in the somber and melancholy world of the indigenous races."[91] In the Indian past, to quote Ignacio Ramírez, "terror made the social body tremble and people consisted of subjects and slaves."[92] "We have become the *'gachupines'* [Spanish masters] of the Indian," tardily confessed a chagrined Prieto.[93]

Closely tied to the land issue, and the jaundiced view of Indians, was the Liberal worship of European colonists. Wanting to stimulate Mexican agriculture, but not at the expense of the hacendados, the Liberals trotted out the hoary idea of inviting Europeans to settle in Mexico. Farmers especially would bring modern techniques to agriculture and, at the same time, stimulate the growth of small, private property. It was also claimed that they would improve the country's racial stock. So in 1875, at the behest of President Lerdo de Tejada, Congress passed a resolution inviting "our European brothers" to settle in Mexico, offering them lands at low cost and easy loans. Once settled, authorities would confer Mexican citizenship on the newcomers. As one ecstatic proponent put it, "We must invite them to come and share with us a wealth that we have been unable to exploit. . . . European colonization opens the door to the development of our country."[94]

IX

The Reforma was both an epic success and a colossal failure. It separated church and state, gave Mexico the trappings of a modern capitalist republic, and conferred political power on a largely mestizo class. All the same, it worsened the iniquitous distribution of wealth and income and bestowed undeserved perks on mining moguls, merchants, and hacendados beholden to the export economy. The dysfunctional colonial heritage of an externally oriented economy closely linked to sources of demand and supply outside its control weathered the winds of independence. This reliance on exports blocked the diversification of the country's productive structure, to cite Aldo Ferrer, the Argentine economist, and stifled the technical and cultural growth required for the development of an internal market.[95]

FIVE Colonialism's Thumb

I

The golden age of capitalism, when the tree of the Industrial Revolution bore ripe fruit, was no time for the peripheral world to free itself from colonialism's thumb. Known as the Gilded Age in the United States, Mexico's new trading partner, it saw the triumph of the world economy of industrial capitalism, when Western Europe, and then the United States, embarked on imperial adventures, acquiring colonies by trade and investments and, if that failed, by rifle and cannon. By 1914, these colonies of the rich and powerful covered nearly 85 percent of the globe's surface. As international commerce expanded, so too did Western capitalists' investments in the peripheral world. Steamships, railroads, the telegraph, and bank loans opened the door for the sale of factory goods in faraway corners of the globe. Western factories now had markets in Asia, Africa, and Latin America for their expanding productive capacity.

The Gilded Age was a time of splendid Western hypocrisy, when deeds and spoken words rarely coincided. Englishmen dressed fastidiously in somber clothes, led the vanguard of this globalization, and saw themselves as the bearers of respectability and Victorian virtue, while caste societies and even slavery prevailed in their colonies. It was a time when dual standards dictated the behavior of upper-class men, usually bearded and sporting drooping mustaches, who gawked at women with breasts, hips, and buttocks swelled huge by perverse and punitive Victorian corsets, demanded chastity from their wives and daughters, but made women of the lower classes fair game for their sexual escapades.[1]

These Englishmen and their cohorts in the West bore in their souls the seeds of a virulent racism.[2] Herbert Spencer and his silly doctrine of social Darwinism made deep inroads in liberal thought, the prevailing dogma of the Gilded Age.[3] A horror of miscegenation spread like wildfire through Western Europe and the United States, prompted by a belief that half-breeds inherited the worst of their parents' races. A horde of Mexicans wishing to deny their mestizo roots, especially the middle class, which was always uncertain of its place on the social ladder, fervently embraced Spencer's nonsense to distant themselves from the Indian and the swarthy poor. As Federico Gamboa had a Spaniard say in his novel *Santa,* the "vices of Mexico sport aboriginal roots, nasty after-tastes of savages and characteristic of pre-Hispanic Indians."[4]

With Spencer as their bible, Europeans, capitalists, and liberals one and all, and soon their cousins in the United States, would dictate events in Mexico and the rest of Spanish America, cementing in place, by trade, finance, and steel, the colonial structure of underdevelopment under the mantel of free trade. As in colonial times, Mexico kept on strumming the same old guitar, relying on an export economy choreographed by hacendados, powerful merchants, foreign mine owners, and a servile *burguesía.* In its relations with the advanced capitalist countries, Mexico served as an adjunct, supplying them with raw materials, industrial metals, cheap labor, fertile soil for investment, and a market for goods.

II

After the restoration of the Republic, another day dawned, calling forth decades of peace and order, all under the Liberal Party banner, an era now remembered as the Porfiriato. At the helm of the ship of state was an elite embracing the Western capitalist values of money, personal success, schooling, and science. Urban growth, a signpost of rising middle-class importance, was a hallmark of the times; the populations of Mexico City, Guadalajara, and León, three of the booming cities, multiplied rapidly. With the Western European hunt for raw materials for industry and markets, investment capital slowly started to come, primarily to Mexico's metropolises and the mining districts of the northern border states. Little of the money found its way into factories, partly because the investors did not want competitors. Despite the flow of capital into Mexico, the poor went from want to want. Dirt farmers and artisans alike swelled the ranks of job seekers, while campesinos who held on to their parcels of land had little money to spend. Designed to supply the needs of the industrial nations, the local economy gave birth to a *burguesía* that blossomed at the cost of its independence. Nor did Mexico, much admired by Westerners, rid itself of the age-old sin of corruption in public office and business. It went on as before, to quote the novelist Gregorio Lopez y Fuentes: "El que tiene chiche mama, y el que no, se cría sanchito" (He who has a tit to suck, sucks; he who hasn't grows up an orphan).[5]

III

To share the benefits of the outsiders, upon whom they came to depend, the Porfiristas bid change a hearty welcome, conceding to foreigners power over their economy and aping their culture. A dependent but prosperous economy of benefit to the few rested on political stability, so law and order took top priority, along with the need for a cheap and docile labor force. In politics, it was a time of lobotomized accommodation, when docile and obedient politicos did the masters' bidding. Out of this concoction of need and circumstance surfaced a strong, centralized state, which rid itself of domestic trade barriers such as the *alcabala.* Banks too made their appearance, mostly with English capital. Trade between Mexico and the West helped establish political stability, the cherished peace and order. Dependency, that of Mexico on the capitalist nations, offered benefits sufficiently lucrative for better-off Mexicans to abandon anarchy.

It befell Porfirio Díaz to preside over this veneer of progress, with its lavish superficiality. *Befell* may be the precise term, given the flowering of Western capitalism, and as the stability and prosperity of Argentina, Uruguay, and Chile testify, what occurred in Mexico, more likely than not, would have taken place no matter who governed. Díaz, to his credit, did everything possible to speed the transformation. For his contemporaries, Don Porfirio was a remarkable man. In an age when men apotheosized Herbert Spencer's social Darwinism, Díaz, his admirers proclaimed, exemplified its truths; his amazing accomplishments verified the axiom of the "survival of the fittest."

If Díaz proved anything, it was the nonsense of Western racial categories. He was not, according to current definitions of race, a white man. His skin the color of the earth, he was the son of a Mixtec woman and a mestizo father. Whether he was proud of his racial heritage is problematic, though he was wont to boast, "Yo soy mexicano porque soy indígena" (I am Mexican because I am Indian). That acknowledged, he also spoke with crocodile tears of the "wickedness of the Yaquis of Sonora," then being robbed of their lands by the federal army.[6] As Díaz aged, especially after his second marriage, persons who saw him up close noticed that, in an effort to look less swarthy, he dusted his face with white powder. The mate a person chooses can tell something of that person's beliefs and values. Little is known of Díaz's first wife, but his second, whom he married at age fifty-two, was a criollo girl of eighteen, white of skin and clearly of European heritage, the daughter of Manuel Romero Rubio, a former cabinet minister. Socially pretentious, Porfirio's wife once attended a ball given by the English minister dressed as Diana the huntress, carrying a bow and arrows.

A self-made man, the type eulogized by social Darwinists, Díaz was only superficially schooled. More shrewd than intelligent, he read poorly and wrote worse, knowing little about grammar and being a poor speller. He preferred to learn by listening and observing. He rose early, worked ten to twelve hours a day, and seldom stayed up late. During the American invasion, he enlisted in the militia of Oaxaca and, finding military life to his taste, fought the Conservatives and the French on the side of the Liberals, whose principles he came to espouse. For his services against the French, he rewarded himself with the Hacienda de la Noria on the outskirts of the city of Oaxaca.

A military man by vocation, Díaz employed force when necessary and could be ruthless. Don Porfirio's worship of power, "a passion impossible to curb," asserted Emilio Rabasa, who knew him well, matched his analysis of Mexico's needs.[7] Mexico, Díaz believed, could not afford the luxury of politics and at the same time enjoy economic growth. If it were to "progress," peace and order had priority. To quote Justo Sierra, one of the adulators, "The political evolution of Mexico had to await economic growth."[8] Partly because of this, critics of Díaz called him a dictator; that epithet ignores his popularity, a fact of life until the turn of the century. He was indeed popular, but nevertheless these Liberals, who earlier had been vociferous critics of the Conservatives, whom they accused of tyranny, once in power resorted to harsh measures and dictatorship. Whether Díaz, who took over the reins of Mexico in 1876, had read Adam Smith or any classical economists is highly doubtful, but his multiple administrations, in theory at least, certainly hewed to them.

During Díaz's thirty years in office, the state bowed to the wishes of the rich and powerful, natives and foreigners alike, both identified with exports. As Octavio Paz wrote, "The past returned, decked out in the trappings of progress, science and republicanism."[9] Paz had truth on his side; the Porfiriato, as the era is known, not only kept alive the old colonial dependency, but foreigners, notably Americans, reaped huge profits. It was a rapacious moral order, of vicious injustices shamelessly flaunting the cruelty of Mexican life for the poor and weak.

As for the church, the traditional enemy of Liberals, Díaz never proclaimed a policy of conciliation. He let others smooth relations with the church for him, and the clergy, fully aware of the rules of the game, hailed him. And well they should have, because during his tenure in office the number of priests and nuns, monasteries and seminaries, multiplied. Officials turned a blind eye to church schools, where priests and nuns taught the children of the well-to-do, to religious processions, and priests who wore black cassocks in public, banned by the Constitution of 1857. In the Indian villages, meanwhile, hybrid forms of Catholicism survived, sometimes within sight of the nearby priest.

How did this stability come about? One irrefutable reason for it is that the times were ripe. Western capitalist expansion, the needs of its industry, that of England, France, and the United States, more than any other factor, explain Mexico's stability and prosperity. Markets for Mexican industrial metals, copper particularly, as well as railroads to transport them north of the border, in turn lured foreign capitalists to invest their money in Mexico. Exports supported the Porfiriato's golden years.[10] Díaz also had the good sense to appoint acolytes of Western capitalism, upon whom he relied for advice and guidance, to his cabinet. The two he chose for the ministry of the economy, the key post, were neither men of the people nor men of Indian blood. Matías Romero, a native of Oaxaca, who had served Benito Juárez, was a criollo so enamored of the United States that he came to be known as the "biggest *pocho*," as Mexicans refer to devotees of American ways. Like many others of that time, Romero believed in the myth of the Mexican cornucopia; one had merely to exploit the country's plentiful, rich resources. He had spent years in Washington as head of the Mexican legation and thought American investments in Mexico to be necessary, regardless of the danger posed by such a weak country being beholden to capital from a powerful neighbor. Romero had scant use for tariffs that hindered the exchange of goods, and he overlooked their need to protect infant industry.[11]

Romero's successor, José Ives Limantour, in office for nineteen years, left heavy footprints on policy. Although not an aristocrat, he never knew what it was like to be poor, to be unable to acquire something he desired. He was the owner of an opulent estate not far from Mexico City. Of French ancestry, an admirer of everything French, he saw Mexico through the eyes of a rich man, a snobbish attitude he barely concealed. When he fled Mexico, he chose to live out his life among the people of Paris, whom he adulated. As a young man, he had spent four years in Europe, had read Spencer, and had accepted his theory of the survival of the fittest. Like Romero, he welcomed foreign capital, believing it the road to Mexico's salvation. A moderate protectionist, Limantour conceded the necessity for some barriers to protect what was produced at home, but not "ones in conflict with sensible economic theories." He confessed that he had been inclined to support free trade, but it could not be implanted over night, without taking into consideration special circumstances, such as geography and "race," that helped mold the character of a people.[12] A politico with his ears finely tuned, he seldom forgot his Porfirista allies and was always alert to the need to shield the enterprises of friends of the regime with tariffs.

Lord Acton, the English sage, once remarked that the bonds of class were stronger than those of nationality; in Mexico this was undoubtedly true. The elites of Mexico sought to identify themselves with the elites of Europe and, later, the United States, rather than with their countrymen. The Mexico of the Porfiriato was a stratified society: the rich, constituting just 1 percent of the population, controlled the lion's share of income and wealth, while a small urban middle class that fed at the public trough spent sleepless nights worrying about making ends meet but nearly always parroted the opinions of the rich. At the bottom of the strata languished the common folk. Acton's wisdom perfectly describes the class society of the Porfiriato, which came to denigrate everything Mexican and sought, wrote the philosopher Samuel Ramos, European models to emulate.

The well-off sent their sons and daughters to private schools, mostly run by the church, and when finances permitted, so did the middle class, while public schools, where they existed, catered to the poor. The rich and middle classes, read Friedrich Nietzsche, Henri-Louis Bergson, and William James and attended plays by George Bernard Shaw and Henrik Ibsen, but would not have been caught reading the Mexican novel *Astucia.*[13] It was all a farce: just one out of five Mexicans could read and write. When the Porfiristas celebrated the centennial of Mexican independence in 1910, an orgy of foreign adulation, things Mexican were conspicuous by their absence. It was an age when art for the sake of art had center stage, when members of "la clase decente" felt shame on seeing the shoddy clothes worn by the poor, dark-skinned, bedraggled compatriots, whom they believed soiled the image of the homeland. No one "embarked on an enterprise without first acquainting himself with what Europeans had done in similar cases," wrote one critic.[14] Certain that peace required a philosophy of order, intellectuals embraced Positivism and Spencer's social Darwinism.[15] As Ramos recalled, the upper classes "dressed in the French Parisian style, and imitated its good and bad customs." The descriptive term for this masquerade was *afrancesado,* referring to a Mexican who imitated the French. Bankers, textile magnates, *empresarios,* and rich hacendados lived in splendor in the *colonias* Juárez, Roma, and Santa María of Mexico City; some even adorned their mansion with mansard roofs, though it never snowed in Mexico City, and decorated their walls with European art.[16]

Perhaps no intellectual better personifies this age of mimics than Francisco Bulnes, prolific author, popular lecturer, and sociologist of sorts.[17] Highly intelligent, he was a keen observer of the human condition and knew Mexico as did few others of his day. As a senator and congressman, he viewed protective tariffs as simply a tool by which to compel consumers to buy goods at inflated prices, and as a friend of foreign investment, he praised opening the petroleum fields to foreign capitalists. An enemy of agrarian reform, and a defender of private property, he called the *ejido* a form of landholding for primitive peoples, not one for those who hungered to belong to the family of civilized nations. Long on assertions but often light on data, for Bulnes, history demonstrated that the wheat eaters of the world had led the march of modernity, while corn eaters had lagged behind. Corn, of course, meant Indian, while Bulnes equated wheat with white men and the world of Western Europe and the United States.[18] Bulnes, of course, merely parroted what good Porfiristas upheld as God's truth, a concept of modernization founded on wheat-based diets.[19]

In his famous pyramid, Karl Marx argued that the economic base dictated the nature of intellectual thought, but he conceded that over time ideas modified it. In Mexico, Marx was only partly right. Literature, which takes its cue from the society that produces it, never got beyond simply parroting the conservative culture of the time. An effete elite poeticized and endlessly debated the obscure points of French literature and put into service their farcical infatuation with impressionist art to cloak themselves from the brutal world of hacendados and *empresarios* busy getting rich off the toil of hapless human beings. However, in one respect, poetry, the reigning art form, departed from the *afrancesado,* though Verlaine, the French bard, influenced it. The Porfirista epoch was that of *modernismo,* the poetry of the swan, a genre given birth by Rubén Darío, a diplomat from Nicaragua who spent most of his life in France.[20] *Modernismo* epitomized an age antithetical to all that Antonio Gramsci, the Italian cultural Marxist, stood for, when intellectuals believed it possible to know without understanding, shorn of any feeling for the basic passions of the people, free of any attachment to them. Writers and poets, the intellectuals of the Porfiriato, became a priesthood at the service of the state. An esoteric poetry of flowery verses, *modernismo* had a host of Mexican disciples, among them Amado Nervo, Manuel Gutiérrez Nájera, and Salvador Díaz Mirón, all of whom served the Porfiristas, usually in the Mexican embassies of the best of the European powers, never losing sleep over the dreadful social conditions of millions of Mexicans. Perhaps the most shameless of the lot was Díaz Mirón, who groveled before the master and whose verse not once touched on the subject of the chicanery and corruption of the Old Regime.

The novel, then just getting off the ground as an art form, had authors of far less talent, although Federico Gamboa's *Santa* stood out. A story of a poor girl done wrong by a scoundrel and who then becomes a prostitute in a house of ill fame, the novel displays the influence of Emile Zola's *Nana* and the school of "naturalism."[21] However, though that literary school asked for faithful attention to reality, that did not unduly trouble Gamboa. The word *syphilis,* a constant companion of prostitutes in Mexico, never mars the pages of *Santa,* nor does the police tactic of returning prostitutes to their bordellos, nor laws forbidding prostitutes to walk the streets in groups. Gamboa served Díaz faithfully, never raising his voice against the inequities of his time. When he wrote *La parcela,* a novel supposedly sympathetic to the plight of the peon, José López Portillo y Rojas had been a congressman, senator, and governor of Jalisco. *La parcela,* which sets out to examine social conditions on a hacienda, ends up defending hacendados.[22]

Art and music were asked to generate sweetness and light, not truculence and disaffection. So José Mará Estrada, father of the pictorial school, painted beautiful landscapes, but with nary a brush stroke to depict inequality and poverty. José Guadalupe Posada, a caricaturist and, at times, a dissident critic, drew for Porfirista journals. Manuel María Ponce, baptized the father of *la música mexicana,* was a composer influenced by European classical music, especially Italian. His "Lejos de ti," "Estrellita," and "Rayando el sol," a good part of the lyrics taken from *modernista* poetry, are icons of Mexican music.

On the international scene, huge changes were afoot. Between 1870 and 1913, the industrial growth of the Atlantic nations led to a rising clamor for the natural resources of the peripheral countries. Speculators made fortunes investing in their export sector, especially mining and railroads. Reliance on exports was a two-edged sword; sales abroad engendered foreign funds that fattened the economy and, ironically but logically, helped promote some industry. All the same, reliance on them made Mexico much more dependent on the markets of the outside world. That reliance marched in step with the belief that salvation depended on the know-how and capital of foreigners. At first, European and English bankers lent the money, and then, over time, Wall Street replaced them. As José Ives Limantour, the minister of hacienda, acknowledged, borrowing from Wall Street bankers, which ultimately converted Mexico into a dependency of the Yankee, carried obvious dangers. Yet Limantour helped convince his countrymen, predisposed to believe him, that the benefits of these investments outweighed the dangers. Limantour and like thinkers predicted confidently that, once Mexicans were wealthier, they would redeem what had been lost to foreigners.

On the assumption of future redemption, the Porfiristas, believing fervently in the "open door," invited the stranger into their home. Slowly Mexico's foreign debt grew beyond its ability to pay. The profits of foreigners, moreover, were rarely reinvested in Mexico.[23] The benefits of this export economy fell into the hands of a small coterie of mine owners and merchants in the import and export trade, a majority of whom were foreigners by 1900. As Mexico became fully integrated into the world market, the engine driving it was the flow of capital from United States. The formation of a national market, though recognized as a proper goal, sat at the rear of the bus. To exacerbate matters, dependency on exports exposed Mexico to the ups and downs of international commerce. It also befell Mexico to suffer the adoption of the gold standard by the United States and the Western capitalist countries, which dealt a heavy blow to sales of silver. While a depreciated currency made Mexican exports cheaper, it also brought inflation and made imports more costly.

For the Porfiristas, foreign capital, as well as exports, embodied the magic bullet of modernization. The challenge, therefore, was how to create the political and economic conditions that would keep foreigners coming to Mexico and, at the same time, find markets for Mexico's goods. So Mexico had peace and order, opened wide its doors to American investors, and courted American markets. So attractive did Yankees find Mexico that they had invested nearly 2 billion dollars by 1911, monopolizing over 80 percent of all foreign investments. U.S. corporations controlled over 80 percent of mining, owned over 100 million acres of land, and provided nearly 60 percent of imports, while taking 75.6 percent of Mexican exports. These investments represented nearly half of all U.S. investments abroad. Of the manufactures purchased by Mexicans, nine out of ten came from across the border.[24]

Signs of modernity made their appearance particularly after the arrival of the railroads in the 1880s, which began the integration of regional markets into a semblance of a national one.[25] The iron horse made profitable the exploitation of previously neglected minerals, such as copper, lead, and zinc, and spurred the birth of a steel industry when rail transport brought the coal of Coahuila to the foundries of Monterrey. The iron horse, likewise, fostered urban and middle-class growth. Despite that, Mexico remained basically an exporter of minerals and, as such, tied its kite to the windy currents of the international market.[26] So long as the United States bought silver, all was well; after that, exports of copper, lead, zinc, graphite, and antimony took over, along with those of henequen. Yet without an uninterrupted flow of foreign capital and technology, a sure sign of underdevelopment, says Enrique Florescano, a Mexican historian, the formula proved unsustainable.[27]

Worshiping at the altar of foreign capital brought other maladies. The French owned most of the banks; Americans the telegraph, railroads, and mines; and the English and Americans the oil wells. Wages paid Mexican workers usually made their way out of the country for the purchase of imported articles, though spending on food kept some home. Yankee owners employed their own engineers, technicians, and foremen to run their enterprises. Nor did all of them behave honorably. Edward L. Doheny, the oil magnate, remembered Americans who came to Mexico as "young, hardy, and impetuous, not to say ruthless."[28] Or, to quote James Stillman, an American investor, "The people of Mexico will have to be supplanted by another race . . . before a great development can be expected."[29] These nonbelievers in the virtues of the Mexican "race" segregated Mexican workers. Tampico, the oil depot, was overcrowded and polluted, and at Cananea, the copper queen, workers and their families were housed in shacks of discarded tin and scrap lumber, while on the railroads Mexicans laid the tracks but American conductors and engineers ran them.[30] At the mines, Mexicans were paid less for jobs also done by Americans. Nor did these Americans lose any sleep when the needs of Mexicans went unmet. In Guanajuato, with Americans at the helm of mining, infant mortality rates reached 84 percent.

Don Porfirio and his supporters believed privatization a panacea for what ailed Mexico. So they set about making sure that individuals owned virtually everything under the sun, even the subsoil. The mining code of 1884 revoked Spanish and Mexican laws declaring the subsoil a national reserve and conferred ownership on owners of surface property, swinging open the doors to Americans who had long yearned to own the mines they operated. The law of 1909 reaffirmed that decision, labeling minerals and petroleum in the subsoil the "exclusive property" of the owner. Most important, the subsoil denoted petroleum, the black gold used to fuel the internal combustion engine of the automobile. Doheny, an American, got the ball rolling in 1900 when he bought

450,000 acres of land in Ebano, not far from Tampico; for part of it, he paid one dollar per acre to campesinos who had no idea that their subsoil had petroleum. Eventually, Doheny's operations controlled 1.5 million acres of subsoil. A bit later, a similar benevolent fate befell the Englishman Weetman Pearson, who discovered oil near Laguna de Tamiahua in Veracruz, the start of El Águila, eventually a pillar of Royal Dutch Shell, while Doheny sold his holdings to the Standard Oil Company.[31]

For the Porfiristas, the railroad was the talisman, a magical formula to unite the Republic; create a national market; resurrect the mining industry; spur the cultivation of cotton, sugar cane, tobacco, and guayule; boost cattle ranching; settle idle lands; and, above all, multiply many times the amount and value of exports. But the dream of a national railway grid never fully materialized; it was replaced by lines that ran from the United States to Mexico City, linking Mexican mines to industry north of the border. Still, Mexico had 24,717 kilometers of railroad tracks by 1910. Lands granted the railroad builders in the form of rights of way reached the grand total of 8,200,000 acres. The steam locomotive, in a nutshell, delivered Mexico into the arms of American merchants. Exports from the United States to Mexico grew rapidly and permanently altered relations between the two dissimilar neighbors.

What the railroads did was to make Mexico more export-oriented. Not only did the iron horse tie the country to the United States; it also revived mining, which had been the key to the export economy since colonial days. It did so largely because of the exploitation of industrial metals, which, concomitantly, brought about a flourishing import trade, including capital goods, paid for by the sale of industrial metals. The recovery of mining occurred almost entirely because of foreign investment, mostly American. The effects were dramatic. In 1800 Sonora was the poorest of the states, but because of its copper mines and rail lines, which joined Guaymas and Hermosillo to Arizona, and trunk lines tying Cananea and Nacozari to the American smelter at Douglas, Sonora became the richest state a century later. By 1910, Sonora exported ores worth 26 million pesos, three-fifths of it copper. During the boom, the population of the mining towns multiplied; Cananea led the way, growing from nine hundred inhabitants in 1900 to twenty-five thousand in 1906. Changed too, because of the Southern Pacific Railroad, were the fertile lands of the Mayo and Yaqui Indians, robbed from them by Díaz henchmen on behalf of American speculators, who turned them, with the help of the rivers running through them, into agricultural emporiums producing cash crops for export to the United States. Concurrently, in Hermosillo, Guaymas, and Alamos, the cities of Sonora, importers of American goods, as well as a middle sector of lawyers, accountants, and office clerks dependent for their livelihood on the mining industry, multiplied, few of them advocates of industry.

IV

As for the industrialization of the Porfiriato, much admired of late by some scholars, that too requires another look. It is now popular to say that under the Porfiristas the torch of Mexico's industrialization had been lit. There is germ of truth in that assertion, above all because the railroads made the transport of goods to a wider public cheaper. The cotton industry enjoyed spurts of growth, doubling in size by 1911, propelled along by tariff walls. Textile mills, many dating from earlier years, turned out cotton and woolen cloth and supplied virtually the entire domestic market, as did paper mills and the cement industry. Established in 1900, the Compañía Fundidora de Fierro y Acero de México, a steel conglomerate, could handle a thousand tons of ore per day; equipped with rolling mills, cranes, and locomotives, it produced finished steel. There were paper mills: one of them operated its own tree farm and a mechanical wood pulp plant, and generated its own electricity. The Cervecería Cuauhtémoc, a brewery, flourished in Monterrey, while the Vidiera de Monterrey, a glass factory, started out making bottles for it. The soap factory in Durango ranked among the biggest in the world. Other enterprises turned out cigarettes, cement, jute, henequen twine, sugar, and sundry explosives. One industry to get a face lift was pulque distilling, once confined to provinces such as Hidalgo but, with the advent of the iron horse, became established in Mexico City.

The truth is, however, as a doubting scholar puts it, that Mexico's infant industries never made it to adulthood. When the Porfiriato collapsed in 1910, Mexican industry, with one or two exceptions, confined its output to consumer goods. Mexican *empresarios* imported the machinery as well as the technology required to make the machines that produce these goods.[32] Foreign technology, as well as the machinery, designed with a mass market in mind, underlay industrialization. Staffed by foreign technicians, the nascent industries were capital-intensive, copies of their foreign counterparts, too advanced for the Mexican market and often operating at less than capacity. In some cases, workers in the textile industry were laid off so that production not exceed demand. No thought was given to the erection of labor-intensive factories; local entrepreneurs copied the Europeans, importing the latest gadgets—into a country with an abundant supply of cheap labor.

In the last fifteen years of the Porfiriato, the labor force employed in industry grew only slowly, below the pace of population growth and below that of agriculture. Inefficient production led to high prices, for steel from the Fundidora Monterrey and cement, to name just two. Overproduction was endemic, making economies of scale impossible.[33] Mexican industry proved unable to compete with imported goods. Hampered by high prices, and the absence of a national merchant marine, *empresarios* were unable to sell their goods abroad. Until the end, profits from mineral exports paid for the purchase of the technology and machinery needed to produce consumer goods. Meanwhile, a shortage of skilled workers hampered industry, multiplying the ills of low productivity and pushing up the cost of manufactures.

In response, entrepreneurs chose to erect monopolies to control the market.[34] No laws barred mergers or consolidations; the influence of *empresarios* in government circles kept out competitors, both Mexicans and foreigners. Monopolies, from textiles to beer, from steel to cement, barred upstarts. In 1910, five cotton textile mills, out of a total of 145 in the Republic, controlled over a third of the country's productive capacity. As justification, the owners pointed to low profits and to the need to band together to withstand competition from outsiders. True, foreign competitors helped make monopolies almost inevitable; with a head start of half a century or more, Europeans and Americans were selling their wares over the entire globe and undercutting Mexican goods. Trying to expand its monopoly over the world market, United States Steel even sold steel at a loss in Mexico.[35]

Still, *empresarios,* though hardly at the forefront of innovation, knew enough not merely to join hands in monopolies, but to band with politicos to erect special tariffs for their industries, textiles and printed paper for one, but as time went on, also cement, iron, and steel.[36] However, these tariffs were not simply protective measures but, as in the past, revenues for the national exchequer.[37] *Empresarios* endeavored to build an industrial edifice in a closed market, first behind these special tariffs and a devalued peso, the result in the fall of silver, and then with the help of incentives, the elimination of taxes for five years to new industries, for example.[38] Not all *empresarios* got help, because, as the pragmatic Limantour explained, they had to prove that their industries benefited the country or would be annihilated by foreign competition. Since Mexican industries operated at high cost, no one would have invested in them without some tariff protection, but these measures also passed on the high cost of local manufactures to the consumer. By bankrupting some of Mexico's *empresarios,* the depression of 1907 further discouraged investment in plants and equipment and put a brake on industrialization. What Mexico built during its Industrial Revolution, to quote one skeptic, "was underdeveloped industrialization."[39]

What went wrong? Why did the effort to build a national industry, one step on the road to independent development, stumble? The answer is complex. For one, the absence of capital hindered industrialization; the funds required for the purchase of machinery, tools, and materials were not in evidence. Largely absent were banking institutions prepared to lend money to industry (or to hacendados); not until the 1880s did they make an appearance. In 1884, Mexico had only eight banks, and by 1911 just forty-seven, but only eleven of them able to lend money for terms of more than a year. Long-term loans were, to call up an old cliché, as scarce as hen's teeth. Manufacturers, in short, could rarely rely on bank financing.[40] Wealthy merchants, mostly foreigners, provided the capital. Few Mexicans were major stockholders of manufacturing companies. In 1910, Mexicans controlled only 20 percent of the money invested in textiles, the oldest of the industries.[41] The Mexican capitalist class had emerged at a snail's pace, one reason being the peculiar nature of the native merchants or financiers of the semicolonial economy, who acted as subordinate collaborators of foreigners. These Mexicans got rich off profits from exports, which paid for the imports they handled, and not by entering into risky ventures.

Above all, it was the nature of the market, too small to support a dynamic and profitable industry, the result of low wages, both in cities and in the countryside, as well as the lopsided nature of income and wealth distribution. As Andrés Molina Enríquez wrote in his eloquent analysis of Mexico's ills, *Los grandes problemas nacionales,* only industries relying on exports profited, such as tobacco and henequen. Those relying on the domestic market faltered upon arriving at a certain stage in their development.[42] The only way to circumvent this barrier was to sell abroad. Failure to do so meant stagnation, since it was impossible to build industry on the buying power of the Mexican masses. But how did one compete with the more efficient industries of the United States and Western Europe? By the same token, the ups and downs of foreign markets, a result of economic currents outside the control of Mexico, made reliance on exports hazardous. This was the nature of dependency. Julio Sesto, the Spanish tourist and poet, recounted that during the bonanza years of henequen a clerk counting money in a store in Mérida accidentally dropped a quarter and, seeing a janitor standing nearby, asked him to pick it up. "Bah! I don't stoop for a *pinche* quarter," he replied. After the bottom fell out of the export market for henequen, that same janitor, if he was lucky to have a job, labored from dawn to dusk for less than a quarter.[43]

This was a strange and illogical world. For its survival and prosperity, Mexico's industry essentially relied on consumers of the lower classes; the better-off purchased foreign goods. If that were so, one would have to conclude that efforts would be made to raise wages in order to multiply the numbers of consumer among the workers. What, if anything, was done? Well, strange to say, nothing—absolutely nothing. Shoe manufacturing, for instance, began only in the twentieth century, because the wearing of shoes was restricted to a small urban sector; campesinos, a majority of the population, by and large, wore homemade huaraches.[44] This in no way suggests that Mexican *empresarios* were ignorant of the problem: to the contrary, they agonized over it, but nonetheless they ruled out paying decent wages. For industrial workers, there were always those waiting to take their place and, concomitantly, keeping their wages low. On a national average, industrial wages seldom exceeded fifty-nine centavos per day, just over three pesos per week. Management, more likely than not, paid wages in "vales," chits redeemable at the company store, notorious for selling low-grade goods at bloated prices. Between 1897 and 1900, wages fell precipitously. As a result, workers could not buy much beyond coarse cotton cloth, cigarettes, soap, and beer. No wonder that the *pulquería* where men and women drank themselves into a stupor became the workers' church.

Lest we forget, Porfirista Mexico was the domain of social Darwinism. Proverbs 28:27, "Whoever gives to the poor will not want," had scant credibility for the Porfiristas. Mexican *burgueses* preferred Mark 14:7: "You always have the poor with you." Labor had to endure a multitude of hardships. The hours of toil were long. Factories opened their doors before the break of day and closed them after dark. Men, women, and children, the industrial labor force, spent their days toiling in sweatshops no better than colonial *obrajes* or risking life and limb in the mines. Employers displayed a callous disregard for human life. Even Guillermo Prieto, that Liberal bellwether, looked upon labor as merchandise subject to the laws of supply and demand, while José López Portillo y Rojas, the Catholic writer, pronounced that labor turmoil was criminal. The penal code of 1872, a Liberal landmark, branded private property sacred and levied a fine or jail sentence on anyone convicted of exerting moral or physical force to modify wages or to impede the "free exercise of industry or labor."[45] A law in Sonora, a haven for Yankees, punished workers who joined labor unions. Article 4 of the textile codes, symbolic of management's attitude, permitted workers to complain only in writing to the head of their department. But then this heartless behavior took its cue from contemporary practices in the rest of the world. To cite Joseph Conrad's acclaimed novel *Heart of Darkness*, depicting European colonialism in the African Congo and the rape of natives in the pursuit of rubber and ivory, malcontents had to be punished: "Pitiless, pitiless. That's the only way. This will prevent all conflagrations for the future."[46]

What held the growth of industry back even more was the penurious buying power of rural inhabitants.[47] Of the total population of the Republic, just over 12 million, some 70 percent dwelled in the countryside, mostly in small communities. Some eleven thousand haciendas monopolized approximately 88 million hectares, an average of eight thousand hectares for each one of them. Two out of three Mexicans survived off some form of farmwork.[48] Of the rural population, 63 percent (9,591,752) dwelled on haciendas. More Mexicans toiled in agriculture than had done so earlier: their percentage had risen from 60.3 percent of the workforce in 1895 to 64.4 percent in 1910. Scholars who study development tell us that for a country to industrialize it must modernize its agriculture, required, they add, to feed a growing population and secondly to provide the export earnings needed to finance imports.[49] The Porfiristas, however, only partially followed that wisdom. They modernized the export sector of Mexican agriculture, that of the northern states, Morelos and Yucatán, while imports of wheat and corn, what campesinos cultivated and most Mexicans ate, shot upward.

The concentration of landownership gave form and substance to the structure of poverty, putting shackles on the buying power of campesinos. On agrarian questions, the Liberal answers of Juárez and Díaz were one and the same. Their tonic was to "privatize" the land. Setting aside rhetoric about preference for small farms, they eulogized "efficiency and productivity," identified with big agricultural units, and exhibited scant concern when their nefarious scheme concentrated the land in the hands of the few. As Francisco Pimentel, one of the stalwarts of the regime, told everyone, the communal system had "robbed the Indian of all feelings of individual enterprise." By 1900, hacendados were the bulwark of the Porfiriato, their numbers swollen from 5,700 in 1876 to more than 8,000 in 1910.[50] Foreigners owned 150 million acres, a majority of them in American hands, roughly one-third of the land of Mexico.[51] Only 4 percent of rural families possessed any land.[52] Yet agricultural output grew by only 0.7 percent, below that of the rate of population growth.

A paradox had dogged the Porfiristas: eager to make Mexico more capitalistic, they had intensified the cultivation of agricultural commodities yet left intact seigneurial relations of production inherited from the colonial hacienda.[53]

On the question of race, it was the old saw again. Mexico, it was proclaimed time and time again, had to bring colonists from Europe, as one *científico* pontificated, "so as to obtain a cross with the indigenous race." Only European blood, he insisted, could "raise the level of civilization" or keep it "from sinking." What he meant, of course, was that Mexico must "whiten" its skin, become more European and less Indian. To lure European colonists, as well as encourage ambitious mestizos to take up farming, Mexico had to hold out the promise of land. In December 1893, the Porfiristas approved the Ley de Terrenos Baldíos, updating the legislation of 1863, which encouraged individuals to blow the whistle on uncultivated lands. Merchants, hacendados, politicos, real estate speculators, and mining moguls rushed to organize bogus surveying companies to take advantage of the legislation that allowed them to keep one-third of the lands surveyed. Legislation passed in 1894 reinforced this policy.

The results were lamentable. Few Europeans arrived, and those who did settled in the cities, usually as merchants. To the delight of the architects of the scheme, however, private individuals gobbled up the land, much of it from the *ejidos*. In less than a decade, over 38 million hectares were mapped out. Of that total, the government kept for sale just over 12 million hectares; private individuals kept the rest. By 1910, the Porfiristas had accomplished what criollo hacendados and mestizo rancheros had attempted after independence and with the Reforma. By 1900, some 82 percent of the country's campesinos were landless; just 1 percent of the population owned 97 percent of the fertile land. Given these conditions, the buying power of rural labor plummeted, averaging between 18 and 30 cents for a day's work. Between 1810 and 1910, wages paid to the peon remained nearly stationary. In the Valley of Toluca, next door to Mexico City, the peon earned a *real y medio,* less than twenty-five centavos for a day's work, not enough to sustain the worker's family. At the end of the week, Gregorio López y Fuentes alleged in his novel *El Indio,* wages could not pay for "unbleached muslin to make pants and shirts."

Worse still was the lot of the Indians. In 1910, Mexico was 70 percent rural, and Indians made up the majority, nearly every one of them illiterate. For all intents and purposes, the Indian as a consumer did not exist. Whether a peon on a hacienda or, theoretically, a free worker in a pueblo, the Indian's life and that of the Indian community were a day-to-day struggle. Survival meant a daily battle against poverty, exacerbated by the racism of mestizos and criollos. Enrique Creel, a Díaz henchman and governor of Chihuahua, claimed that "100,000 Europeans were worth more than a million Indians."[54] To quote Francisco Bulnes, "The Indian is disinterested, stoical and unenlightened" and "loves only four things: the idols of his former religion, the land that feeds him, personal freedom, and alcohol."[55] More and more bereft of lands, the Indians sank into dismal poverty, compelling them to labor for ever-lower wages. Aside from cotton cloth and a bit of leather for huaraches, they purchased little. In their frenzied exploitation, the Porfiristas went so far as to sell as slaves Yaquis and Mayos from Sonora to the henequen lords of Yucatán. Only now and then did a lonely voice speak up in the Indians' defense, one being that of Heriberto Frías in his novel *Tomochic,* which movingly describes the resistance of the Tarahumaras of Chihuahua to the Díaz regime.[56]

Over this scene, Mexico's national debt hung like the sword of Damocles. Despite the flow of capital from abroad and at times a favorable balance of trade, the cost of servicing the foreign debt could not be covered and was made worse by the loss of profits and interests on investment sent home by foreigners. On four occasions, Mexico had to turn to foreign lenders lest the economy capsize. It was a vicious cycle, as Limantour explained: each new wave of foreign investment meant more money leaving the country in the form of profits. On the heels of these difficulties came the financial panic of 1907, the swan song of prosperity, revealing flaws in Mexico's economic and social fabric. Until the crisis paralyzed the economy, Americans and Europeans alike paid homage to the Mexican success story. With the onset of the panic, Mexico's adulators began to abandon ship.

SIX Lost Opportunity

I

Modern Mexico, according to sundry scholars of that country, both nationals and foreigners, starts with the Porfiriato, a regime that went on for ever and ever, or so it seemed to a multitude of Mexicans. Many of these same scholars, turned contortionists, then go on to swear allegiance to the Revolution of 1910, a social upheaval, in their opinion, that toppled Don Porfirio from his throne and put a fresh face on Mexico. This view, however, presents a problem. It's like a mixed metaphor in which a figure of speech is used in place of another to suggest a likeness but fails to withstand close scrutiny. Did the Porfiriato give life to modern Mexico, or was it the Revolution of 1910? If the latter, then modern Mexico owes its origins not to the Old Regime, but to the men who toppled it. Both views, paradoxically, are correct, because the changes ushered in by the upheaval of 1910 were hardly revolutionary. The wisdom of David Ricardo and his disciples, though somewhat modified, continued to be espoused. The export economy of yesteryear became the export economy of "revolutionary" Mexico, as did dependency on outside markets. The chance to alter Mexico's path was squandered.

One reason the opportunity was missed is the class leadership of the Revolution, which from start to finish arose from the northern hacendados, an export-oriented bunch. Nary a one had a national industry on his mind, and no one spoke up in favor of a national market for homemade goods. Only a minority at Querétaro, site of the Constitutional Convention of 1917, embraced any radical doctrines, and none dealt with the pitfalls of dependent development. Despite high-sounding rhetoric, which at times exalted socialist doctrine, a majority of the rebels had reform on their minds, not the burial of capitalism. The ambivalent progeny of the Old Regime wanted entrance into the portals of government and business. Radical declarations aside, none of them seriously considered adopting a platform of independent development.

The rebels, after all, marched in step with their times. These were the years of the Progressive movement in the Unite States, when Theodore Roosevelt and particularly Woodrow Wilson opened doors to middle-class reform but left untouched the economic edifice. Much the same occurred in Argentina, where the Radical Party, foe of the Conservatives, did not tamper with the old reliance on exports of beef and grain to Great Britain. Next door, José Batlle y Ordóñez, a remarkable politico, was trying to inject a bit of social justice into laissez-faire doctrines in tiny Uruguay, installing public schooling and adopting higher-revenue tariffs. The Revolution, which Francisco I. Madero ignited, stepped out of this context. Except for the issue of land reform, which neither Batlle y Ordóñez nor the Radicals of Argentina tackled, the Revolution had brotherly links to the reform currents sweeping the Western Hemisphere.

Of course, the Mexican Constitution of 1917, the Magna Carta of the upheaval, prominently featured labor and agrarian legislation that, if carried out, might have led to a national market. But its enactment was fleeting. No one seriously questioned the age-old dependency on exports of metals. The absence of any serious discussion of industrial goals is striking. The legislation, while modifying some of the ideals of Porfiristas, tampered only mildly with traditional dogmas. Its ideals accepted the principles of the French Revolution, as well as those of England and the United States. The raison d'être remained the capitalist formula, updated to meet the Mexican needs of the twentieth century. The framers of the charter of 1917 wanted to modernize the system and, certainly in the thinking of their left wing, to maximize its benefits for labor and the campesinos. This Magna Carta revised its predecessor of 1857, adding a more comprehensive political and economic platform. Many of these middle-class reformers, a generation of twentieth-century liberals, had no basic quarrel with the old charter, wanting only to modify and update it. Even positivism somehow found itself part of the intellectual baggage of revolutionary Mexico.

II

Why the collapse of the Porfiriato? Popular interpretations point an accusing finger at the "agrarian question." The landless and their champions, the enemies of the octopus-like hacienda, kindled the protest. However, as an embittered José Ives Limantour recalled from exile in Paris, the nature of the agrarian question underwent a transformation in retrospect.[1] The old Porfirista bellwether had ample reason to complain. To credit the discontent of the landless for the upheaval simplifies, if not distorts, the nature of the upheaval. Francisco Bulnes phrased it succinctly. Before Francisco Madero, who challenged Porfirio Díaz's long tenure in office, the apostles of agrarian reform had called the country to arms; yet its proponents merely got themselves jailed. The landless failed to answer their call. A few months later, Madero, no archenemy of hacendados, uncovered fervent rebels in the northern provinces. If hunger for land had put the match to the tinderbox, asked Bulnes, why had the northerners not rushed to enlist in the earlier uprising?[2] Similarly, the tragic course of the rebellion, bizarre and cruel at times, records the death of apostles of agrarian reform at the hands of their companions in arms. This in no way denies the existence of rural maladies, which, statistics document, were endemic and complex. The uprising offered a plethora of opportunities to landless and exploited campesinos to settle old scores with hacendados, to throw off, if only momentarily, the yoke of oppression. More to the point, the rebellion flared up in the provinces most identified with the export sector, namely Sonora, Chihuahua, and Coahuila, and to the south Yucatán and, interestingly, Morelos, where the crisis of 1907 upset the status quo between owners of sugar haciendas and their peons.

One factor that stands out, and that only indirectly touches on the exploitation of campesinos, is a mounting concern with the low productivity of agriculture. For twenty years Mexico had imported corn and wheat from Argentina and the United States. From Bulnes's perspective, this fact documented Mexico's inability to feed itself. Others placed the blame at the feet of the hacienda system. The emphasis on an agriculture for export had encouraged hacendados to cultivate cash crops, as they were doing with garbanzos in the Yaqui and Mayo valleys of Sonora. Reliance on food imports grew worse during the final years of the Díaz regime, bringing about rising public expenditures on food: 5 million pesos for corn imports in 1908, 15 million in 1909, and 12 million in 1910.[3]

Then, to exacerbate matters, Tlaloc, that flighty deity, forgot to water the lands of his worshipers. From 1907 to 1911, Tlaloc failed to make an appearance, and droughts struck with devastating fury and wreaked havoc on the countryside. The drought of 1890 was the most severe of the century. One of the regions hit hardest was the Bajío, the Republic's breadbasket. The fickle hand of Tlaloc punished unevenly. The droughts crippled rancheros, tenant farmers, and sharecroppers, who depended on the heavens to water their fields. Few of them cultivated irrigated lands. Rancheros, most of whom also raised cattle and other barnyard animals, and *medieros,* the tenant farmers or sharecroppers, blamed their plight on the hacendados, who monopolized irrigated lands. Shortages of corn and wheat reflected the predicament of *medieros* and rancheros. By 1910, as Andrés Molina Enríquez, an acerbic critic of the Porfiriato, explained, they harvested the bulk of the grains for local markets, though haciendas occupied nine-tenths of the fertile lands.[4] Grain shortages occurred at the expense of dirt farmers. But few at Querétaro linked the food issue to the moribund market, a large segment of it composed of penniless peons, whether indebted or not.

Droughts hurt the northern provinces especially hard. Cotton output fell in Coahuila, inflicting heavy damage on its textile mill, where wages fell and unemployment rose. In Chihuahua, the last plentiful rain fell in 1906; by May of the following year, newspapers had begun to report an "alarming drought with terrible consequences for nearly the entire state." The drought lingered on through 1908 and into 1909, severely damaging the wheat crop and leaving the countryside parched and dry, without a blade of grass for the cattle to feed on. By April, the livestock industry, mainly for export to the United States, and a leading source of Chihuahua's wealth, confronted a crisis of major proportions. One apocryphal story sums up the severity of the situation: In Miñaca, a town in the district of Guerrero, saloons, faced with a grave shortage of water, put up the following sign: "Whiskey solo, twenty centavos; con agua, fifty centavos."

Ironically, the labor arm of industry, still in its infancy, had a hand in the downfall of the Old Regime. Until 1900, some industrial workers had benefited from an ever-so-slight rise in real wages. All the same, between 1891 and 1908, food prices rose alarmingly, with markups for corn, beans, and wheat, staples of the Mexican diet.[5] The drop in the price of silver, the resulting inflation, and the panic of 1907 wiped out labor's gains. Already, by the turn of the century, industrial workers had started to fend for themselves. Mutual aid societies, which buried the dead and cured the sick, met with considerable success. Sadly, but logically, given the nature of Mexican politics, the Gran Círculo de Obreros, the first of the labor organizations, split into warring camps, one answering the siren call of Díaz. Anarchism, a potent element in labor's indoctrination, infiltrated labor's ranks by way of Spain and the French thinker Pierre Joseph Proudhon, whose book *What Is Property?* Mexicans read avidly. Also from France appeared the work of Elisée Reclus, *Evolution, Revolution, and the Anarchist Ideal,* followed by the writings of Pyotr A. Kropotkin, the Russian revolutionary, and Mikhail Bakunin, a fellow anarchist. From their wisdom, Mexicans learned that human beings are by nature good, but institutions, primarily the state and private property, corrupt and enslave them. Unexpectedly, Americans, too, planted the seeds of the labor union in Mexico. The railroads, mines, and oil industry employed American workers affiliated with labor organizations across the border, specifically the Knights of Labor, and in Tampico the Industrial Workers of the World. Imitating the Americans, Mexicans began to organize brotherhoods, largely on the railroads.

The tug-of-war between Mexican workers and their foreign bosses intensified the sense of class struggle. Responding to the loss of jobs and cuts in wages, harbingers of hunger for their families, Mexicans engaged in a wildcat strike at an isolated mining camp in Sonora in 1889, then in San Luis Potosí, followed by a massive strike of railway workers that paralyzed the cities of San Luis Potosí, Torreón, Monterrey, and Aguascalientes. The workers had organized themselves into La Gran Liga de Ferrocarrileros Mexicanos, demanding that Mexicans, not "gringos," run the railroads; fifteen thousand railroad workers had joined by 1908.

Management, just the same, refused to have anything to do with the labor unions. Of the sundry strikes, three set the stage for the downfall of the Porfiriato. The north hosted two: the violence at Cananea, Sonora's copper kingdom, in 1906 and the railroad walkout of 1908. The other occurred in the textile mills at Río Blanco in Veracruz. The strikes had common threads. Declining exports linked two of them: copper and the railroad running north from San Luis Potosí relied on Yankee customers. The American debacle of 1907, felt early in Mexico, hurt copper exports and the transport industry. On the railroads, the lag in business kept wages low in the face of the spiraling cost of living and intensifying competition for jobs between Mexicans and foreigners. Price gouging by the French owners of the *tienda de raya,* who paid their foreign workers higher wages, lit the fuse at Río Blanco. Foreign control of the best jobs as well as better wages for foreign workers applied the torch on the railroads. At Cananea, the American company paid its American workers five pesos in gold for a day's labor but paid Mexicans less than half of that. Soldiers put down the strike at Río Blanco, while Rurales, mounted Mexican police, and American rangers quelled the uprising at Cananea.

As so often happens, one event ignited the fuse of rebellion. The disastrous financial panic of 1907, its roots in the United States, marked the swan song of prosperity and became the watershed of rebellion.

The panic of 1907 headed the list of culprits because, for all intents and purposes, the United States, the chief customer of Mexico, determined the welfare of the local economy.[6] Proximity to the big and wealthy northern neighbor, helped along by the railroad network and by heavy investments of American capital in mining, had transformed Mexico into a tributary of the United States. By reducing the value of Mexico's exports, the crisis, Don Porfirio informed Congress, had rocked the foundations of prosperity.[7] His message had special relevance for the northern provinces, since their economies rested almost entirely on customers across the border. The railroad carried copper northward from Sonora to factories in the northeast: cattle from Chihuahua for the Kansas City stockyards, mineral ores too, and cotton and guayule from Coahuila. Plummeting prices for mineral ores savaged the national economy. When the bottom dropped out of the copper market in the United States, the mining industry suffered a staggering blow, crippling Sonora and Chihuahua. As Cananea shut its mines, the jobless filled the streets. Once the biggest city in Sonora, Cananea lost two-fifths of its inhabitants. In summary, Mexican mining, the principal foundation of the export economy, was hit hardest by the financial crisis of 1907. Its debacle thrashed the rest of the economies of the mining states, particularly Sonora, Chihuahua, Durango, and Sinaloa.

To rub salt into the wound, the depression touched off a banking panic. For decades Mexico had come to depend on foreign investors, whether speculators or bankers. Prior to 1907, more than 50 million pesos had entered Mexico annually. When the financial debacle engulfed the United States, the principal source of funds, Mexico had no one to turn to for money to shore up its crumbling economy.[8] With its capital tied up in long-term loans, usually to hacendados, Mexico's rickety banking system could not come to the rescue of merchants, businessmen, shopkeepers, and rancheros. Partly responsible for the banking debacle were debtors who had borrowed large sums of money from the banks and then defaulted. The shortage of loans severely punished small entrepreneurs. There followed an epidemic of bank failures, most of them accompanied by charges of mismanagement and wrongdoing.

Even the Banco Nacional de México, according to Bulnes, had "water in its wine barrels."

Such a fate befell Yucatán, where exports of henequen to the United States, purchased by International Harvester, dictated activity. The region's prosperity had largely rested on credit. The buying and selling, the imports of machinery as well as luxury articles by the henequen barons, the expansion of commerce, and the bank loans counted on ever-widening markets abroad for henequen. It was an era of frenzied speculation in haciendas and urban real estate at inflated prices. By 1907, the landed barons of Yucatán, as well as the merchants and bankers dependent on them for their well-being, were deeply in debt. When the henequen market shrank, partly as a result of the crisis of 1907 as well as competition of manila hemp from the Philippines, the speculative bubble burst. With money no longer available to fill their empty coffers, banks started to foreclose on their loans to merchants and planters. The banks that weathered the storm had to occupy bankrupt properties. The incapacity of planters, the principal beneficiaries of the bankers' largesse, to meet payments on their mortgages touched off widespread banking failures.

"Do not bite the hand that feeds you," runs the old adage. For Mexico, that hand was a Yankee one. Because of its export economy, and the Porfirista belief in the miracles of foreign capital, Mexico, for all intents and purposes, had become a colony of the colossus next door. The American presence was ubiquitous. In Coahuila, a hotbed of revolutionary fervor, one company, United States Rubber, controlled the guayule industry, the second-largest in the state after cotton. The Carbonífera del Norte, an American enterprise, owned the major coal mines, another the railroads, the biggest investment in the state. Large tracts of land were in American hands; Piedra Blanca, one of the holdings, embraced 1.2 million acres; San José de Piedras, 460,000 acres. That Mexicans might come to fear and resent this powerful alien presence seems logical if not inevitable.

Nationalism, a telling factor in the rebellion of 1910, contained a striking paradox. Mexico won acclaim in the Western world, as Bulnes warned cogently, because of foreign investments and markets.[9] Eventually, Mexicans, denied a place at the banquet table, put the blame for their exclusion on their guests. Their bitterness sparked a wave of xenophobia that colored the twilight years of the Old Regime and set the stage for the rebellion. Nationalist firebrands accused Díaz of selling off Mexico to foreigners, most of them Americans. From the cherished dream of ridding the country of alien potentates surfaced a strident cry of "México para los Mexicanos!" In its origins, the rebellion of 1910, wrote Bulnes, "had a marked Boxer character . . . against the influence and prestige of the United States." The battle against the Old Regime and that against foreign domination were one and the same.

Too late did Díaz, José Ives Limantour, and others of the school of "the need for foreign capitalists" come to realize what a mess they had on their hands. The charges of betrayal stung the old rulers, who from exile rushed to defend themselves and, by doing so, inadvertently testified to the truth of the charges levied against them. Unquestionably, Don Porfirio lived to regret the faith he had had in American capitalists. To the day of his death in France, he endeavored to vindicate himself. He told an Argentine reporter, "I was never a darling of the Yankee." To the contrary, his policies had advanced the Americans' desire to dominate Mexico. So too did Limantour, the man who set economic policy, come to question the wisdom of Mexico's reliance on its next-door neighbor. Americans, he concluded, wanted to transform Mexico into an economic and intellectual clone of the United States. He even wrote that Theodore Roosevelt, when president of the United States, had wanted to acquire Baja California and, if Mexico did not sell it, was willing to wage war to get it. Nor did Limantour believe that the Americans had stationed troops along the Mexican border just to halt the clandestine sale of arms to Mexican rebels. Moreover, Limantour wrote, he had opposed signing a new reciprocity agreement with the United States as demanded by its ambassador, as well as refusing to modify Mexico's banking and commercial legislation to conform to American practices.[10] On Limantour's advice, in 1906 Mexico purchased the controlling interest in the national railway system, thus closing the barn door after the horses had fled. After all, the railroads, more than any other institution, had solidified Mexico's export dependency.

III

Superficially, the Revolution, as it came to be called by its admirers, changed some things, but if one closely examines its aftermath, it was a failure in a major way, a lost opportunity because it left untouched the basic structure of dependency. Whatever the character of the revolt against Díaz, whether a collection of disparate uprisings, each responding to local and regional needs, or a national crusade, it failed to put to death what some Mexican scholars call the capitalism of underdevelopment, that is, reliance on foreign investment and markets for the export of primary goods.[11] The men at the tiller of the regime, the "revolutionary generals," some primitive and brutal though claiming to be civilized, were welcomed quickly by merchants, textile magnates, and *empresarios*, as well as hacendados who learned early that they had little to fear. Declarations of loyalty to the *Revolución* were soon forthcoming. Neither did the small "middle class" wish to upset the apple cart; it just wanted a piece of the pie. The rebel leaders, nonetheless, wanted to rid the country of the old political oligarchy and its military stooges, and doing this required the support of campesinos and workers, the men asked to fight and die in the battle against Díaz's soldiers. Frequently these men did not know for whom the bells tolled. To win their backing, concessions were made, but not on too large a scale, and the concessions ceased once the lower classes were subsumed into the modified system.[12]

Is this a cynical view, or a realistic one? For an answer, let's start by looking at the caudillos of the *Revolución*. Three men stand out: Francisco I. Madero, Venustiano Carranza, and Álvaro Obregón. On the surface, they were different, certainly in personalities. Be that as it may, they shared common characteristics. All came from the hacendado class. Madero, the scion of wealth, was more typical of the Porfirista hacendados, while Carranza and Obregón were less so. All three were natives of border states, Sonora and Coahuila, export-oriented provinces with economies joined to their northern neighbor. Neither of these two states had major industries; the men from Sonora, the ultimate winners, came from a state entirely dependent on its export-oriented economy, which relied for its prosperity on the sale of copper and other industrial metals to the United States and also on the sale of cash crops from the Mayo and Yaqui valleys to American consumers. None of the three was a complete outsider: the Maderos had been allies of Díaz, Carranza had been governor of his state, and Obregón, an up-and-coming garbanzo planter who never tired of casting aspersions on *los calzonudos,* the campesinos, hobnobbed with the gang in power in Sonora. Of the three, only Obregón was mildly liberal, though pragmatic. None championed agrarian reform, though Obregón and to some extent Carranza too went along with the need for it when it suited their purpose. So far as we know, none had industrialization and high tariffs high on his list of priorities, though Carranza, a fervent nationalist, stood for Mexican ownership of the country's natural resources, petroleum in particular.

We can begin with Madero; after all, he was the father of the Revolution. His wealthy family had a stake in the cotton plantations of La Laguna, banks, coal and silver mines, the wine and grape industry, guayule, and even a textile mill. Madero and his family had strong ties to the Porfiristas. None had made any attempt to hide their admiration for Díaz. You "honor me," Madero told Don Porfirio, "when you think of me as a friend." In 1908, he admitted that "our economic, industrial, commercial, and mining progress is undeniable." A laissez-faire capitalist, he believed in the rights of property, scorned the communal system of landholding, and admired the efficient and modern hacienda.[13] His economic policies differed little from those of the Porfiriato. When confronted with an empty treasury, like the Porfiristas before him, he negotiated a loan with New York banks. Nowhere, in either his writings or his speeches, did Madero call for a large internal market, without which no national industry can prosper.

Madero thought in terms reminiscent of nineteenth-century liberals, the admirers of Adam Smith and Edmund Burke. His cry of "effective suffrage and no reelection" failed to stir the hearts of landless campesinos.[14] Before an audience of workers, he declared that the "people did not ask for bread but for liberty," a pronouncement that surely fell on deaf ears. His platform hailed the ideals of the Constitution of 1857, spoke of free and honest elections, and banged the drums for municipal autonomy. The silence of Madero's Plan de San Luis Potosí on the land question was ominous. On social issues, Madero spoke of the need to uplift the material, intellectual, and moral condition of the worker, focused on the need to curb his drinking and gambling, and cited schools as a cure-all for public evils. Without revolutionary theory, to quote Vladimir Ilyich Lenin, on this subject a man of impeccable credentials, there can be no revolution. By this rule of thumb, Madero was woefully unprepared to lead a revolution or inspire social change designed to dismantle the old order.

Elected president in the first honest election in Mexican history, Madero lasted just long enough to get himself killed by the ruthless and brutal General Victoriano Huerta, with whom Madero had entrusted his life. Madero was well meaning but inept as a politico and leader. His demise set off a race to succeed him. Nearly three years of violence was unleashed by the "revolutionary" caudillos, as they came to be known, caudillos immortalized by Jorge Ibargüengoitia in his satiric novel *Los relámpagos de agosto,* who fought first to avenge Madero's murder by the rascally Huerta and then among themselves. By 1915, the Revolution had degenerated into a veritable state of anarchy. Out of the chaos Venustiano Carranza, with the help of Álvaro Obregón, emerged the victor, but not before untold enemies of the Revolution were left to die hung from telegraph poles, their tongues hanging out of their mouths. Among the vanquished were Emiliano Zapata, the agrarian chieftain, shot in the back by one of Carranza's lackeys, and Francisco Villa, whose revolutionary credentials are still being debated.

An old-fashioned Liberal, Carranza endorsed the ideals of Benito Juárez and José María Luis Mora, but he shaped them to fit the mold of a northern hacendado. A conservative, he believed in law and order and wanted men of his own ilk around him. Extremists of the left never won his confidence; Luis Cabrera, a close confidant and a lawyer with abiding faith in private property, best represented his chosen men. In his famous speech on September 1913, before an audience in Hermosillo, Carranza rated the loss of liberty the worst of Díaz's crimes and pledged a return to constitutional order. Without respect for life, liberty, and property, he told Congress in 1917, morality and individual rights, the substance of order, withered and died.[15]

Having matured amid the language of free trade and eulogies to Herbert Spencer, Carranza lived by the tenets of capitalist doctrine, believing that a healthy society thrived on competition. To him, the "protected industry, rather than an asset, was a burden," because, assured of easy profits, it grew fat and flabby. Competition hardened muscles and imbued industry with vigor and drive. Some industries might fall by the wayside, but they would have been of negligible benefit anyway. Nationalist considerations, for all that, tempered his admiration for classical dogma.[16] A nationalist at heart, Carranza awaited the day when Mexicans would own their natural resources. Out of necessity more than out of conviction, he embraced some tariffs advocated by protectionists. Nor did he ever ask for a foreign loan or take money from private individuals that might jeopardize Mexico's sovereignty.[17]

IV

In the winter of 1916, Carranza and his supporters, the rulers of Mexico, sat down in the city of Querétaro to write a national charter. When they convened, the moderate wing of the rebel factions answered the roll call; extremists, purged by their former allies, sat on the sidelines. The Constitutionalists at Querétaro, a small, urban middle class mainly, affixed their ideological seal on "revolutionary" Mexico. They were, above all, *licenciados,* lawyers, but also generals, schoolteachers, engineers, journalists, poets, writers, physicians, and store clerks, as well as Singer sewing machine salesmen. So far as it is known, no proponent of industrialization sat among them; the textile barons, solidly Porfiristas, had foolishly applauded the Huerta coup that had toppled Madero.[18] The Constitution of 1917, which these architects hailed as a brilliant political success, signaled the victory of moderates, descendents of the

Reforma and the Porfiriato. After weeks of debate, the delegates hammered out a blueprint that was often at odds with the dreams of Carranza, who wanted just to update the charter of 1857. Many of the ideals of nineteenth-century liberalism survived. On one fundamental point they differed: from then on an all-powerful state, the new Leviathan, would set the economic tone.

At the Convention of 1917, industrialization, tariffs, and the idea of a national market never topped the list of priorities. Rafael Nieto, undersecretary of the economy for Carranza and author of Article 28, the one reference to industry and monopolies, regarded himself as something of a free trader. He considered protectionist measures, the brainchild of monopolists, partly to blame for the plight of the consumer.[19] At his urging, the delegates banished tariffs and custom duties. Article 28 upheld free competition, banned monopolies, and warned that authorities would punish any attempt to raise the price of consumer goods.[20] Ironically, industrialists were given free rein to band together in monopolies for the purpose of exporting their goods to foreign customers. For a while the Carranza regime, hewing to a free-trade policy, lowered tariffs on certain types of cotton cloth, but at the behest of the textile industry, it backed down and restored the Porfirista system of selective duties.

The agrarian question, more than the future of industry, set the agenda at Querétaro. For the delegates, the turbulence and unrest in the countryside unleashed by the war against Huerta would disappear only by resolving the land issue. But in drafting the legislation for land reform, specifically Article 27, a prerequisite if Mexico were to have a large internal market and not a puny one, the constitutionalists were more orthodox than not. Even Francisco Mújica, who led the forces for change, shared Carranza's belief in private property; both looked upon it as the pillar of society. As Andrés Molina Enríquez, an acerbic consultant, pointed out, for these men the objective was to "defend, develop, and multiply small property," which would be the nucleus of a big and strong rural middle class. They consigned the *ejido*, the one exception to private property, to a secondary role, a tool, as one scholar writes, to pacify campesinos and establish communities of cheap labor for nearby haciendas.[21] Only a fringe demanded the expropriation and redistribution of the lands of hacendados and foreign landlords. Nearly every one of the delegates wanted the state to pay for property taken. Article 27, the land reform provision, excluded *peones acasillados* from the right to petition for land and called for the subdivision but not the disappearance of large property. The states would set the limits of private property; hacendados had to divest themselves of excess lands. If hacendados refused to sell, state officials had the authority to expropriate them, a hypocritical bit of hocus-pocus since the locals were usually in cahoots with hacendados. Congress and the state legislatures were to enact laws setting up guidelines for the subdivision of large property.

Article 27 also marched in tune with the slogan "México para los Mexicanos." In a return to Spanish legislation, both the land and the subsoil belonged to the Mexican nation. Foreigners had to obey Mexican laws, while government wielded the authority to review contracts and concessions made since 1876 that gave individuals and corporations monopolies of land, water, and mines and to nullify them when they were in conflict with the public interest. Only Mexicans, by birth or citizenship, and national corporations had the right to acquire mines or water or to exploit the subsoil. The state, nonetheless, had the power to grant concessions to anyone who agreed to abide by Mexican legislation.

Article 123, the labor code, whose enforcement would indirectly stimulate the internal market, called for a minimum wage and an eight-hour day, limited the type of work that could be done by women and children, and set aside Sunday as a day of rest, among other guarantees. It set up boards of arbitration and conciliation to oversee labor relations and gave workers the right to organize and join unions and the right to strike. Article 123 sought to establish an equilibrium between labor and capital. The state would supervise relations between labor and capital and decide what was in the public interest. Article 123 did not do away with classes, but simply made the state the protector of the worker, who presumably would be better off, although still a worker in a capitalist world.

On other issues, the revolutionaries of 1917, were no less "liberal" than their 1857 mentors. For its sin of coexisting with Don Porfirio's regime, the church got its comeuppance; Article 130 reaffirmed the separation of church and state, denied the church jurisdictional personality, and declared priests to be members of a profession. From then on, the church was subordinate to civil authority. States were authorized to regulate the number of priests, who had to be Mexicans by birth. Disappointingly, Article 3, the school provision, stated merely that "primary instruction in public institutions shall be free." Nothing guaranteed a national network of public schools or, incredibly, obligatory attendance. Worse yet, Justo Sierra's ministry of public instruction, an innovation of the final years of the Porfiriato, was thrown into the trash can. Supporting a concoction of centralized authority and regional autonomy, the delegates placed the implementation of Article 3 in the hands of states and municipalities, the least able or willing to carry it out.

V

The postrevolutionary era, the years from 1917 to the early thirties, did not alter the model of externally induced development. Mexico survived or, if you wish, endeavored to survive, relying, as before, on the production of minerals and raw materials for export, primarily to the United States, and employed profits to purchase manufactured goods, again mostly from the United States.

The revolutionaries inherited a troubled economy.[22] Paper currency, a legacy of the years of fighting, most of it not worth the paper it was printed on, flooded the country. A banking system in distress weakened the financial edifice, making a shambles of Mexico's international credit rating. Huge debts piled up, partly the result of damages claimed by foreigners, mainly Americans, who demanded repayment. Twice Mexico declared moratoriums on debt payments. Mining production, including copper, had dropped by a whopping 65 percent. Wages fell and unemployment rose, while shortages of food, part of the crisis in agriculture, drove prices skyward. Caught in the spiral of inflation, city dwellers never knew from one day to the next if they could make ends meet. The railroads, which carried the country's goods, lay wrecked, testimony to the ability of rival armies to blow up bridges and tear up track and rolling stock.

To the good fortune of Mexico's leaders, the copper industry began to recover by 1916, largely because of the demands of World War I, which also spurred exports of petroleum and the rise of an electrical industry.[23] During the 1920s, petroleum, copper, lead, and zinc, along with henequen, topped the list of exports. For most of these years, Alberto Pani, a fun-loving orthodox economist who collected European art, as well as women, served as economic czar and placed mining at the top of national priorities. Mining was an industry, he testified, that supplied jobs and salaries as well as revenue for the national treasury, but he overlooked, conveniently, that its owners, nearly all Americans, enjoyed the lion's share of the profits.[24]

The new rulers, recognizing that their survival required some concessions to the people, spoke of a government by and for the people, of a *revolución* considered unique in Mexican annals. Official jargon, all the same, neglected to spell out what was meant by *revolución,* beyond speaking of an uprising of hungry campesinos and angry workers led by noble leaders against an evil empire of rapacious hacendados, a greedy *burguesía,* and "imperialistic foreigners." As a term, *revolución* was left in a state of flux, employed to justify and explain government policy. Official propaganda pronounced the "revolutionary regimes" not to be *burgués* (bourgeois), without explaining what that meant, especially since the capitalist trappings of the Old Regime weathered the bombast.

To the despair of Mexicans, the European war ended in 1918. Sales of henequen toppled, and only oil and copper exports stayed up. Then an upturn in the economies of the United States and Western Europe helped Mexico to overcome its slump. Good times, however, proved fleeting; by 1926, Mexico had again fallen on hard times as the winds of the approaching Great Depression started to blow. In July, exports of petroleum fell, while Tlaloc again forgot to water the crops, making 1929 a terrible year for agriculture; one-fourth of the lands planted never yielded crops. Foreign investors sent their money home, spurring a wave of capital flight and a monetary crisis.

A cautious politician as well as a crafty poker player, Álvaro Obregón, who had lost an arm to a musket ball at the battle of Celaya (he would steal less, it was said, because he had only one hand with which to pilfer the till) and was president of Mexico in the early twenties, expressed sympathy for the underdog. But he believed in the survival of the fittest, wrote Martín Luis Guzmán in *El águila y la serpiente*.[25] His goal was to update Mexican capitalism. In its pursuit, he welcomed *empresarios*, bankers, merchants, and especially hacendados into the "revolutionary family." He looked upon Mexico and its neighbor across the Río Grande as sister nations, and he believed in private enterprise and the sacredness of property. It was time to let bygones be bygones; time had gone by and much water had flowed under the bridge. The Obregonistas, like their leader, acquired fortunes and, little by little, identified with the status quo, not destroying what was left of the Porfirista edifice but upholding it.

Corruption, whether in the old Porfirista style or in the revolutionary mold, had a field day.[26] Politicians as well as businessmen made fortunes on shady deals. In 1923, one of Obregón's cohorts told a journalist that of the twenty eight-governors, only two were honest, two were doubtful, and the rest corrupt. "*Compadre*," went a popular saying of that time, "I don't ask that you give me anything; just show me where the loot is." All the same, Obregón's administration was the first to enforce the articles of social content of the Constitution of 1917, albeit timidly. Former Zapatistas were allowed back into the ranks, but their ideals were placed on the back burner. Meanwhile, revolutionary Mexico was filled with former soldiers making a living off politics, their pockets stuffed with ill-gotten gains.

Plutarco Elías Calles, the next president by edict of Obregón, had deep roots in Sonora, where agrarian reform, outside of the Yaqui pueblos, had scant popular appeal. Despite his radical talk, he had little sympathy for campesinos. He looked with a jaundiced eye upon any attack on the tenets of capitalism. His successors, puppet rulers under him, endeavored to promote capitalist growth, warmly welcomed foreign investors, and sought to repair Mexico's tarnished credit rating and expand the country's trade with the outside world. What emerged was a plan to spur the familiar exports, an economy dependent on foreigners.

During these turbulent years, Mexicans had to deal with a truculent Uncle Sam.[27] From the days of William H. Taft's presidency, Washington had warily watched the unfolding Mexican drama and had set limits on the degree of reform the rebels might expect to carry out without outside interference. Any attack on international capital, Woodrow Wilson told Carranza, "was no less than an attack on democracy and civilization itself." Carranza would be well advised not to attempt to enforce the Constitution of 1917. Regardless of what Mexican law might say, Washington, along with London and Paris, claimed the right to intervene on behalf of their nationals. Ironically, with few exceptions, the revolutionaries had no quarrel with the principle of foreign investment; they coveted it. At no time did they ask Americans, the principal investors, to leave or to stop investing their money in Mexico.

Oil was the eye of the hurricane.[28] The Carrancistas, voicing nationalist sentiments, had started to step on foreign toes. Needing funds, they raised the tax on petroleum, but timidly, to merely a fourth of what the oil companies paid in the United States; a subsequent hike in 1917 made it clear that Mexico had ended Díaz's exemptions. Between 1911 and 1921, the golden age of Mexican oil, only the United States produced more. The bonanza spelled trouble for Mexico because as petroleum revenues spiraled upward, so did national dependency on them. Meanwhile, Carranza attempted to enforce Article 27 of the Constitution, which declared that the subsoil, including petroleum, belonged to Mexico. But Washington rejected this interpretation, refusing to exchange, as Carranza asked, titles to petroleum properties for state concessions. When Uncle Sam labeled Mexico's decision confiscation, Carranza, fearful of armed intervention, left his edict unenforced.

Washington did not shed tears when Carranza was ambushed and killed in cold blood by Obregón's lackeys in a forlorn village, but neither did it embrace the "Sonorenses," as the dynasty from that state came to be known. It refused to recognize the interim administration of Adolfo de la Huertas, a would-be opera singer and ally of Obregón from Sonora, unless the administration rejected Carranza's interpretation of Article 27. Cowed by Washington's bellicose behavior, the Sonorenses capitulated but said that they would accede to the demands only after receiving formal recognition. The Americans, knowing they held the high cards in this poker game, rejected the compromise, leaving the Sonorenses in a quandary; lacking Washington's blessings, they could not repair Mexico's international credit rating. Without a repaired credit rating, their government had not a ghost of a chance of survival. By the same token, to bow to Washington's demand in the face of Mexican nationalist fervor would mean, most likely, the end of the Sonorenses. The clan had to assure the United States "through sovereign acts that its acquired rights would be respected" and thus convince it that no need existed for a formal treaty, which would have been anathema to Mexican nationalists. The Sonorenses had to resolve the petroleum impasse and begin payments on Mexico's debt, owed mainly to American banks. They were dealing from weakness because the rocky economy of the early twenties, which cut into exports, put the burden on petroleum. Using the pliant Mexican Supreme Court to unveil the government's conciliatory stance, the justices declared Article 27 nonretroactive. The ruling, nonetheless, failed to convince the American oil tycoons, who asked Washington to withhold recognition of Obregón's government, which by now had replaced De la Huerta's.

Failing to win over Washington, which spoke for the stubborn oil barons, the Obregonistas decided to court American bankers and merchants, dangling markets and pledges of repayment before them. By the terms of the De la Huerta–Lamont Agreements of June 1922, Mexico had acknowledged an obligation of 500 million dollars and promised to pay 30 million dollars annually for four years, almost a fourth of the yearly national income, and to pay more after that. The pledge cut deeply into social reform. Despite this, Washington held out for a formal treaty of capitulation. By the Bucareli Agreements of 1923, Washington got it. The Obregonistas declared Article 27 nonretroactive when owners of the oil fields had taken "positive" acts before 1917, and they also acknowledged the validity of American claims against Mexico, dating as far back as 1868. As a concession, Washington let stand Mexico's insistence that titles to oil properties be exchanged for almost indefinite concessions. Uncle Sam then conferred diplomatic recognition on Obregón, but at the cost of subverting further Mexican sovereignty and undermining reform.[29]

The embrace of the Yankee lasted only briefly. Petroleum output had begun to decline by 1922, and when it took a nosedive after 1925, Plutarco Elías Calles, another Sonorense and now president, blamed the oil barons, believing that their companies, unhappy with Mexican nationalists, had decided to punish his country by shifting the focus of their activities to Venezuela, in that way telling Mexico to make additional concessions or face the consequences. In response, the Callistas declared Mexico's ownership of the subsoil "inalienable" and limited concessions to fifty years. Unable to get its way, Washington, until then a vociferous bully, turned sly fox, sending to Mexico Dwight Morrow from the house of J. P. Morgan of Wall Street. As a banker, he wanted Mexico to pay its debts and shelve talk of social reform at the expense of foreign capitalists. Oil was not uppermost on his mind; on that issue Morrow could be flexible. So in 1928, Calles, in those days confronted with an uprising of Catholic fanatics known as Cristeros, had the always pliant Mexican Supreme Court uphold an appeal from the oil companies and rule Article 27 nonretroactive and limits on property concessions unlawful. Morrow went on to persuade Calles to downplay nationalistic legislation, to open wide the doors to foreign investors, to curb labor demands, to balance the budget, and to pay off Mexico's international debt. This relegated social reform to limbo. When the Great Depression cut into Mexico's revenues and the cost of putting down a military revolt in 1929 drove it to the edge of bankruptcy, which jeopardized repayment of its debts, Morrow, with the aid of Wall Street bankers, proffered a loan. For forty-five years, Mexico would make annual payments of 12.5 million dollars. So improved were relations between Mexico and the United States that Herbert Hoover, a businessman's president, likened them to the friendly ties of Don Porfirio.

While all of this was taking place, what there was of Mexican industry, despite a brief downturn from 1914 to 1916, had recovered from the slight damage wrought by rebels. The violence of the war years had left intact the country's industrial plant, perhaps because of its unimportance in the eyes of the revolutionaries. The swift recovery of industrial output evidenced the nonradical nature of the heralded *Revolución.* So too did the resurgence of foreign investment, along with the arrival of an assembly plant of the Ford Motor Company, plus DuPont and Palmolive plants, all looking for ways to surmount tariff walls. All of the old monopolies survived, as did their reliance on foreign machinery and technology. Foreigners controlled nearly all of the textile industry, the oldest and most developed. The old monopolies still held sway. The *Revolución,* writes one scholar, "rather than tearing down the industrial structure of the Porfiriato, reinforced it."[30] From 1918 to 1925, industrialists reaped big profits, roughly twice that of earlier years. Until the eve of the Great Depression, the barons of industry, though unwilling to invest in their factories, simply went on being rich.

During these decades, Alberto Pani, as head of the ministry of hacienda, had the tiller of the economy in his hands, and he nearly became president in 1932. A classical economist, but not a devotee of laissez-faire, so he claimed, he believed in capitalism but not in the right of voracious *empresarios* to exploit others. A free trader, he thought it a mistake to protect industries that could not survive on their own. Unhampered competition, he explained in *Política hacendaria de la Revolución,* would rid Mexican industry of its "diapers." Industries built behind tariff walls would be given time to stand on their own feet but sooner or later had to compete on the international market. Still, tariffs on imports were a much-needed source of federal revenue. And for all of his criticism of the Old Regime, Pani, like José Ives Limantour, the old Porfirista, wanted foreign capital to help develop Mexico, a blueprint that surely limited the ability of Mexican officials to enact basic social change.[31] For his part, Calles, who ran Mexican affairs for a decade as president and then as *Jefe Máximo,* saw no future for a capital goods industry. Rather, he believed in a future, like the past, based on the exports of industrial and precious metals, agricultural produce, and petroleum. To help this future along, Pani, as head of hacienda, devalued the peso, thus spurring exports, and by making foreign goods more costly, he curtailed imports.

But Calles's ideas, which Pani either authored or carried out, were a self-fulfilling prophecy: they not only discouraged the development of a modern industry but, along with the failure to rid the country of the notorious hacienda, left the rural population, the majority of Mexicans, desperately poor, unable to help form the internal market that a national industry required. Ironically, in a *Revolución* fought supposedly on behalf of exploited campesinos, agrarian reform was more dream than reality. Haciendas still dotted the countryside, and debt peonage was alive and well. The neglect dated from the days of Venustiano Carranza, who had manipulated the promise of land reform for political ends. To triumph, Carranza and his followers had to win over campesinos, firmly in Zapata's camp. Largely out of necessity, Carranza gave his blessings to a measure of land reform, but for all intents and purposes, he safeguarded haciendas from expropriation. Obregón and Calles, more inclined to heed pleas for land, did so when compelled to do so by circumstances beyond their control, Obregón to help quell the revolt of his generals in 1923 and Calles to squelch the Cristero rebellion. Neither wanted to break up the big estates. In the census of 1930, just 1.5 percent of the landlords owned 97 percent of rural property. In that year, Calles returned from a trip to Europe convinced that agrarian reform had been a terrible mistake. It was time to call a halt to the nonsense. In his *Política hacendaria,* Pani, ready to speak the truth when it suited his purposes, admitted that little had been done to help the poor, who might have strengthened the internal market.[32]

SEVEN Internal Market

I

An international crisis may, if the powerful bleed from their own wounds, provide a chance, especially for peripheral countries, to reshape policies. Such a chance befell Mexico in the 1930s, when, thanks to the Great Depression—a malady of the capitalist West and a sledgehammer blow to the economy of the almighty Uncle Sam—Mexico had the opportunity to rethink old habits and, more important, to change course.

The international debacle, long before it wreaked havoc in other Western nations, savaged Mexico, turning topsy-turvy an economy reeling from years of strife. Export earnings plummeted, with petroleum and mining hit hardest. A similar catastrophe struck the country's farms. As exports dropped, so did the national income, by 25 percent between 1929 and 1933, and consequently the value of the peso also dropped. Not only did exports decline by almost 50 percent between 1928 and 1930, but a downturn in the term of trade, particularly for agricultural products, slashed revenues more.[1] For the poor, particularly those whose livelihood depended on the export sector, the times were catastrophic. At Cananea, the copper emporium of the Republic, half of the miners were unemployed. At Nacozari and Pilares, two other camps in Sonora, all the miners lost their jobs when the Moctezuma Copper Company shut down. When sales collapsed, factories closed their doors, leaving the jobless to fend for themselves. In Toluca, capital of the big state of Mexico, the Toluca y México brewery went out of business, one of many to do so, as did the textile mills in María de Otzolotepec, San Ildefonso de Nicolás Romero, and San Pedro de Zinacatepec. In the towns and cities of Jalisco, armies of the jobless begged for work, while the return of Mexicans deported from the United States exacerbated the unemployment rate. Facing a budget deficit, authorities cut salaries of bureaucrats, adding to middle-class unrest. The ranks of the jobless tripled between 1930 and 1932.[2] The poor were not merely worse off than before but more numerous.

To complicate matters, the harvests of Mexico's two basic crops fell on hard times. In 1933, Mexico produced 30 percent less corn and 22 percent fewer beans than in 1907, the last of the good years. Per capita consumption of corn, the mainstay of the popular diet, dropped from 136 kilograms to 88. Meanwhile, commercial agriculture took a nose dive. With the end of the war in Europe, demand for cotton and henequen petered out. As their markets shrunk, so did lands under cultivation. When textile mills slashed production and let workers go, cotton planters reduced the size of their crops and cut their labor force, a formula adopted by henequen hacendados, their difficulties augmented by competing fibers from Africa and the Philippines. The brunt of this decline fell on the backs of labor. Hardest hit were commercial zones with the bulk of jobs. Difficult times spawned labor unrest. Strikes flared from one end of the Republic to the other. In Mexico State, a skip and jump from the National Palace, workers, risking the ire of politicos and business owners, went on strike, while campesinos occupied hacienda lands.[3]

Reluctantly at first, after it became virtually impossible to borrow from foreigners and markets for exports dried up, Mexico's leaders began to reassess the export-oriented model, one that like drug addiction requires constant infusions.[4] These were years when Mexican economists avidly read Karl Marx and John Maynard Keynes and learned that full employment required state intervention. Mexican social reform, however, is one of those national oxymorons, like Italian Protestantism or British cooking, of which nothing much is expected. But somehow, once in a while that threadbare tradition finds a spokesman who reaches out beyond the narrow confines of his adherents to strike a chord in the larger society. Such a man was Lázaro Cárdenas, called upon to rethink the model of external development and replace it with an internally driven one.

Why did Cárdenas modify or, better still, alter course? Given his background, an answer is hard to find, because he was neither well read nor a master of economic theory. He had no schooling beyond the primary grades, nor were the men he relied on always economists. A singular man in many respects, he loved horses, plants, and water. Neither tall nor short of stature, he did not smoke, drink liquor, or dress stylishly, and unless far from home, he ate breakfast and dinner with his family. He hailed from Jiquilpan, a town in Michoacán, its name signifying "a place of flowers" in Purépecha, the local Indian tongue. Jiquilpan lived off the weaving of *rebozos* (shawls) in blue and black, tightly knit woolen sarapes, leather huaraches, and the tanning of hides, all done at home. It was a poor town; many of its one thousand inhabitants farmed lands as sharecroppers or cultivated tiny parcels of rocky soil of their own. The people of Jiquilpan, like most natives of Michoacán, including Cárdenas's mother, worshiped at the Catholic altar. Yet Cárdenas, neither an intellectual nor a flaming radical by any means, somehow had an incredible clarity about what was right. There were things in Mexican society that were rotten to the core and needed fixing.

Jiquilpan had a land problem. On the road to Chapala and Guadalajara stood the hacienda of Guaracha, the property of Don Diego Moreno. One of the richest haciendas in Mexico, Guaracha dated from colonial times, when African slaves cultivated sugar cane on its lands. On its outskirts lay the haciendas of Cerro Pelón, Platanal, Cerrito Colorado, Guarachita, San Antonio, Las Arquillas, El Sabino, Guadalupe, Las Ordeñas, and Capadero—all more or less part of Guaracha. Don Diego did not know exactly how much land he owned. His holdings included a sugar mill, twenty thousand head of cattle, as well as horses, mules, and sheep. Don Diego's labor force, which largely consisted of sharecroppers, cultivated sugar cane for the manufacture of sugar and alcohol, as well as wheat, corn, and alfalfa for the markets of Guadalajara and Mexico City. Don Diego, and afterward his son, spent little time on the hacienda, preferring Guadalajara and Europe.

On March 25, 1895, Cárdenas was born into this world. His father, Dámaso, was the son of a soldier, a native of Jalisco, who married a girl from Jiquilpan and stayed there, at first making his living as a campesino and weaver of *rebozos.* In time, Dámaso became the proprietor of La Reunión de Amigos, a small store, and because he could read, he also became a *curandero,* or healer. By then Dámaso had married and sired a family; the eldest was Lázaro. The family resided on San Francisco, the main street in Jiquilpan, in one of the biggest houses in town, the bequest of a well-off grandmother and distant aunt of Felicitas del Río, mother of the Cárdenas clan.

At the age of six, Lázaro enrolled in a private school, but after two years he transferred to a public one in Jiquilpan, where its sole teacher, Don Hilario de Jesús Fajardo, worshiped José María Morelos and Benito Juárez and talked of the heroes who fought against the clergy and the French invaders. To Fajardo's school came the sons of the artisans, merchants, and rancheros of Jiquilpan, the better-off. Shy and not talkative, qualities that earned him the sobriquet the Sphinx of Jiquilpan, young Cárdenas preferred the company of older men, known as *banqueros,* who spent their time seated on the benches of the Plaza Zaragoza, the town square. As he grew older, Cárdenas found a job in the tax collector's office in Jiquilpan. After his father's death, he became the assistant to the secretary of the prefect, the political boss of the district. In June 1913, Cárdenas, then sixteen years old, went off to fight Victoriano Huerta, the usurper, and had a long and distinguished military career, fighting under many of the Revolution's famous military chieftains, including Plutarco Elías Calles. From then on, Cárdenas rode the coattails of Calles, who considered him one of his loyal *muchachos,* and he should have, because Cárdenas served at his master's pleasure.

Cárdenas had few peers as a politico. He always knew which way the winds blew. He was a *politico a la mexicana;* when necessary, he bent with the wind, looked the other way when his companions dipped their hands into the public coffer, and rarely questioned the wisdom of his superiors. With intimate knowledge of the jungle of Mexican politics, he kept his guard up and spoke only when spoken to. Cárdenas, the people who knew him say, was *desconfiado,* wary and distrustful, a man who wanted to control his own decisions. All the same, he felt the poverty and exploitation of the poor profoundly, the condition of campesinos above all. His policies as governor of Michoacán, a term he began in 1928, provide an insight into this complex man.

When Cárdenas arrived in Morelia, the capital of the state, he faced the united opposition of hacendados, clergy, and Cristeros, the Catholic fanatics then battling the federal government. To deal with them, and bring his allies under one roof, Cárdenas organized the Confederación Regional Michoacana del Trabajo. Made up mainly of campesinos, it included a smattering of workers, public employees, university students, and teachers. By 1932, Cárdenas's last year as governor, the *confederación* had one hundred thousand members, plus four thousand agrarian committees. Beyond that, Cárdenas organized the *ejidos,* many the result of his land reform program, into armed rural defense units.

But Cárdenas kept political power to himself. As "honorary president," he presided over the meetings of the *confederación* and helped finance it. Both profited: Cárdenas won a popular base of support in Michoacán, which he could use against Mexico City, and the members of the *confederación,* in turn, had agrarian and labor reform. In reality, Cárdenas co-opted the leaders of the *confederación.* They became members of the state legislature, the national Congress, or *ayuntamientos* (town councils), and on occasion they sat on the courts. The backing of the *confederación* converted Cárdenas into one of the provincial caudillos to be reckoned with in an era when rifles often ran politics. With the *confederación* behind him, Cárdenas climbed the political ladder to become head of the Partido Nacional Revolucionario (PNR) and then became the secretary of war. By 1932 he was one of that select body of men who, with Calles, governed Mexico.

Cárdenas won the presidency with an eclectic band of supporters. Despite his reform credential, he had antagonized no major rival on the political scene. He had the backing of key caudillos, among them

Saturnino Cedillo, boss of San Luis Potosí. Thanks to him, Cárdenas's quest for the presidency received the blessings of the Confederación Nacional Campesina, the most important in Mexico. When Cárdenas became the popular favorite, Calles, the *Jefe Máximo,* chose to back him. His election was a foregone conclusion; the PNR ruled, not the people. Just the same, Cárdenas, despite being certain of election, traveled the length and breadth of the Republic, the first political candidate to do so. His travels took him by horseback to countless villages, to pueblos whose inhabitants spoke no Spanish. The times, meanwhile, had taken on a rosy hue for the Cardenistas: sales of cash crops for export rose, the gross national product climbed upward, and the economy improved.

The job ahead was formidable. Despite the Revolution, the traditional interests had stayed alive, if not in the saddle, determined to keep their wealth and privileges. Hacendados, kingpins under the Old Regime, controlled rural Mexico, and they were now joined by "revolutionary generals" turned hacendados, many of whom were now governors or military heads of provinces and were as opposed to agrarian reform as the most reactionary of the Porfiristas. Landless peons with negligible buying power inhabited much of the countryside, and Indian campesinos were no less penniless.[5] Corrupt bosses headed what passed for labor unions, one and all beholden to politicos in Mexico City and *empresarios* who admired the dictates of the Old Regime. Over this scene presided Plutarco Elías Calles, the *Jefe Máximo,* who had made his peace with the rich and powerful, Washington among them, and now looked askance at any sign of revolutionary unrest. If change were to come, Cárdenas must rid Mexico of Calles and his henchmen, roll back the power of the hacendados, curb Washington's meddling, and revive the dormant Revolution. It was a herculean challenge.

Under the Cardenistas, big government sat at the tiller of the ship of state. The formula adopted led to a "mixed economy," using state intervention to promote economic growth and retool the productive structure so that it would respond to internal demand. Believing that it could not be implemented without his consent, Calles, the *Jefe Máximo,* accepted the Plan Sexenal of 1934, an ambitious six-year plan of reform, because of rising labor unrest. One goal of the plan was to build up the internal market and thus give a boost to industry.[6] Mexico would have land reform, an *ejido* system, and loans for *ejidatarios* and small farmers. The plan also provided guarantees for "authentic small property." Of tremendous importance, the plan gave *peones acasillados* the right to petition for the lands of their haciendas, which sounded the death knell of the haciendas. The plan also upheld labor's right to organize and strike. Highly nationalistic, it called for the enforcement of legislation dealing with the subsoil, specifically petroleum and mining. For Cárdenas, agrarian reform was an integral part of a model of economic development, but hardly revolutionary. The future, Cárdenas affirmed, would be capitalistic but with a soul.[7]

Cárdenas inherited a Mexico where nearly three out of every four economically active Mexicans labored in rural areas. Fewer than 15 percent had jobs in industry, which included mining and petroleum, and only 5.5 percent in commerce. Just 3.5 percent of the farmland had been given to campesinos. Land reform started in the Laguna, a cotton belt lying mainly in Coahuila, where the Nazas and Aguanaval rivers watered rich alluvial soil, ideal for planting cotton. The Tlahualilo and Rapp-Sommer y Purcell companies were the biggest of the conglomerates in the Laguna. "Revolutionary" generals had also acquired haciendas, among them Eulogio Ortiz, who, after being stripped of his ill-acquired lands, uttered the much-quoted statement "The Revolution gave me my lands and the Revolution took them away." Aside from Torreón, two more cities straddled the Laguna: San Pedro, once home to Francisco I. Madero, and Gómez Palacio; 125,000 inhabitants dwelled in the area, nearly all, in one way or another, linked to the cotton industry. The hacendados employed, in about equal numbers, both wage workers, many of whom lived in the nearby cities, and *peones acasillados.*

The time was ripe for change. The Great Depression and a prolonged drought had led to social unrest; workers had gone on strike, threatening the cotton harvest. In response, the hacendados had imported *esquiroles* (scabs). Cárdenas spent the summer of 1936 in Torreón, supervising the expropriation of the haciendas. When it was over, more than thirty-four thousand campesinos had land; 73 percent of the irrigated lands had been given to them. The rest, about 70,000 hectares, were subdivided into plots of 150 hectares for distribution among dispossessed hacendados, sharecroppers, and *colonos*. The Cardenistas did not simply carve up the Laguna. They organized it into a giant collective *ejido;* the goal was to redistribute the land of the haciendas but leave their productive capacity undisturbed, keeping intact the economies of scale. The *Banco Ejidal* would provide credit, offer technical assistance, and oversee operations. The collective *ejido* of the Laguna became the forerunner of similar ones, "islands of socialism floating in a sea of capitalism."[8]

Yucatán's turn came next. Henequen, once the state's golden crop, sat in the doldrums; with markets closing and prices falling, production had dropped. Not illogically, private investors, both Mexicans and foreigners, showed no interest in Yucatán, to the sorrow of its three hundred thousand inhabitants, a multitude of them jobless. To alleviate discontent, state authorities had earlier redistributed 30 percent of the henequen lands. In the biggest single act of land redistribution in the history of Mexico, Cárdenas granted the campesinos more of the *henequenales,* as the fields were called. The henequen haciendas had been banished from the face of Yucatán, replaced, in the manner of the Laguna, by 272 collective *ejidos.* The *desfibradoras,* the rasping machines that shredded henequen into fiber, went with them. To maintain the unity of henequen production, the Cardenistas established a henequen "trust" run by campesinos and "small farmers," the former hacendados.

Cárdenas was not through altering the Republic's landownership map. In Mexicali, capital of Baja California Norte, Cárdenas expropriated the cotton plantations of the Colorado River Land Company, converting it into *ejidos.* In 1937, too, El Mante and Santa Barbara, the haciendas of Calles in Tamaulipas, went to their workers. Then the axe fell on the hacendados of Los Mochis, the rich Fuerte River valley of Sinaloa. In 1938, the Dante Cusi family, originally from Italy, lost Nueva Lombardía and Nueva Italia, haciendas growing rice and citrus fruits in Michoacán. Guaracha, fiefdom of Diego Moreno, also felt the axe. Both Nueva Lombardía and Nueva Italia became collective *ejidos.* In 1939, some of the coffee planters of Chiapas, notorious for their ill treatment of their workers, lost their lands.[9]

When Cárdenas entered the National Palace, just 6 percent of the Republic's land had been redistributed; in six years, he added another

12 percent, a good part of it fertile. Virtually by his own hand, Cárdenas had distributed nearly 18.4 million hectares of land to over 1 million campesino families. By 1940, there were over 1.5 million *ejidatarios.* They were the owners of nearly half of the arable land and constituted nearly 42 percent of the agricultural population. At the same time, the percentage of landless laborers dropped from 68 to 36 percent. Of equal importance, the farmers on the collective *ejidos,* as well as those on lands restored to pueblos, had doubled the value of the country's agricultural output. Given equal access to fertile land, water, credit, and the right equipment, the *ejido,* as well as the small farm, could be more productive than the hacienda.[10]

But Cárdenas also made social justice a priority, not the least for the Indian.[11] The case of Sonora, where he returned to the Yaquis seventeen thousand hectares of irrigated lands stolen from them at the point of a rifle by the Porfiristas, serves as an example. Also, wanting closer ties with the indigenous population, and to show them that the president of Mexico cared, Cárdenas convoked regional meetings of Indian groups and never failed to attend, listening and asking questions. For the first time in Mexico's history, a national leader had taken an interest in the forgotten Indian. Dirt farmers, many of them Indians, needed schools, according to an axiom of the Cardenistas, so rural education, neglected since the twenties, became a priority once again. A "hungry Indian cannot be turned into a good scholar," it was said, nor, it can be added, into a consumer. Indian parents, once enamored of schooling, had started to question its efficacy. In isolated pueblos, children either dropped out of school early or stayed home to help with the chores. Because children must eat, an old Indian told the teacher in Gregorio Lopez y Fuentes's *El India,* a popular novel of those days, time "was wasted going back and forth to school." When "there is not enough to eat, schools are a luxury."[12] Familiar with their plight, Cárdenas sought to improve the quality of the special schools for Indians. Then, in a bold departure from past practices, he organized the Autonomous Department of Indian Affairs, a cabinet-level office, to handle all of their needs.

A dynamic capitalist sector in the countryside emerged out of agrarian reform, adding thousands of consumers to the country's rolls.[13] Formerly landless campesinos had money to spend and, along with a multiplying number of urban dwellers, enlarged the size of the home market. Consequently, the possibility of a home industry emerged, opening the way for the process known as import substitution. The government's role—enlarged many times by the needs of the rejuvenated agrarian sector and, after 1938, management of the petroleum industry, which was nationalized by Cárdenas—added to the federal payroll agronomists, engineers, architects, physicians, clerks, and secretaries. Intellectuals, never ones to reject public jobs, seldom failed to proffer their wisdom in return for one of them. Some of the recipients of land went on to swell the ranks of a rural middle class. Economic growth, which, with the exception of the World War I years, had stagnated until 1935, hovered around 8 percent during the Cardenista years.

Industry, too, profited. Cárdenas believed that Mexico had to industrialize; to that I can attest. In 1950, when I was doing research for a doctoral thesis, I had been in Michoacán visiting Indian schools with the help of Angélica Castro, an anthropologist and head of the Indian language program of the ministry of education. We were in Pátzcuaro at the home of a teacher in one of the Indian schools, who one day remarked that he had just seen General Cárdenas in Uruapan, a nearby city. Angélica asked if I would like to meet El General. Of course, I replied, jumping at the chance to talk to the man I so much admired. The next day we drove to Uruapan. Cárdenas then headed the Comisión del Río Balsas, a federal water agency in Michoacán. When we arrived, just about noon, we found ourselves among hundreds of campesinos and politicos from Mexico City waiting to talk to El General. How, I wondered, would I ever get the opportunity to see him? Angélica, however, was not fazed. She made her way through the crowd to the office of a *licenciado* (lawyer) in charge of appointments, as it turned out a close friend of both Cárdenas and Angélica. "Don't worry," he assured us. "I will speak to El General." That done, he disappeared to return to tell us that I had an appointment for that afternoon and that El General had asked him to take us to lunch.

At the much-anticipated meeting, I shook hands with General Cárdenas and spent an hour or so asking questions about contemporary Mexico. These were the days of the presidency of Miguel Alemán, held in high esteem by the *burguesía,* who had tossed into the wastebasket the agrarian promises of the Revolution and had given free rein to business owners who wanted to industrialize Mexico. In the opinion of the old Cardenistas, Alemán had betrayed the Revolution. These were also the days when new industrial blueprints were being hotly debated, when men such as Luis Chávez Orozco, a rabid Cardenista, distinguished historian, and former head of the Autonomous Department of Indian Affairs, wanted Cárdenas to speak up and call for a return to an agrarian elixir. I asked General Cárdenas what he thought of current policy. An astute politico, and loyal to the political party he helped form, Cárdenas, no friend of Alemán, did not speak ill of him, but insisted that Mexico must industrialize, though, he emphasized, not in the manner that it was being done. What he lamented, obviously, was that Alemán had given corrupt politicos and grasping, profit-hungry business owners, the monopolists of yesterday and today, a free hand to exploit the people of Mexico. Cárdenas also had by his side Narciso Bassols as minister of hacienda, a fierce critic of nineteenth-century Liberalism, who believed that a national industry had scant chance of taking root in Mexico unless the purchasing power of rural Mexicans took on new life. Nor did Bassols think highly of the idea that foreign investment offered Mexicans a way out of the economic doldrums, especially if investors took home more than they brought in. Cárdenas and his advisors wanted to put the horse, the consumer, before the manufacturer's cart. Industrialization needed to be built from the bottom up, by creating a mass of consumers. Agrarian reform was a step on the path toward that goal.[14]

That Cárdenas, an agrarian reformer, espoused industrialization should not shock anyone. He had witnessed time and time again the poverty and misery of landless campesinos dependent for their livelihood on an antiquated agrarian structure of heartless hacendados and their allies. He was a fierce nationalist, perhaps because he recalled his days as military commander of the Huasteca, a region rich in petroleum, where Americans flouted Mexican laws and exploited Mexican workers. At the time of the petroleum expropriation, Cárdenas said that he wished to free Mexico from its reliance on "imperialistic capital." He wanted limits set on the foreign ownership of Mexican resources and recognized that reliance on the exports of primary goods placed Mexico at the mercy of outsiders. Nor did Cárdenas believe that paying off the foreign debt should take precedence over the needs of Mexicans.[15]

Ironically, during the Cardenista years, manufacturing was a star performer, the fastest-growing sector of the economy, with a 25 percent increase in industrial production.[16] The devaluation of the peso made imports more expensive, helping protect domestic industries from outside competition and also spurring local manufacturing. For example, Mexican cement drove foreign competitors out of the local market. From then on, theoretically at least, the internal market would help propel the economy. Funds spent on public works—roads and irrigation projects, a feature of the Cardenista years—helped industry prosper, especially cement and steel. Earlier, the Nacional Financiera, a kind of development bank, had been established by the Callistas.[17] Cárdenas added the Instituto Politécnico Nacional, a rival of the stodgy National University, to prepare engineers, chemists, physicists, and others to advance the technology of Mexico. That said, the character of exports did not change: minerals and petroleum made up two-thirds of them.

Not unexpectedly, the Cardenista reforms sparked angry opposition from conservatives. One unexpected but logical antagonist was the embittered Calles, no longer enamored of revolutionary change. Cárdenas, to the surprise of nearly everyone, sent him packing. *Empresarios,* unwilling to make the slightest concessions to labor, were up in arms, especially in Monterrey, their heartland. In 1936, when a strike, partly over low wages, broke out in the Vidriera de Monterrey, the Republic's biggest glass factory, its owners, the Garza-Sada clan, mounted antilabor demonstrations, calling both labor and the Cardenistas Communists. Local business magnates, clasping hands with the Garza-Sadas, locked out their workers, despite a ruling to the contrary by the Department of Labor. When Cárdenas, who sided with the workers, confronted the *empresarios,* he told them that if they were tired of the social struggle, they could hand over their factories to the workers or to the government.[18]

Later, when workers in the petroleum fields asked for higher wages and benefits, a strike erupted after the foreign oil companies said no.

When the companies refused to budge, Cárdenas, by the stroke of his pen, expropriated the properties of Royal Dutch Shell and Standard Oil; for the first time, the nationalist vows of Article 27 had carried the day. Whether the oil barons thought Cárdenas a Communist, as the *empresarios* of Monterrey apparently did, is not known, but they surely had no desire to eat crow handed to them by the chief of a peripheral country. Washington and the oil barons took their pound of flesh, doing what they could to prevent the sale of Mexican petroleum to Latin America and stopping the purchase of Mexican silver by their Treasury Department. From the two confrontations, Mexican workers emerged with higher wages and better benefits, and the internal market enjoyed a shot of adrenalin. The dream of domestic growth helped drive Cárdenas and his allies. Petroleum would spur national development; supply gasoline for autos assembled in Mexico and as well as trucks; power water, electrical and fertilizer plants; help produce plastics and chemicals; and update the railroads.

As to Cárdenas's political views, he was no more of a Communist than was Franklin Delano Roosevelt. Neither was he anticapitalist; rather, he was a nationalist with a social conscience who wanted capitalism with a human face. The times were ripe for him to stand up to both the bully *empresarios* and the arrogant oil companies. As a young man, José López Portillo, destined to be president, proudly recalled how Cárdenas had expropriated the petroleum properties of Standard Oil and Royal Dutch Shell, but he lamented how much of the middle class, even students at the national university, who applauded the move initially, had subsequently turned against Cárdenas.[19] Unable to visualize a Mexico independent of Uncle Sam, the *burgueses* were terribly frightened.

II

Hopes for a less dependent economy, one less inclined to worship at the shrine of the markets of others, a society with a bit of social justice for campesinos and workers, gave birth to an artistic and literary renaissance. Its writers and artists antedated the Cardenista years, the "revolutionary" ones; their endeavors saw the light of day during the ambivalent times of the Sonorenses. They were ahead of their times. Not until the Cardenista regime did economists and politicos join hands with artists, writers, and intellectuals.

As I have argued earlier, the behavior of intellectuals reflects and reinforces the contours of a society. Intellectuals are a barometer of their society, as Diego Rivera, the great muralist, asserted. It is only when people rebel, whether with paint or in print, that they emerge to stand alongside the exploited. What they say, what they write, and what they paint provide insights into the nature of a society. We learn much about a society by analyzing its literature and art. One advocate of such a view was Antonio Gramsci, whose thoughts on intellectuals in capitalist societies pervade his *Prison Notebooks*.[20] As one critic theorized, this may, in part, reflect the special conditions in Italy before the advent of the unified state in 1870. Given those conditions, Italian language, literature, and culture, the offspring of intellectuals, took on greater importance, perhaps greater than in the history of other countries. Gramsci argued that before Italian national unity had been achieved, the behavior and thought of intellectuals tended to embody a universal spirit, akin to that of the Roman Catholic Church.[21] That spirit was hardly nationalistic. Rather than helping to build national unity, the Italian intellectuals blocked it.

What Gramsci said of Italy, the implications of its tardy arrival as a nation, applies to Mexico. The Reforma and the Porfiriato pieced together parts of what would become the Mexican nation, but it was not until the Revolution of 1910 that Mexico truly started to become a nation. Mexican intellectuals helped bring about this transformation. Earlier, with only a few exceptions, Mexican intellectuals, in their writings, aped European culture, turning their backs on pre-Columbian and Spanish inheritances alike, their minds gobbled up by foreign models. They worshiped at the altar of English and French thinkers, then later at the feet of Anglo Americans and, under the Porfiriato, added, in flowery poetry, an escapist mumbo jumbo that turned a blind eye to the horrific social inequities of society. This literary movement was called *Modernismo* and was the brainchild of Ruben Darío, a poet from Nicaragua who rarely set foot in his native land, preferring to hobnob with the upper crust of Paris. Salvador Díaz Mirón, one of Mexico's much-lauded *Modernistas,* even applauded the Victoriano Huerta military coup of 1913, which toppled the democratically elected Francisco Madero.

But, as Gramsci explained, when a people break with their past, intellectuals can no longer simply sit on their hands and rely on oratory eloquence; they have to actively participate as organizers and persuaders. In Mexico, the earlier error of intellectuals came from believing it possible to be detached from the passions of the people. When they did so, they became a caste, a priestly brotherhood akin to the colonial clergy. The Revolution opened the eyes of Mexican artists and writers to the necessity of fighting for the independence of their country, the seedbed of an authentic national culture, to cite Frantz Fanon. The abandonment of the Europeanized ideal signaled the defeat of the old system. As Gramsci explained, since society was full of complexities and contradictions, the intellectual had to explain and justify its nature. If intellectuals, one of the social groups most responsible for change, led, the people would follow.

In Mexico, it was the muralists who most fully embodied Gramsci's thoughts, and in the 1930s they were joined by Cárdenas and his band of reformers. As Guillermo Bonfil Batalla writes, the muralists of the *escuela nacional* (national school) assumed the role played by Tlacaelel, the priest servant of Cihuacoatl who, at his master's command, burned the ancient books so they could be replaced by others depicting the glory of the *mexica* (ancient Mexicans).[22] What captured the spotlight for Mexico was the Revolution as a cultural event, the epic of a people searching for its soul, tossing aside centuries of adoration for the European. It was in mural art, a form largely ignored since the days of the Italian masters of the sixteenth century, where Mexicans saw visions of a new day and in so doing gave meaning and substance to the dream of a Mexico standing on its own feet. In these murals, indigenous roots were everywhere, glorifying a pre-Columbian Mexico.[23]

Overwhelmingly powerful and, both in theme and color, Mexican, the mural was conceived as a popular art for a people untrained in looking at objects of art, to cite Diego Rivera, who most epitomized Gramsci's dictum. The artist had to provide an understandable art, interesting at first sight. An art for the people, it was also an epic art, dealing with momentous themes and controversial subjects. Above all, it was art with a message; this was particularly true of the work of Rivera. Rivera, José Clemente Orozco, and David Siqueiros were known as the "Big Three."

Why the renaissance? Why at this time in Mexican history? I believe there are two answers. As stated earlier, artists, writers, and intellectuals are barometers of their times; with either the written word or design, they embody the mood of the people. Gerardo Murillo, the artist most responsible for the muralist outburst, offered the classic answer. For Murillo, or Dr. Atl, as he called himself, the Revolution held the secret to the renaissance. Before 1910, art had been both Spanish and Christian, basically an architectural art, orphaned by the culture that had produced it. Imitation was the result. To overcome the cycle of mediocre art, a sharp break with the past was necessary; that rupture, said Atl, must be Mexican and pagan. The Revolution made such a break possible; it was an anticlerical crusade that acquired a religion of its own, becoming a facsimile of the Counter-Reformation, the mother, as Atl rightly pointed out, of Spanish art. The Revolution symbolized the struggle for social justice; from it a spiritual renewal arose, conferring importance on the common Mexican and rediscovering the Indian and Mexico's pre-Hispanic heritage. Unlike Europe, ancient Mexico had had "no art for the sake of art," no artistic elite. Everyone was an artist, while the useful and beautiful were one and the same. Folk art, which had survived the tastes of the Porfiristas, provided examples for others to emulate, such as murals in the *pulquerías,* where the poor went to drink, and in the *retablos* of churches, artistic testimonials to miracles. These things, Atl concluded, explained the renaissance.[24]

A second, equally plausible answer also explains this outburst of art and its ideas. Atl's theory sheds only partial light on the renaissance. Bertram Wolfe, one Rivera's biographers, provided the other answer, and it also reflected the changing character of Mexico. For Wolfe the answer lay in the official patronage of mural art. When talented painters like Orozco and Rivera did not have to depend for their livelihood on the sale of their art to *burgueses*, previously closed channels opened to them. No longer captive to the tastes of private buyers, artists were free to experiment, to paint in a novel fashion. No longer dependent on the goodwill of the rich, they could refuse to paint a wealthy Mexican wife or mistress; the horizons of their art were thus liberated from the dictates of critics in the European mold.

Over and beyond that, the pragmatic politicians of the twenties had risen to power partly on their revolutionary rhetoric, and now they had to make good on it. Since they had little inclination to do so, they had to offer something on account, a promise of better things to come. If contemporary Mexico had changed ever so slightly, tomorrow, politicos swore, would be different. Mural art—which evoked nationalistic aspirations, hailed the bronze native, took comfort in the fall of tyrants, and pictured, in the drawings of Rivera, happy campesinos tilling land of their own—filled that need. If the people believed, they would have their banquet. Walls for the muralists to paint, similarly, beckoned everywhere, on the buildings of government ministries, the National Palace, schools, and *mercados*. By encouraging artists to cover the walls of public buildings, the government, by association, gained for itself a "revolutionary" and nationalistic veneer.

Artists had radical ideas on their minds. As early as 1917, Siqueiros, already conversant with socialist theories, had met in Guadalajara with artists of similar views to define, as they phrased it, the "social purpose" of art. By 1923, after they had walls to paint on, their thinking had jelled. The *manifiesto* of the Sindicato de Pintores y Escultores founded by Rivera and Orozco, among others, called on "soldiers, workers, campesinos, and intellectuals" to quote Orozco, to "socialize art, to destroy bourgeois individualism, to repudiate easel painting and any other art that emanated from ultra-intellectual and aristocratic circles." It asked artists to "produce monumental works for the public domain," demanding, "at this historic moment of a transition from a decrepit order to a new one, . . . a rich art for the people instead of expressions of individual pleasure." Many artists came to believe that pre-Columbian art was their "true heritage," even talking of a "renaissance of indigenous art."

Radicals, whether artists or writers, are an odd lot. Some, through a process of indoctrination, turn left, but others, for unexplained reasons, break with established norms on their own. Such is the case of Diego Rivera, the son of a *burgués* who worshiped the memory of Benito Juárez; yet his son went on to become the spokesman for an independent and socially just Mexico. Big and fat, with bulging eyes like those of a frog but with tiny hands, Rivera was an intellectual of brilliant mind. A picturesque character who craved public acclaim, he painted on a scaffold with a pistol at his waist, "to orient the critics," he was fond of saying. Educated in Catholic schools, Rivera was never an orthodox pupil, once shocking the nuns by questioning the truth of the Immaculate Conception. In 1907, Rivera departed for Europe, where he spent fifteen years, initially in Spain and then in Paris, earning fame as a cubist painter but then abandoning the style, looking for inspiration to Renoir, Matisse, Cézanne, and Juan Gris.

Over the course of the years, Rivera started to wonder why artists separated themselves from the community; he studied the history of art, trying to learn how this had come about. Until the European Renaissance, he concluded, artists were not isolated from society but were artisans working among other artisans who taught their neighbors the importance of art and beauty. That was also true for pre-Hispanic artists. The rupture with society occurred during the Renaissance, a break prolonged by the commercial and industrial revolutions, birthplaces of capitalism. At this juncture, easel art, the prerogative of wealthy patrons, came to dominate, and artists catered to the whims of their customers and became outcasts in society and pawns of the rich. Rivera's visit to Italy, where he saw the murals of Michelangelo, provided the answers to these questions. To integrate the artist into society, Rivera deduced, art, like that of the Italian masters, must be for the people. As he saw it, the Russian revolution, which had brought the Communists to power, had ended the era of "modern Christian art," which dated from the French Revolution. Socialist Russia opened up a new era, a Marxist world asking artists to give birth to a social art, accessible to the people, nourishing and reforming their tastes.

Determined to be a Mexican artist, Rivera made the Indian the centerpiece of his art. Everything of value in Mexico, he insisted, had Indian roots; without the inspiration of the Indian, he insisted, "we cannot be authentic." Show me, he declared, "one original Hispanic-American . . . idea and I will . . . beg forgiveness from the Virgin of Guadalupe." An ideologue who scoffed at the "neutrality of art," Rivera believed "all of it to be propaganda" and, as a nationalist, scorned the *burguesía* of Latin America, labeling it *malinchista,* a class fawning on foreigners, evidencing a colonial inferiority complex. He warned time and time again against imitating "whites and blonds," saying that such behavior led to feelings of shame for the native.[25]

Literature, too, embodied the attempt to break out of the colonial mold. The genre was the "novel of the Mexican Revolution," a neorealistic account of the deeds of campesinos and, at times, their chieftains. Like mural art, it enjoyed the patronage of the public coffer. In December 1924, Manuel Puig Casauranc, a politico in the ministry of public education, dangled a carrot before Mexican writers. If they accepted certain premises, he implied, the government would find jobs for them. For Puig, who thought of himself as a writer, literature had to be shorn of affectation and sham, which had to be replaced by a somber and austere style, faithful to "our way of life." He wanted fiction to portray anguish and selfless and sincere grief, and he urged writers to spotlight despair and link it to "our terrible social situation, thus lifting the curtains that hide from sight the misery of the damned."[26]

The novel of the Revolution made its appearance in 1925, when the soothsayers eulogized Mariano Azuela's *Los de abajo.* Few had read Azuela's other novels, some dealing with prostitution, alcoholism, and tragic death, themes that appealed to the *burguesía.* In *Los de Abajo,* however, he broke with old formulas. A tale of the Revolution, *Los de abajo* told of "brutal acts," to quote a Mexican scholar, in "brutal style." With the discovery of Azuela, old literary formulas lost their popularity. Like easel art, they had gone out of style. Ironically, Azuela, a physician with Francisco Villa's armies, had not written a sympathetic account of the Revolution, but probably a realistic one. Focusing on the "underdogs," it described primitiveness and brutality and told of waiters, barbers, and thieves, as well as campesinos, who had turned warriors, as well as unscrupulous intellectuals looking out for themselves. He described the story's antiheroes not merely as cruel and grasping but as ignorant of why they fought. As one Mexican reviewer confessed in 1925, "This is not a revolutionary novel because it detests the Revolution," nor, paradoxically, "is it reactionary because it reveals no zest for the past."[27] Still, Azuela's fiction met Puig's demands; in *Los de abajo,* readers found Mexican life portrayed in somber colors, depicting, in a style that packed a wallop, the agony of the poor.

Azuela opened the floodgates. In 1928, Martín Luis Guzmán published *El águila y la serpiente,* both fiction and historical memoir. A journalist by trade, Guzmán, who had no love for Venustiano Carranza and Álvaro Obregón, wrote about the caudillos of the upheaval of 1910. As early as 1915, this "revolutionary novelist shed no tears for the Indian who, he claimed, lacked 'pride in race,' judging him, because of an 'irritating docility,' a weight and burden" on Mexico. Quite different are the novels of Gregorio López y Fuentes, an author who championed the exploited campesino. In *Campamento,* a vivid account of nameless revolutionary soldiers spending one night in a nameless village, Lopez y Fuentes used vignettes to express the humor, melancholy, and tragedy of Mexican peasant life. *El indio,* another of his novels, tells the story of an Indian village that comes into contact with the outside world through a school, roads, and a church, and *Tierra* tells of Indian villages robbed of their lands by laws dating from the Juárez era.

A change had taken place in Mexicans' attitudes toward the white world, wrote, Samuel Ramos, author of *Perfil del hombre y la cultura en México,* a pathbreaking book first published in 1934. Mexicans began to appreciate their own life, to take pride in their own values, and to stop bowing before the European. Mexicans had learned a painful lesson, that imitating a foreign civilization led nowhere, and that they had values and a character of their own, as well as a unique destiny. As Ramos wrote, it was natural that Mexicans should come to resent Europe, because their dependence on its cultural leadership had caused them to belittle national values as well as themselves. The only legitimate course was "to think Mexican."[28]

EIGHT False Miracle

I

Miracles, as everyone knows, are hard to come by. Only zealots, skepticism cast aside, can believe that even the parched desert will bloom with flowers. Yet, according to a plethora of pundits and scholars, Mexico enjoyed a miracle starting in the 1940s. The miracle, growth of the gross domestic product (GDP), was indeed a miracle. Not only did the GDP triple from 1940 to 1960, but it did so again in the seventies, with, miracle of all miracles, manufacturing taking the lead. It was a time when bumper stickers on autos and trucks proclaimed, "Lo hecho en México está bien hecho" (What Mexico makes is well made). Much of this heady progress stemmed from the adoption of import substitution, begun earlier as simple ad hoc measures taken to shield particular local industries, and then blessed as theory by a strategy advocated by CEPAL, the Economic Commission for Latin America of the United Nations, which encouraged Latin American countries to manufacture goods that had previously been imported.

Euphoric Mexicans, the rich and the middle class, feasted. Bureaucrats, university professors, storekeepers, and the like could buy automobiles, acquire homes of their own, and take vacations in Acapulco, the mecca of the affluent. Not since the 1880s, the golden years of the Porfiriato, had middle- and upper-class Mexicans basked in the glow of such good times. As Joan Robinson recalled, "The great slump of the 1930s was a nightmare forgotten in the dawn of a seemingly permanent prosperity."[1] The architects of these halcyon days were the magnates of industry and banking, and their allies in politics, out to prove that a business-run economy could give Mexico a face-lift.

With industrialization, Mexico would be proudly capitalistic, a paradise for private enterprise and a haven for the laws of supply and demand. Some observers, however, particularly American ones, saw a mixed economy, implying that they detected a bit of socialist planning. This was nonsense. What they had in mind were the *paraestatales*, industries owned and run by the government, but these were often positioned as aids to private business. Many of these state-run enterprises, scores of which had been on the verge of bankruptcy, were purchased by the government from their owners; others performed tasks of no interest to private investors. A popular saying sums up this sweetheart deal between government and *empresarios:* "If they invest, we will subsidized them; if they lose their shirts, we will bail them out; if they go belly up, we will buy their bankrupt enterprises."[2] The trickle-down theory held sway. Business owners were part and parcel of the government entourage. As early as 1942, industrialists from Monterrey, the most conservative of conservative bastions, joined the parade when the Garza-Sada clan, the local kingpins, made their pilgrimage to Mexico City to pay homage to the nation's authorities.

II

Manuel Ávila Camacho, the first of the "miracle presidents," a disciple of the "free market" and an unabashed foe of government tutelage, went out of his way to restore the confidence of foreign investors, scared out of their wits by the Cardenistas' expropriation of the petroleum industry. To assure conservatives, as well as American investors, that his heart was in the right place, Ávila Camacho feigned ignorance when his subordinates lambasted nefarious Communist influences, a veiled reference to Cardenista policies.[3] To check the power of labor and campesinos, Ávila Camacho reorganized what under Cárdenas had been merely a "fourth constituency" of middle-class representatives in Congress, replacing it with the Confederación Nacional de Organizaciones Públicas (CNOP), which then became a counterweight to the labor and campesino blocs in Congress. A devout Catholic, Ávila Camacho let religious schools run free of government interference, and soon, according to the novelist and critic José Agustín, they were teaching the men who by the 1980s would be the kingpins of government.

Thus began an era of government largesse for Mexican capitalists, when politicos big and small proclaimed tongue-in-cheek allegiance to the old adage "The less government the better." Bankers and business tycoons applauded the annual reports of sympathetic presidents and won entrance into their cabinets, their influence enhanced by personal ties to public officials, by their role in the economy, and because they came to own the press, radio, and television. It was a rosy era for the *burguesía,* when admirers saw Mexican capitalism on the front lines of the battle against underdevelopment.

All the same, the road was rocky. Old ills survived. It was the old dependency, now cloaked differently. Corruption, never absent from the Mexican scene, took on a life of its own. The rot infiltrated the ranks of politics, business, commerce, industry, and labor. Not since the days of the Porfiriato had corruption had such a bountiful day, transforming *empresarios* and politicos of the inner circles into millionaires.[4] Senators and deputies, the ruling *Priistas* (members of the Partido Revolucionario Institucional, or PRI) in the national legislature, turned themselves into servile eunuchs of the president, who dictated the laws Congress should have written, while judges, from the Supreme Court down to the lowest magistrate, rarely challenged the president's dictates. It was claimed that no "leaf of a tree moved without presidential blessings." Official lies, in which *el presidente* and his allies sang the praises of their supposed gifts, became hackneyed expressions. It was the patronage model of politics: loyalty exchanged for access to the holy grail. Nearly everyone hungered after "the crumbs of the Priista banquet," wrote one observer, a scene "reminiscent of the days of the Porfiriato."[5] The Partido Acción Nacional (PAN), the opposition party, challenged the government but not the system, encouraging middle-class Mexicans to believe that one day they would have the banquet table for themselves. To quote one Mexican writer, the Panistas (members of PAN) wanted to get the Priistas out of the way "so that they could take their place."[6] The system was, to quote the novelist Mario Vargas Llosa, "the perfect dictatorship."

Why so much corruption? There is no one answer; the problem is complex. The seeds of corruption had been planted with the Conquest, when Spaniards had their way with Crown officials, who turned the other cheek when royal laws were bypassed. The first viceroy fattened his pocketbook selling off Crown lands; history recalls that no viceroy returned home a poor man. That precedent survived independence, as the chicanery of politicos as well as military brass reveals. Antonio López de Santa Anna was corrupt, but he was not alone; nor were the Porfiristas, either in government or in business, free of the malady. Generals of the Revolution, Álvaro Obregón and Plutarco Elías Calles among them, acquired haciendas and died millionaires. Should the public be above the use of the *mordida* (bribe) to avoid a traffic ticket or get a passport from a bureaucrat? Corruption flourishes under authoritarian regimes, and Priista control of Mexican politics was certainly undemocratic. Without watchdogs to call attention to chicanery in high places, politicos fattened their pocketbooks, nor were *empresarios* inclined to be above board in their dealings, particularly since bribes cut official red tape, an ever-present obstacle because it ensured the need for bribes. No bureaucrat blows the horn on corrupt colleagues without knowing whether those higher up are on the take. When bureaucracies stand in the way of what citizens want, bribes cut the red tape; they motivate bureaucrats to act, especially since those bureaucrats earn piddling salaries.

The most notoriously corrupt of the presidents, Miguel Alemán (1946–52), successor to Ávila Camacho, charged José Vasconcelos, "had rejuvenated the grandeur of the Porfiriato."[7] Always on the side of the well-off, Alemán made himself and his friends rich, whether in politics or business, relying on *obras públicas,* public works, as a cover. This son of a "revolutionary general" acquired hotels and mansions in Acapulco and erected a business empire that included *Novedades,* a national newspaper, and Televisa, the country's television network. Ill-gotten gains were as Mexican as the tortilla, but they were condemned in the past; now efforts were made to justify them on the grounds that tribute must be paid to the builders of modern Mexico. "We laid the basis for Mexican capitalism," Carlos Fuentes had the banker Federico Robles say in *La región más transparente.* "What if we did get our percentage from every contract?" Would you, he asked, "prefer that in order to avoid these ills we had done nothing at all?" A man had to take advantage of his opportunities. "And if I hadn't," Robles continued, "someone would have seized what I have seized, stand where I stand, and do what I do."

Just when boasts like that of Robles started to sound hollow, the Korean War revived the economy, faltering from the effects of Europe's recovery from World War II. A horde of Yankee tourists brought welcomed dollars, especially to Tijuana and sister towns, their money spent on curios, drink, food, and ladies of the night. Affluent politicos and their allies in business sank millions of pesos into Acapulco, the first of the international resorts, which paved the way for Cancún, Ixtapa-Zihuatanejo, Puerto Vallarta, and Mazatlán. When campesinos stood in the way, they were driven out, to become gardeners, janitors, and handymen, their wives and daughters kitchen workers and hotel maids. Until 1964, braceros, their ranks swollen by "wetbacks," sent checks home and added more dollars to the Mexican economy. When the Korean War ended, a recession struck the United States and the Mexican boom sputtered. The year 1952 brought to a close Alemán's tenure in office and saw the end of his popularity, as Mexicans who had closed their eyes to his peccadilloes had by then had their fill of corruption, inflation, stagnant wages, and his brutal repression of dissent. As he left office, Alemán called on soldiers to squash a challenge from Miguel Enríquez Guzmán, a general of Cardenista leanings and aspirant to the presidency. When a huge public protest on Guzmán's behalf broke out in Mexico City, soldiers and thugs broke it up, using tear gas, beatings, and killing.[8]

III

World War II had set the stage for this drama. With the United States off fighting, Mexicans were left to fend for themselves. The miracle of a rising GDP had a life span of approximately thirty years, from 1940 to 1970. The new rulers of Mexico, increasingly conservative, adopted an economic model that theoretically replaced the export-led blueprint. It was an industrialization geared to the demands of the internal market, a policy known as "import substitution," reflecting the thinking of business owners who believed that their manufactures would never find extensive markets abroad. They saw themselves as noncompetitive high-cost producers. This was an industrialization run by and for the benefit of Mexican businessmen. Private capitalism coexisted with state capitalism. As José López Portillo, later president of Mexico, put it, it was development within the system of dependent capitalism.[9] The critics of Alemán, who took credit for much of the new policy, said he wanted to bury the Mexican Revolution and replace it with a satellite capitalism of the United States.[10] That observation may have been true, because Alemán never saw an American capitalist he did not like. Men such as Alemán, their critics remind us, were more closely identified, both culturally and economically, with the United States than with their fellow Mexicans.[11] The new blueprints, unlike those of the Cardenistas, had no place for any socialist planning, now laden with sundry negative connotations.

The architects of this policy did not just march off on their own; World War II made the policy almost inevitable, because it cut Mexico off from the goods it had formerly imported; capital goods were especially hard to obtain. As Claudio Véliz, the Chilean economist writes, industrialization came, not as a result of a deliberate policy, but because of a historical accident, not the upshot of a reformist middle class, nor that of a rising industrial class on the European model.[12] This interpretation is mostly true, but not entirely. Also responsible for the model's vigor was the rise of organized labor, the Confederación de Trabajadores Mexicanos (CTM), a national federation blessed by Cárdenas that demanded better working conditions, stable jobs, and less costly domestic goods—trade protection, in short. The war, too, made it possible for Mexico to escape from the devastating competition of the United States and other industrialized nations and thereby free itself from the chronic drain of funds originating in the repatriation of profits by investors and an unfavorable balance of trade. Fortunately for the rulers of Mexico, World War II doubled traditional exports between 1939 and 1945.

So a blueprint for industrialization was adopted, one based on import substitution carried out under the tutelage of the state, whose job was to promote economic development. This policy rested on the industrial edifice of the Porfiristas, which the "revolutionaries" had left intact. Without it, no miracle would have occurred, because capital goods were unattainable. According to one expert, industrial growth was largely the result of "the running of the nation's already installed plant night and day."[13] This brought to center stage a manufacturing sector of big, capital-intensive, monopolistic firms, hiding behind tariff walls and relying on cheap labor to produce shoddy goods for captive, mostly middle-class consumers. Productivity growth was modest. The *empresarios,* the movers and shakers behind this enterprise, displayed the ability to make a great deal of money in a particular way, a talent highly advantageous to them, but time made clear that it implied no virtue beyond expertise in a lucrative activity. As the economist Paul Baran noted, "Monopolistic control became an additional factor preventing the widening of the market." The *empresarios* did not welcome intruders but employed their monopoly to harass and exclude them. This *capitalismo salvaje*" writes Guillermo Bonfil Batalla, rewarded a handful of *empresarios,* largely the manufacturing and commercial sectors as well the big commercial farms.[14]

The end of World War II did not bring with it an alteration in policy. On the contrary, efforts were redoubled to spur industrialization. To get wealthy Mexicans to invest in factories, without much risk and with promises of lucrative profits, the government dangled inducements before their eyes: import licenses, protective tariffs, tax breaks, and loans at low interest rates. Foreign investors were also invited to the banquet table. The network of highways was expanded, and plants were built to provide electricity, cement, and sundry items at low cost to industry. A commercial agriculture for export, designed to earn dollars to pay for the creation of the industrial edifice, an old Porfirista remedy, received similar blessings. By the 1950s, growth in the gross national product (GNP) was averaging 6 percent or better. All the same, the end of the war left Mexico more than ever at the mercy of markets north of the border: over 80 percent of its foreign trade was with the United States.

IV

What went awry? The failure was hardly an exclusive Mexican phenomenon. Other peripheral countries, usually with poor long-term results, had adopted import substitution as a panacea for their ills. Traditional economists say that the model ran aground because it pushed against the "natural tendency" of the market, that is, it relied on tariffs, subsidies, and similar measures to protect industries from outside challenges. Yet Western nations, England in particular, had relied on similar measures to get their industrial plants off the ground. But the world had a distinct hue then. When the English started, the technological gaps between itself and the outside world were small; what gaps existed were not protected by internationally recognized patents, and few production processes required immense amounts of investment capital, while transport costs offered natural tariff walls.[15]

The Mexican debacle has other explanations. For Daniel Cosío Villegas, a respected scholar, Mexico's economists had mistakenly entrusted the enterprise to a new, inexperienced capitalist class. Amiya Kumar Bagchi goes further: he believes that the fault lay with an economic blueprint "geared to private needs and private profit." Selfish at heart, to recall the opinion of José López Portillo, the system's architects did not have the national welfare in mind; their primary goal was private gain. They were not once bothered by the fact that they "enjoyed good times at the expense of others."[16] It could be argued, in defense of Alemán and his cohorts, that they strongly believed that people are generally selfish, but that selfishness can ultimately benefit people. In any case, their strategy embraced the old, discredited trickle-down theory: when a country's output climbs upward, some of the benefits filter down to the poorest of society. But even in halcyon days, the trickle-down process takes time because, to maximize growth, profits must not be shared immediately with workers in the form of higher wages.

Structural change, too, such as industrialization, tends to exacerbate the poverty of the poorest members of society. Taxes on income, on interests from investment, and on profits from production were kept low for fear that *empresarios* might lose their incentive. Given the absence of state planning and the stimulus of tariff walls and state patronage, industrialization took place in a haphazard fashion, in a pattern of demand laid out by the earlier history of export-led exploitation. This was economic growth euphemistically labeled *desarrollo estabilizador* (stabilized development), to be achieved by keeping taxes down, industrial wages low, and inflation under control. For a while, the formula worked, with growth financed from internal sources. But the need to buy capital goods, and the unwillingness to tax the rich, led to growth financed by borrowing from outsiders, with inflation a steady companion. As López Portillo complained, "stabilized development" eventually became anything but stable because, in order to finance the cost of import substitution, Mexico had to borrow to pay for the necessary machinery, equipment, and supplies.[17] More and more economists came from the United States, while would-be Mexican economists went there to study and on their return boasted that they spoke English fluently.

From the start, industrial development had a lopsided look, as it was concentrated chiefly in Mexico City, with lesser buildups in the cities of Monterrey and Guadalajara; This was a development largely dictated by the size of the consumer market. Even in these cities industrial growth was small and progressed slowly. The neglect of the small farm drove campesinos to the cities in search of jobs, providing a source of cheap labor for industry but hampering the expansion of a consumer market.

Industry never became competitive, as it was, with few exceptions, unable to sell its products abroad. As late as 1982, after three decades of the "miracle," manufacturing represented 20 percent of the gross domestic product, but only 3 percent of exports, which largely consisted of minerals and agricultural products. Additionally, the miracle economy had come to be dominated by its tertiary sector: commerce, transportation, and services such as health, education, and finance.[18]

To exacerbate matters, the population ballooned, from less than 20 million in 1940 to over 100 million by 2000, partly because of medical advances but also because the battle against poverty had been put on the back burner. The growth in population was a sure sign of underdevelopment. When human survival is at risk, high fertility rates are necessary; when not, big families become a burden. Mexicans and their offspring were living longer because of vaccinations for smallpox, measles, and other maladies, but not necessarily because they were better off. Malthus had it backward: a population does not outrun its food supply. Poverty, more than any other factor, breeds population surges.[19] I recall Manuel Gamio, the distinguished Mexican anthropologist, telling me that when darkness descends on an isolated rural village, procreation takes off. "What else is there to do?" he would ask. Even after Mexican authorities awakened to the looming disaster, the population kept surging. Over a hundred million Mexicans begot more Mexicans, although birth rates did drop. Poverty aside, other reasons also explain the failure to halt the run-away train. Business owners and politicians, dreaming of more cheap labor and more consumers, forgot that Mexicans required adequate wages in order to become consumers. Meanwhile, the Catholic hierarchy, among the most conservative in Latin America, opposed any type of family planning; any whiff of birth control sent it into hysterics. Not until 1974 did officials reverse course; fearing that a large mass of unemployed or poorly paid workers might cause trouble, they established a National Population Council and a network of clinics to help couples plan their families.[20] Still, family planning, though helpful, did not by itself not halt runaway birth rates.[21]

Along with the population boom came the hemorrhaging of rural people to industrial cities, causing urban population growth rates to surpass economic growth rates. By 1960, for the first time in its history, Mexico was more urban than rural. The cities grew, as Guillermo Bonfil Batalla lamented, "like mushrooms when it rained," and with them came shantytowns, belts of hunger and poverty, as well as pollution, unemployment, and crime. Among the unskilled, fierce fights ensued over menial jobs that paid ever-lower wages.[22] More funds had to be spent to enlarge health care facilities, build schools, provide housing, and build roads. Mexicans were younger, consumers primarily of food and essential services such as health and schooling, so the burden for their upkeep fell on others and diverted funds that might have been used elsewhere.[23]

The miracle workers set out not just to industrialize but to copy the models of the core nations. Mexican *empresarios* imported the latest technology in the belief, according to economists of the day, that highly mechanized means of production resulted in high rates of capital accumulation and, ultimately, high growth rates. Much of the money went for the purchase of machinery, chemicals, and semiprocessed manufactures from the United States.[24] By 1960, goods for use in industrial production made up 83 percent of the value of imports. The policy led to unforeseen obstacles. One was an unfavorable balance of trade. Profits from traditional exports did not cover the cost of imported technology and machinery; since local industries proved unable to compete on the international market, Mexico had to borrow from foreign banks.[25] Western technology exacerbated unemployment because, designed for countries with a relatively high cost of labor, it served as a labor-saving device.[26] Neither the Mexican nor the foreign capitalists lost any sleep because of unemployment brought about by the new machinery. The goal, after all, was to keep wages low and profits high, on the assumption that money in the pockets of the *burguesía* would fatten domestic savings and spur reinvestment in productive enterprises. Industry magnates reaped huge profits; the National University of Mexico reported that the sixty-nine major industries had watched their profits rise by an incredible 295 percent between 1977 and 1981. Those huge profit margins did not stem from either greater efficiency or more productivity but essentially from milking the public with high prices.[27]

The inability of Mexican industry to get beyond just manufacturing consumer goods brought sundry maladies. It was a catch-22 situation, since as industry expanded, more and more money had to be spent on the purchase of capital goods, which made borrowing from abroad necessary to finance the enterprise and consequently added to Mexico's foreign debt and made its economy even more dependent on outsiders. Mexico had simply substituted one type of import for another, renewing the old dependency on the industrialized West and exacerbating the need for foreign capital.[28] Since Mexico's high-profit industry was noncompetitive, largely because of its monopolistic character and reliance on government largesse, it survived by producing costly and shoddy merchandise. To get the less wealthy to buy it, the government had to subsidize the working class's food purchases, lest they have nothing to spend. The subsidies led to chronic inflation. Worse still, the prevalence of monopoly, which conferred "privileged sanctuaries" on certain firms, to quote Paul Baran, and the concentration of industry in central Mexico drove scores of medium-sized industries out of business, as well as smaller ones.[29] By stealing the market away from these small-scale labor-intensive industries, scores of them in the provinces, monopolists added thousands of workers to the ranks of the unemployed. Also hit hard were the artisans, who once upon a time had made toys, dishes, huaraches, *rebozos,* and cotton and woolen cloth for sale at local markets. At the same time, exorbitant profits and bloated salaries for executives exacerbated inequality.

V

The euphemistically labeled *desarrollo estabilizador,* which followed on the heels of the former wild spending, enjoyed limited success. The goal was to rein in inflation, banishing it by borrowing money for development from foreign bankers. But this borrowing led to an astronomical rise in Mexico's foreign debt. By the 1970s, as López Portillo recalled in his memoirs, the ills of inflation had hit the economy hard, partly owing to foreign factors but also because of the nature of Mexican industry: the need to buy costly machinery, equipment, and supplies at inflated prices and the reliance of *empresarios* on price gouging to multiply profits from the sale of inferior goods. So bad did inflation become that in the days of López Portillo it reached the astronomical figure of 32.2 percent. Local *empresarios* had learned that one way to deal with the workers' wage demands was to raise prices. The more you got for your product, the more you could pay your employees, within limits; you simply transferred the cost of wages to the consumer.[30]

So were Mexican industrial workers paid handsomely? The answer is a qualified yes, but not when one considers wages in Western Europe or the United States. Mexican employers had an abundant pool of cheap, unskilled labor to exploit, which kept wages low. In 1993, workers at the Ford assembly plant in Hermosillo earned 6 pesos an hour (about 2 dollars), while their counterparts in the United States earned 15 dollars an hour for exactly the same job. At the Volkswagen plant in Puebla, the best-paid auto assembly plant, employees earned 28 dollars for a day's labor, but unionized assembly workers in the United States took home between 120 and 180 dollars per day. Unable to compete on the international market, *empresarios* put the blame on labor: it cost too much. So they got the government to sit tight on wages. They were helped by the fact that industry never produced enough jobs; unemployed men and women were always available.[31] The Mexican economy needed a million new jobs each year, but Mexican industry produced only half of them.[32] With politicos in Mexico City in cahoots with *empresarios* and with a labor surplus at hand, it was not difficult to keep wages under control, so much so that between 1977 and 1981 real wages dropped by 22 percent and unemployment rose.[33] Before 1976, one Mexican in three had a job, but now only one in four was employed.[34] When President Luis Echeverría attempted to marginally raise wages, industrialists and business owners accused him of being a populist and, worse still, of sympathizing with Communists. Frightened by his so-called populist policies, the wealthy, *empresarios* among them, took their savings out of Mexico.

At the table of labor sat Judas: *charros*, supposedly defenders of workers' rights, kept labor leaders beholden to industry and government. In cahoots with the *empresarios*, *charros*, labor leaders hand-picked by politicos, made unionization a mockery, kept wages in check, and protected industry from the threat of worker strikes.[35] This behavior, of course, was not entirely new; it dated from the days when Venustiano Carranza, then president of Mexico, gave his blessings to the first national labor organization but, before doing so, had the good sense to make sure that Luis Morones, the chief of labor, stood at his beck and call. This development, hailed by Alemán's admirers, blunted labor's more radical aspirations; one result was the appearance of *sindicatos blancos,* for all intents and purposes company unions. Alemán and his cronies, say some observers, accorded Mexico the honor of being one of the countries in the world with the lowest wages.

The false miracle provides a lesson. High rates of economic growth, a phenomenon of the miracle years, do not guarantee more jobs, lower the unemployment rate, ensure a better distribution of income, or alleviate poverty.[36] In the case of Mexico, which boasted 6 percent growth or more during the heydays of the miracle, not only did the ranks of the jobless climb, but the gap between the poor and the rich widened. Nor did welfare expenditures, specifically for schooling, increase with the boom. Money set aside for education never kept pace with the rise in national income, even though school facilities were inadequate. Was the goal of industrialization the culprit? Not at all, though doubts about its ability to solve the problems of the peripheral world began to emerge in the late fifties. To cite the advice of the economist Raymond Vernon, "The developmental model . . . no longer functioned, needing new directions and new policies." From then on, he continued, substitution would have to "take place mostly in intermediate goods—in steel instead of bed springs, aluminum instead of kitchen pans, in engine blocks instead of assembled cars, and so on," requiring bigger investments, different technology, and a larger, more dynamic market.[37] If economic growth is the goal, manufacturing is undoubtedly the means, but, equally certain, a goodly slice of the population must also come along, lest development bypass it. Distortions flow not from industrialization but, to quote Joan Robinson, from the "choice of investment projects . . . and secondly from imitating Western industry and allowing Western industry to organize industry for them."[38]

Mexican manufacturing sat atop a pyramid of protective walls. Higher than those of earlier years, they dated from the administration of Ávila Camacho.[39] Until then, tariffs had been limited to the protection of specific industries. In the forties, high tariffs began to be set up to keep out foreign goods, with the exception of capital goods. With the end of World War II, tariffs protected what could be produced locally, and by the 1960s Mexico had some of the highest tariffs in the world.[40] The protectionists added import licenses, designed, like tariffs, to confer on Mexican manufacturers a competitive edge, but also to discourage internal competition against old stalwarts. *Empresarios* took an eclectic view of protectionist policy: absolute protection for what they manufactured and the free importation of what they needed. Later, under López Portillo, subsidies were instituted to make exports more competitive; on the railroads, for example, the cost of transporting minerals was kept low in order to facilitate their sale abroad, even though foreigners, who profited from this measure, made up the majority of mine owners. The miracle workers also put in place a regressive tax structure.

The Noah's ark of industrialization rested on the export trade, the traditional foundation of the Mexican economy. Devaluations of the peso in 1954 and 1975, for instance, sought to curb imports and encourage exports. As López Portillo recalled in his memoirs, Mexico's financial welfare required a healthy dose of exports, necessary because the change from an agrarian economy to an industrialized one required costly machinery. Moreover, obstacles lay ahead. American tariffs hurt the local economy because a large percentage of the exports were sold north of the border. During the 1940s, Mexican officials had encouraged the cultivation of cotton, investing millions in irrigation projects.[41] By 1956, cotton exports represented 33 percent of sales abroad. When the United States dumped surplus cotton on the international market, Mexican planters lost their shirts. Equally alarming, Europe no longer relied on Mexican raw materials, mostly because of its use of synthetic fibers. Moreover, little had been done to diversify exports. The mining industry, nationalized in 1971, still predominated. By the advent of the López Portillo regime, Mexico had not only discarded the *desarrollo estabilizador* formula, but had once again come to rely on sales of petroleum, which represented three-fourths of all export earnings and over 40 percent of government revenues.[42] But petroleum exploration and exploitation were costly and led to huge increases in Mexico's foreign debt. With oil selling at exorbitant prices, Mexico had gone on borrowing and spending; when the price of oil collapsed, so did the Mexican economy. Not all of this was Mexico's fault. The Western spending boom of the post–World War II era had run its course. During 1974, stagnation had reared its ugly head, and recession, as it was labeled, had made its debut, in the worst economic downturn since the Great Depression.

The nationalist rhetoric behind import substitution, too, had a hollow ring. To produce intermediate goods required bigger plants, more machines, and costly technology, which exceeded the ability of Mexicans to finance. If Mexico were to industrialize, the government had to shoulder a larger share of the financial burden. Freezing industrial wages even more than had already been done was out of the question, as was raising income taxes, which would have antagonized the *burguesía.* The solution adopted further opened the door to foreign capital. Outside money, it was thought, would help finance the industrial effort and keep inflation in check. Between 1955 and 1958, direct foreign investment rose by over 400 million dollars, most of it going into industry. As a consequence, foreigners widened their beachhead, often with the help of *prestanombres,* Mexican front men who sold their names to foreign firms to give the appearance of Mexican ownership.[43] Foreign-owned companies also paid off government officials or threatened to depart if their demands went unheeded. Chrysler threatened to leave Mexico if not allowed to circumvent the 49 percent legislation, a stance that opened the doors to Ford, General Motors, General Electric, Anderson Clayton, and Monsanto.[44] With the government turning a blind eye to their activities, foreigners, mostly Americans, made a joke out of Mexican nationalistic legislation. As José Agustín, the novelist, writes, Mexicans virtually begged for foreign capitalists to come invest in Mexico. However, many of these same businessmen, so eager for foreign dollars, usually kept sizable sums of money tucked away in Swiss banks, so fearful were they of a Mexican economic collapse.

To circumvent the rhetoric of import substitution, which theoretically shut the door to foreign manufactures, foreign firms seeking access to the Mexican market opened plants in Mexico, thus evading barriers. Sears, Roebuck, the first of the retailers to do so, opened a store in Mexico City in the early fifties. Since it sold goods on credit, an unheard-of business practice in Mexico, Sears became a staple of middle-class consumers. Its merchandise, the same sold in the United States, was cheaper and of better quality than comparable articles of Mexican manufacture. Sears was the first of the retail chains to open a store, but not the only one. These transnational corporations, which began to displace Mexican small and medium-sized industries, set the tone for the character of industrial growth and, as one critic claims, "even the culture, values and aspirations of ordinary people." To quote López Portillo, the "middle and upper classes began to identify themselves with the interests of the transnationals." On their heels came a frenzied adoption of American buying habits. Before long, hamburgers and hotdogs were outselling tacos and tamales.

The men who set policy had also gone on borrowing from foreigners, a policy spurred by the downturn of the economy at the end of the Korean war, as well as Washington's shift in its lending policies, thanks partly to the Cuban revolution and its supposed threat to American hegemony in Latin America. It was a time when American salesmen urged Mexicans to borrow and pay later. When international lending agencies cooled their ardor, private banks in the United States took up the slack. In 1960, the Prudential Insurance Company lent Mexico 100 million dollars, not once asking how it would be spent. By 1980, two-thirds of the 80-billion-dollar debt was owed to private banks, largely American, among them Bank of America, Chase Manhattan, and Citibank.[45] Direct investment in Mexico had soared from just over 900 million dollars in 1959 to nearly 1.3 billion dollars by 1964. These funds, said Mexicans, were "indispensable"; without them economic development stood still, a view that ignored the advice of Lázaro Cárdenas, who more than once warned of the pitfalls that awaited Mexico were it to be indebted to foreigners. Nonetheless, more of the cost of industrialization was being paid by foreign funds, with the Mexican foreign debt the highest on record.

Then, in the early 1970s, the first major crisis befell Mexico. During the Vietnam War, exports to the United States had risen, but when the conflict ended, the United States economy went into a tailspin and Mexico's went belly up. Exports fell, a blow made worse by a drop in tourism, the instability of the dollar, and worldwide inflation. To encourage exports, Mexico had to keep its prices in check, but the benefits of the 1954 devaluation had evaporated. Meanwhile, inflation, which cut into workers' buying power, had planted the seeds of labor unrest. The unions, *charro* bosses and all, began to demand higher wages. National policy had brought this trouble on itself; since little had been done to stimulate the production of food crops, their prices had risen, putting a large dent in the paycheck of workers. The trade deficit with the United States, a goodly share to pay for imported foodstuffs, ballooned. By 1975, debt obligations totaled nearly 20 billion dollars, so Mexico, its pantry empty, had to go begging to the International Monetary Fund (IMF), an institution dominated by Washington. The IMF largely controlled poor countries' access to credit; in return for a loan the recipient had to embrace austerity, abide by the whims of the market, let the peso float, and relegate solutions to social problems to the future.[46]

Then providence stepped in, only now, instead of the savior being silver and copper, it was "black gold," for poor countries, the "devil's excrement." Recovery came swiftly with the discovery of huge deposits of petroleum in Campeche, Tabasco, Chiapas, Tamaulipas, and Veracruz. Petroleum would anchor Mexico's export economy. Forgotten in the euphoria was Cárdenas's dream of using petroleum for domestic development. The export past had reappeared: once it had been decades of oil for Standard and Royal Dutch Shell, and now again it was Mexican oil for others. "For the first time since the mining glory of colonial years," Jorge Díaz Serrano, the head of PEMEX, the national oil monopoly, boasted, "Mexico, because of its oil, could plot its own destiny."[47] Clouds, nonetheless, darkened the horizon. Rather than loosen Mexico's ties to the United States, oil cemented them; to pump its oil, Mexico turned to the United States for help with costly equipment and technical assistance, paying for it with oil and natural gas. By 1982, oil represented three-fourths of exports.[48] With pockets full of money from the oil bonanza, Mexicans went on a buying spree, feverishly importing even food. Plugging the gap in the balance of trade and paying off the debt required additional oil exports. No one in government gave any thought to raising taxes on the rich to reduce the deficit. Prices leaped upward, fueling inflation. Graft and corruption multiplied. The *mordida* thrived, its size determined by what had to be done and the level of employee one had to deal with. Corruption was an "ingredient of doing business."

Then, suddenly, in 1982, a catastrophe struck. A worldwide depression, the likes of which had not been seen since the great crash of 1929, turned the economies of the United States and Western Europe inside out. The oil glut was partially responsible. With less demand for oil, Mexico's chief export, its price tumbled, causing a loss of billions of dollars. The crisis savaged the price of raw materials and mineral ores. Exports dropped off, and inflation soared. Mexico's foreign debt multiplied eightfold, far beyond its capacity to pay. When revenues from oil sales shriveled up, Mexico once again could not meet its obligations. American confidence in the Mexican economy toppled, leading to drastic cutbacks in investments and to capital flight. Money lenders, frightened by the Mexican debacle, stopped offering loans and raised interest rates. As money fled, Mexican authorities devalued the peso, despite a public oath by President José López Portillo "to defend it like a dog." Big industry weathered the crisis, but countless small firms went under. By the summer of 1982, Mexico was again bankrupt, compelling Jesús Silva Herzog, minister of finance, to journey hat in hand to Washington and New York. After much haggling, the IMF put together a "rescue package" of 4 billion dollars, and the chance for Mexico to negotiate 4 billion more. Private banks gave Mexico a three-month reprieve from debt payments. In return, the Mexicans agreed to sell the bulk of their oil and natural gas to Americans at favorable rates.[49]

Mexican bankruptcy was not simply a government debacle. Those who ran the private sector were no wiser than government officials. Grupo Alfa, previously held up as an example of a successful business, all the same ended up broke. In October 1986, Mexicans learned to their astonishment that foreign banks, most of them American, had acquired half of Alfa. Bernardo Garza-Sada, a principal owner, acknowledged that Alfa "owed more that it was worth," having lavishly spent funds borrowed from foreign bankers in its haste to expand. With the crash of 1982, partly brought about by the peso devaluation and the subsequent failure of the Mexican stock market, Alfa collapsed, owing more than 2.3 billion dollars.[50]

The rescue package postponed once more Mexico's fall from grace. Again, debt negotiations took center stage, and new agreements were signed in 1983, 1984, and 1985. The debt now stood at 102 billion dollars, and yearly payments of billions of dollars, half of the national budget, went just to pay the interest. To no one's surprise, in the fall of 1988, Mexico asked for yet another loan, this time for 3.5 billion dollars, to pay interest on its debt. At the behest of the IMF, spending on social services, already the lowest in Latin America, felt the axe again. The goal was to right Mexico's balance of payments and stabilize the economy, not to address the needs of the indigent.

VI

Ultimately, the limited size of the Mexican market, more than any other roadblock, drove the spike into the heart of the miracle. Mexico's economic architects had gambled, mistakenly, on a market of middle- and upper-class consumers, less than a third of the population. Its small size, with its low buying power, limited opportunities for profitable investments in industries catering to the home market. Paul Baran called this catch-22 situation a regime of "industrial infanticide."[51] Left out of the blueprint were most rural Mexicans. Including them in the national blueprint would have lessened internal tensions, provided an outlet for cheaper goods of domestic manufacture, and kept campesinos at home by keeping them employed on the land. As Immanuel Wallerstein reminds us, a successful industrial effort in peripheral countries rests on a market large enough to justify expenditures on technology.[52] In Mexico, that included the urban proletariat and also a goodly segment of the rural population.

Auto assembly, considered the backbone of the industrial effort, was a prime example of this truth. Neither it nor its allies in the steel, glass, and tire industries had spurred the growth of well-paying jobs, which would have created auto buyers. The limited number of autos assembled proved overpriced except for a puny number of local customers.[53] Clearly, accelerating the expansion of industry required an improvement in the income of a large segment of the population. To complicate the picture, industrialization had exacerbated the problem because it was unable to provide jobs for a labor force whose ranks had been swelled by rapid urbanization.

In a country still heavily rural, talk of a national market that excluded campesinos bordered on insanity. Yet planning did just that. Little thought, if any, was given to the need to incorporate campesinos into a national consumer market so as to have reasonable hope for the success of industrialization. The import substitution craze had neglected rural Mexicans. This mistake put a brake on market growth. Yet nearly half of the labor force was in agriculture, which accounted for the high percentage of Mexicans in the low-income brackets. A poverty-ridden countryside, and the puny buying power of its inhabitants, stifled the development of a dynamic internal market, which the sometime high wages of industrial workers failed to offset.[54]

VII

In the 1940s, when the architects of the miracle took over, Mexico essentially had two types of agriculture. Despite the agrarian reforms of Lázaro Cárdenas, many of the big estates survived, especially in the northwest; these were farms that produced cash crops for export, mostly to buyers across the border. Commercial agriculture, carried on by big farmers, had received the lion's share of federal benefits, at the expense of small farmers, whether rancheros or campesinos, who harvested much of the food for the dinner table. The agrarian reforms of Lázaro Cárdenas had attempted to alter this picture. Starting with Ávila Camacho, and particularly with Alemán, national policy changed.

No ally of *ejidatarios,* Ávila Camacho started to turn back the clock, to when private landowners ruled the roost. His administration began the neglect of the collectivized *ejidos* and, while conceding the need to dole out land, launched the hoary cry that nearly all of the land held by hacendados had been distributed. Pushed to do something, the administration dealt out marginal lands, but it did little, if anything, to help campesinos till them. To quote a popular campesino saying: "Land without water is like a woman without a man—it won't produce." When haciendas were broken up, their lands, supposedly subdivided, in reality went to the hacendados' family members—sons, daughters, uncles, cousins—thus enabling the hacendados to keep their lands. As depicted in Juan Rulfo's novel *Pedro Páramo,* the hacendados organized *guardias blancas* (armed guards) to protect them from encroachments.[55] Thus campesinos, considered inefficient farmers, were once again neglected, and a deliberate attempt was made to rid Mexico of them in the belief that large, mechanized farms paved the way to the future. It was also believed that, once industry had taken hold, campesinos would find jobs in urban factories. Instead of being a drag on the economy, they would thus become part of an urban labor force. So the technical and financial help proffered campesinos by the Cardenistas was no longer available, and its absence drove more and more campesinos into urban slums or across the northern border to labor as field hands.

It was Alemán who was most responsible for this retreat. In 1946 he pushed a reform of Article 27 through Congress: big landowners now had the right to use the *amparo* (right of habeas corpus) to protect their holdings from expropriation. The public expenditures of the Alemán years went into gigantic irrigation projects, nearly all for the benefit of big farmers, particularly in the north and northwest. Scores of the new *latifundistas* were either high government officials or former "public servants."[56] Despite Cárdenas's land reforms, nearly half of the national real estate remained in the hands of big landlords. For a while, Alemán even stopped the distribution of land, and it was not revived until after campesino protests threatened to upset national stability. The landless campesinos of 1960 outnumbered those of 1930.[57]

Heberto Castillo, the old crusader, told a wonderful anecdote that spells out what this change meant to thousands of campesinos. During a tour of rural Guerrero, Lázaro Cárdenas, no longer president, stopped at the village of Altamirano, where ragged, dirty, hungry campesinos met him. They came carrying a presidential decree, signed by Cárdenas when president, granting them lands, but the decree had never been enforced by state authorities. The oldest of the campesinos handed the document to Cárdenas, who asked Castillo to read it. When Castillo finished, he turn to watch the faces of the campesinos, whose eyes were riveted on Cárdenas. Then, he said, "I looked at General Cárdenas and thought I saw tears in his eyes and anger on his face."[58] When President Echeverría briefly and half-heartedly attempted to imitate Cárdenas in the late 1970s, he hit a stone wall of resistance from the powerful.

This counterreform, as critics called it, gave life to "nylon" hacendados, as they were called by a less than gullible public, when it restored a semblance of the peonage of earlier years. Slowly, the *milpa chica* (small farm), with its cultivation of beans, squash, and chiles, gave way to the commercial farm of soy beans, alfalfa, oats, and sorghum for animal feed, much of it for export. Three-fourths of the total cultivated land in 1940 went to food crops, and less than half by 1980. While of the irrigated lands, just 22 percent grew beans and corn. Mexico now imported up to one-fifth of its food, and it had to borrow money to pay for it.[59] Mexican scholars of the 1960s and 1970s began to write of hunger in the countryside, while guerrillas, led by Lucio Cabañas and Genaro Vázquez, both schoolteachers, and Rubén Jaramillo, a campesino, became active in Guerrero and other states.

In reprisal, police and the army launched what is now known as the *guerra sucia* (dirty war), wantonly killing campesinos, university students, and others who dared protest, at times dumping their bodies, whether dead or alive, into the ocean from army airplanes. Prisoners were tortured, women were stripped naked and raped, as one woman later testified, and their husbands were compelled to watch. When soldiers killed Jaramillo's wife, she was pregnant; it is claimed that the thug who killed her fired a bullet into her womb to make certain the unborn child died.[60] Earlier, at the behest of President Gustavo Díaz Ordaz, soldiers had killed hundreds of university students at the Plaza de Tlaltelolco in Mexico City, and later, on orders of Echeverría, beat and killed others as they marched down the streets of the city. "That which occurred . . . in 1968," charged Octavio Paz, "was simultaneously a negation of what we wanted to be since the Revolution and an affirmation of what we have been since the Conquest."[61]

One episode highlights the ups and downs of this era. Its name is the Green Revolution, an experiment that lasted sixteen years and that endeavored to raise the agricultural output of corn and wheat in northwest Mexico, a region of large, irrigated farms, at a time of growing food scarcity.[62] According to the accepted wisdom, a measure of economic development was the percentage of the labor force employed outside of agriculture; in those days, agriculture and related activities employed nearly six out of ten Mexicans. The lower this number, so went the argument, the higher the level of economic development. To upgrade the economy, one had to transfer labor from agriculture to industry. However, by intensifying production, paradoxically, tractors and other types of mechanized equipment led to the use of more labor.[63] The Green Revolution in Mexico was propelled by the Rockefeller and Ford Foundations and was quickly endorsed by the Mexican people.

The formula of the Green Revolution was that of a capital-intensive agriculture, which dovetailed with Alemán's wish to encourage the cultivation of export crops in order to defray the cost of industrialization. This meant the cultivation of basic grains by use of hybrid seeds, chemical fertilizers, and pesticides, as well as tractors, mechanical harrows, and harvesters. This formula replicated techniques used on American commercial farms. What was good for the United States was good for Mexico.[64] The Green Revolution benefited big landowners in the irrigated zones of Mexico's northwest, who were already favored by the government and whose crops were sold on a large scale.

The results proved contradictory. By raising productivity, by making it possible to grow two or three crops on the same land in one year, Mexicans had more surpluses to export. Farmworkers, too, had jobs for the entire year; yet this job security encouraged migration from less favored regions to more prosperous ones, intensifying the disparities between regions.[65] But the Green Revolution failed to raise the output of staples consumed by the poor. Wheat yields, especially in the northwest, rose dramatically; by 1956, Mexico was self-sufficient in wheat, with average yields four times that of 1940.[66] Corn yields, the staple of the poor, did not keep pace. Under the Green Revolution, Mexico became the Latin American country with the highest degree of agricultural mechanization, but encouraging the use of labor-saving devices placed the benefits primarily in the hands of wealthy landowners.[67] The Green Revolution created new jobs, but mechanical innovations also wiped out jobs, as many as were created. Mechanization, at the same time, exacerbated human relations in the countryside by widening the gap between the haves and the have-nots. Benefits were distributed unevenly, since seeds, fertilizers, and machines went largely to the big farms, widening the gap between small and big landowners and simultaneously depriving multitudes of campesinos of their means of subsistence.

VIII

As national barometers, literature, art, and, for the first time in a major way, film mirrored the contradictions of this era. Art and film particularly spotlighted the values of the day. A victim was the cultural nationalism of the Revolution, reduced, as Carlos Monsiváis writes, to stereotypes, the "macho," "la madre sufrida" (long-suffering mother), "Si me han de matar mañana" (If they are to kill me, kill me now), channeled through film, radio, and the newborn television and, with it, the loss of a sense of Mexican uniqueness.[68] Alfonso Caso, a noted intellectual, lauded European and American thought, as the Porfiristas had done before him, and he made little effort to hide his disdain for the pre-Columbian world. When Samuel Ramos died in 1959, few intellectuals lamented his death: the study of the *mexicano* no longer held sway. The *mexicano,* writes José Agustín, was "out of fashion."[69] Ramos no longer interested most intellectuals, who in keeping with the times proclaimed their cosmopolitism. They were attuned to European and

American currents, and the popularity of Indians and huaraches was diminished. The death of Alfonso Reyes, a Europeanized thinker who died at the same time as Ramos, drew cries of anguish from these intellectuals. The urbanized Mexico of José Gorostiza and Jaime Torres Bodet, who wrote flowery poetry, said good-bye to the *charro* and *china poblana,* while welcoming not just an urban culture but a profound transformation in the definition of the national identity.[70]

For critics, what took place was a cultural colonialism, the embrace of more and more American customs, as Guillermo Bonfil Batalla argued eloquently in *México profundo.*[71] The old plutocracy had imported European models of behavior and thought; today's middle class, the focus of Bonfil's ire, turned northward, self-deprecatingly casting aside what was Mexican in order to copy what they could of the Yankee's way of life. That change, despite Bonfil's assertion, did not come about overnight because, though the radio blared the music of Glenn Miller and Tommy Dorsey, to cite José Agustín, Mexico was not yet totally *agringado* (Americanized). Though the better-off might smoke Lucky Strikes, Chesterfields, and Camels and drink Coca-Cola, most Mexicans still preferred to drink *aguas frutas* (fruit juices), *horchata* (a rice drink), Mexican beer, and tequila. That acknowledged, urban Mexicans also started to eat hot dogs, hamburgers, sandwiches, and hot cakes, and they began shopping for groceries in American-style supermarkets. Music suffered a similar fate, particularly with the deaths of Silvestre Revueltas, Carlos Chávez, and Blas Galindo, venerated Mexican composers. By the 1960s, the Beatles and rock 'n' roll had captured the hearts of Mexican teenagers.[72]

When Lázaro Cárdenas died in 1970, hopes for a better, more just society faded. Those hopes were displaced by public campaigns announcing the need to be realistic: the utopian days had ended. Efforts to remove glaring inequities in the social and economic system could not be sustained. Class differences, which had always existed, became more pronounced, says Agustín. Birth and family status gained privileges for the elect few that were denied to the poor, the "ignorant and dirty." The privileged displayed an arrogance and contempt for the lower-class underdogs, who, Agustín believes, accepted this racist attitude because of centuries of conditioning. Money meant status, success, and social standing, regardless of whether it was obtained honestly or by corruption. The rich paid homage to what they labeled "natural laws," a justification of the rampant inequities in society. As F. Scott Fitzgerald remarked, the rich "are different from you and me," but not because they had more money, as Ernest Hemingway joked, but because wealth confers power and power changes people. The Mexican rich, like so many of their foreign cohorts, were selfish and vicious. Racism, never absent in Mexican society, reared its ugly head. Society held dear the fair of skin, the *güeritos* (light complexioned), and looked down on the *prietos* (swarthy) in a revival of *malinchismo,* admiration for white people. When television made its debut, most of the actors in the popular *telenovelas* (soap operas) enshrining the "American way of life"—fancy autos, luxurious homes, and women in Oscar de la Renta and Ralph Lauren fashions—had white skin and European profiles. The on-screen maids, cooks, and servants reminded viewers that Mexico had mestizos and Indians. Not until the days of Luis Echeverría did the film industry employ, to quote Agustín, "dark-skinned and Indian-looking actors." José López Portillo, when president of Mexico, embarked on a much-ballyhooed journey to "mother" Spain to find, he announced, his ancestral roots.

All the same, urbanization and the expanding middle class, the accouterments of industrialization, spurred a vibrant literary mood, but one seldom in touch with the poor. From it emerged a literature unmatched in Mexican history, part and parcel of the heralded Latin American "literary boom" of the 1950s. During the 1940s, Mexicans had started to experiment with fresh techniques, among them stream of consciousness, unusual time sequences, and complex structures. Their work, setting aside realism, so much a part of earlier novels, focused on the imagination and used a vibrant, rich language. The best of this literature cast contemporary Mexico in a dim light. Rodolfo Usigli, the dramatist, wrote *El gesticulador,* a play about the "big lie," a Mexico of people in the days of Alemán who believed either everything or nothing at all. The principal character, the *gesticulador,* impersonates a dead revolutionary general, but when he eventually confesses his deception, no one believes him, because, said Usigli, Mexicans "prefer myth to reality."[73]

The new literature broke with the novels of the Revolution. With an exception here and there—the novels of José Revueltas come to mind—it was an urban literature, rarely exploring campesino themes. Writers, moreover, had little admiration for the Revolution. This was especially true of the novels of Jorge Ibargüengoita. In *Relámpagos de agosto,* a satiric comedy, the main character, a cowardly "revolutionary general," lies, steals, abuses his power, and mocks everything once claimed for the men who fought to rid Mexico of the Old Regime. In the new novels, characters were usually upper middle class or rich, young, sophisticated, and disenchanted urbanites. They were criollo types, well educated and seldom of Indian ancestry. In their stylized novels, Juan Rulfo, a native of Jalisco, and Carlos Fuentes, son of a diplomat, made the most damning indictment of society. Rulfo's *Pedro Páramo,* perhaps the best of Mexico's novels, depicts a young man who inherited an hacienda, married well, and died a wealthy chief of revolutionaries. From the first, Pedro Páramo, the hacendado, was dead, as were all the people he knew. Juan Preciado, the son sent to search for Pedro, his father, dies without finding him. The dead of Mexico, the novel seems to say, linger on and on, as do the myths about them. Nor did Rulfo put much faith in campesino revolutionaries, preferring to believe that they took up arms not to fight for goals but to defend what they had. Rulfo used the fantasy world to chronicle the frustrations many Mexicans felt after the Revolution failed to break up the country's ruling class.

Carlos Fuentes did the best job of discrediting the legend of revolutionary Mexico. In *La región más transparente,* a story written with visceral power about people in Mexico City, Fuentes included a host of characters, from ranchers turned plutocrats to aristocrats despoiled of their lands by the upheaval of 1910 yet still atop society. Drawing most of the author's ire were members of the middle class, which spawned selfish politicos who, according to Fuentes, betrayed the Revolution. The novel was set in Mexico City, a place of slums, gaudy suburbs for the rich, and cafés where business tycoons hatched shady deals. In *La muerte de Artemio Cruz,* Fuentes bored deeply and singled-mindedly into the marrow of the Mexican tragedy. In the story an illegitimate boy grows up to fight in the Revolution and then betrays it, becoming rich, powerful, and corrupt. He dies in Mexico City a lonely and embittered old man. Mexico, said Fuentes in this powerful novel, was an unfortunate land, "where each generation must destroy its masters and replace them with new masters equally ambitious and rapacious." "Look around," he wrote, and "find intolerable incompetence, misery, dirt, the weakness and nakedness of the impoverished countryside." We are all responsible for this state of affairs, he went to say, because "we have allowed ourselves to be divided by the ruthless and ambitious, and the mediocre." The literate, he lamented, "want only a half revolution compatible with what interests them, their only interest, getting on in the world, living well, replacing" Don Porfirio's elite. Fuentes laments "rapine in the name of the Revolution"; Cruz says, "Today you fuck them because tomorrow, fatally, those you fuck today will fuck you." Then Fuentes has a *burgués,* in a burst of cynical honesty, admit that Mexico "can't make it any longer without American investments."[74] No Mexican writer of our time has so deeply conjured up so many of the mysteries of the pulsating life of his compatriots.

For art, the era represented a return to the prerevolutionary past, when Mexicans sought inspiration in foreign masters. As one critic boasted, in a reference to Orozco, "Today I rarely thirst for his art." Mural painting had fallen from favor, as urban Mexicans took to vilifying Orozco, especially his murals in the Supreme Court, which were decried as a "travesty," "art out of touch with the tastes of the Mexican people." When Orozco died, during the days of the Cold War he detested, few came to his funeral, least of all Miguel Alemán, then president of the Republic, though Pablo Neruda, the Chilean poet who read the eulogy, reminded the mourners that Orozco's art had never lost touch with the people. The official artist of the miracle workers was Rufino Tamayo, who, some claimed, had woven together strands of Mexican and American art with European modernism. Tamayo had synthesized aspects of the abstract expressionists and of Mexican muralists with his own themes. Art, we have to remind ourselves, is anything but autonomous: rather than speaking for itself, it mainly says what we want it to say. As Tamayo acknowledged, "The artist is an antenna who picks up the truth of the moment, who is living his time." So a distinct art, a mirror of its times, gained prominence; to quote José Luis Cuevas, its most notable exponent, that art was alien to the "cactus curtain" of mural art.[75]

For the film industry, World War II opened the doors of opportunity. When Hollywood began making propaganda films on behalf of the war effort, Mexicans, unable to watch Clark Gable, Carole Lombard, and sundry Hollywood stars, turned to films of their own. That opportunity, if artistic films are the measure of quality, was largely squandered during the so-called golden age of Mexican film, despite the majestic photography of Gabriel Figueroa, who brought Mexican literature to the screen, using for his settings shades of gray and highlighting the maguey plant in his rural scenes in an effort to define *mexicanidad,* the essence of Mexican life. For most filmmakers, the promise of profits drove cinematic decisions. There were, however, a handful of exceptions, such as Luis Buñuel, whose socially conscious and majestic *Los olvidados,* graphically depicting the life of poor, urban youth, not surprisingly raised the hackles of *burgueses* unwilling to see the glaring inequities around them.[76] Most films, their stars usually creole types, exhibited a sterile and hypocritical interest in the life of the poor, depicting cabaret girls and life in the slums, as well as singing *charros,* among them the hugely popular Jorge Negrete, wooing damsels in distress. These films generated a black-and-white version of the poor, circumscribed by a range of prototypes no broader than the one laid out by Francisco Bulnes and his *Porfirista* cohorts. They focused on peculiarities and negative behaviors and upheld supposed natural laws, whereby the poor owed the rich submission, loyalty, respect, reverence, and docility. A virulent anti-Communism reinforced the tendency to uphold the morals and Christian values of the Spanish colony.[77]

IX

Here, I add a note on Mexican politics, lest I be accused of neglecting what some may argue is a key element of Mexican development. I do so hesitantly, for it was an age of marionettes: the politicos who ran Mexican affairs during the "false miracle" were cut from the same ideological cloth as the *empresarios* and their kin who helped set economic policy; they were peas from the same pod, allies of the reigning economic interests, with an ear cocked for Washington's solicitude. For a short span of time, they were punctilious beacons of import substitution, but they were hardly steadfast loyalists. All were Priistas, loyal to one party, if in fact it was a political party; they espoused identical principles and were beholden to the same class interests. It was not just a dictatorship but an oligarchy of wealthy Mexicans: *empresarios,* bankers, financial tycoons, big land owners, mining moguls, and merchants, all more or less in accord with North American interests, as "dependency theorists" assert. Cynics argue that the ambassador of the United States must also be included as a member of the oligarchy.

Over this apparatus presided the president, and according to political folklore, he was virtually sovereign. But how can a president elected for a six-year term hold sway when the powerful and wealthy have the upper hand? The answer is that he cannot.[78] In the game of politics, he wielded a heavy hand; economic policy, however, was a different matter. The men who rose to the presidency came from the PRI; they were politicians trained to play by the rules, to keep things on course. A president "picked" his successor, but only after consulting the "official family." In office, he wielded impressive authority. His powers, nonetheless, were mainly political; he could remove governors, discipline labor bosses, appoint "spokesmen" for campesinos, and he always appeared to speak for the nation. All of this was within reason, so as not to endanger the status quo. Loyal politicos were not promoted to the presidency to become mavericks, advocating, for instance, taxes on the rich. To hide reality from public scrutiny, rule by the wealthy and powerful required that presidents appear omnipotent and govern for everyone.

Still, not all presidents were the same. National circumstances determined that they behave according to the needs of the time. Concessions, on occasion, were made to the underclass, but never radical ones. Adolfo Ruiz Cortines, who replaced Alemán, exemplified austerity, the need to halt wild spending and control inflation. In his youth he was an ally of the Americans who occupied the port of Veracruz in 1914, and he loved to dance rumbas and *danzones* with the prostitutes of Veracruz. He became a collaborator of Alemán and ran politics with an iron fist. Scandalmongers recounted that his successor, the handsome Adolfo López Mateos, a likable Don Juan, would ask on arrival at the National Palace, "What is on my schedule for today—*viejas o viaje* [a woman or a state trip]?" He appeared more flexible than the austere Ruiz Cortines, but he dealt harshly with labor. Gustavo Díaz Ordaz, without a whiff of brilliance and the next chief of state, arrived to quell discontent, and he did so using military thugs to kill university students. Luis Echeverría, a long-winded politico who, as Díaz Ordaz's secretary of *gobernación,* soiled his hands in the nefarious deed, became the next president, replaced by José López Portillo, a bon vivant. None of these presidents altered the contours of Mexican economics, though Echeverría, to his credit, sought to reduce Mexico's reliance on American dollars and markets by forging ties with Canada, Japan, China, and the Soviet Union. Yet this man, who supposedly admired Lázaro Cárdenas, left undisturbed the privileges of the wealthy, advised Richard Nixon, the rabid anti-Communist, to be wary of Fidel Castro, warned him of Cuban communism, and distrusted Salvador Allende's socialist regime in Chile.

NINE Death of a Dream

I

By 1982, Mexico's *empresarios* and politicos, with the enthusiastic help of outsiders, had made a mess of the Mexican economy. They then proceeded to throw the baby out with the bathwater, tossing away a domestically oriented blueprint in order to resurrect Adam Smith's old ideas, now packaged as mathematical axioms. Ronald Reagan, the Hollywood actor, and Margaret Thatcher, the fire-eating right-wing English prophet, had orchestrated its revival. These preachers bamboozled the public into believing in the sham of laissez-faire and free trade, that somehow struggling against one another and elbowing and shoving would create efficiency and progress. So died the remnants of the dream.

Under the revived gospel, technocrats replaced politicians at the rudder, basking in the glow of the national spotlight with the election of the colorless Miguel de la Madrid (1982–88). The technocrats, business majors from the University of Chicago, Harvard, and Stanford, quaffed the neoliberal nectar and hurried to woo the old sweetheart of the export economy, once again thought to be the tonic for Mexico's ills.[1] These graduates of elite American business schools had sat at the feet of the oracles who trotted out the hoary theories of David Ricardo, saying that a country does best by allowing the market, Adam Smith's "invisible hand," to determine its comparative advantage. Their Mexican disciples came to believe that every time the oracles spoke, something extraordinary would come out of their mouths.

Tragically for the peripheral world, this free market ideology collided with the facts of history. The United States, now the paragon of open markets, had from early on imposed high tariffs to bar textiles, steel, and other English goods, over time becoming the world's minister of the gospel of protectionism. Not until after World War II, when the American economy had overwhelmed all others, did Washington become the patron saint of "free competition." This new gospel had dire consequences for the peripheral world, encouraging one and all to cultivate salable crops as well as to dig out of the bowels of the earth coveted minerals, and so there arose a deadly competition for the markets of the West. As surpluses piled up, buyers paid less, resulting in a drop in the terms of trade for countries on the margin. The *empresarios,* who it seemed at first glance would be hit hardest by this return to the past, acquiesced, much like ladies of the night at a bordello when told by the madam to take to bed an especially unappetizing but wealthy client.

Economic growth, said the savants at the International Monetary Fund (IMF), to whom the technocrats paid allegiance, required a competitive and untrammeled free market, guided by the notorious "invisible hand." Following this advice had foreseeable consequences: inviting wealthy and powerful transnational corporations into the Mexican home was tantamount to putting the fox in the henhouse. Mexico, so this thinking went, could not make it alone, but must look beyond its borders for allies. How to account for Mexico's capitulation? An old Mexican saying—"de tal palo tal astilla" (a chip off the old block)—is a good place to start. This was Mexico, the descendent of four centuries of doing things in this same way, following an export formula that dated from the discovery of silver in the sixteenth century. To fall back on the wisdom of Samuel Ramos, in evidence was the Mexican sense of inferiority before North Americans and Europeans. This was also the nature of the classical liberalism that had been adopted wholeheartedly by the Mexican Liberals of the nineteenth century; in its renewed form it was essentially unchanged. More than likely, the *empresarios* who watched over industrial policy had come to believe that if they climbed into bed with American capitalists, big profits awaited them. That this behavior would destroy small and medium-sized industry mattered little; money in an alliance with foreigners superseded national unity. This decision cost Mexico dearly, because growth at a snail's pace, if at all, ballooning trade imbalances, and worsening social conditions colored the neoliberal era.

What exactly was this liberalism? *Webster's Dictionary* tell us that "neo" stands for a "revival or adaptation" of a system or formula employed earlier. This was a revival of nineteenth-century dogma, to which modern-day economists added new frills. The goal was to eliminate barriers to the free flow of capital across the globe, as well as to guarantee profits. The removal of those barriers, so goes this theory, allowed a country to concentrate on what it did best; Mexico needed to focus its efforts on mining, a commercial agriculture for export, and, to give one other example, the manufacture of cement. With profits from these sales, Mexico could then purchase what it needed and, with the surplus, build roads, enhance port facilities, and even build factories. One more reason given to pursue the neoliberal revival was the stagnant domestic and global economy of the 1970s, whereas the 1980s for all intents and purposes was a "lost decade" for Mexico. Yet judging by the economic performance of the major Western nations, as well as Japan, the 1950s and 1960s had been something of a golden age for capitalism.

An article of neoliberal faith held that exports, if they eclipsed the value of imports, pumped fuel into the engine of economic growth. Exports had to be diversified and, by whatever measures necessary, made to grow, even by lowering the price of Mexican petroleum below that of the Organization of Petroleum Exporting Countries (OPEC). As Amiya Kumar Bagchi points out, since most world trade originated as exports to and imports from capitalist countries, trade integrated the peripheral countries more fully into the economies of the advanced nations.[2]

But exports alone would not do the job; foreign investment was also needed, and the more the merrier.[3] Mexico had to be made supremely attractive for foreign capitalists. It was like a bordello: attractive ladies entice paying customers. But the capitalists came to make money, so they invested in the industrialized zones of Mexico and polarized regional differences. Then, too, foreign money tended to generate debt and cause currency crises, mostly because of heavy borrowing by peripheral countries and the repatriation of profits. Direct foreign investment is a two-edged sword: it reduces the need for internal taxation but provides fewer government funds for social expenditures, and it becomes a drain on local resources through the repatriation of profits.

Neoliberalism also meant deregulation, putting the private sector at the helm, on the assumption that private ownership was some kind of magic elixir. It meant fighting inflation, no matter what the cost, holding back wages, and privatizing municipal services.[4] These measures, to cite Bagchi, simply aped the techniques and methods of advanced capitalist nations.[5] As the Mexican economist Victor L. Urquidi observed, they were "contrary to the country's best interests"; they weakened "national sovereignty because the borrower sells out to the lender."[6] Neoliberalism came with cuts in welfare, education, and health care and eliminated food subsidies for the poor. Austerity, an old tenet, held that hungry creditors, among them Mexico, should curtail government spending as a cure-all for chronic inflation. When the World Bank perversely insisted that Mexico tighten its belt, it was, said Arturo Escobar, as "if the majority of its inhabitants had not known anything but hardship and self-discipline as a fundamental fact of their daily life."[7] Austerity and the market jeopardized small and medium-sized industries, which required protection for their survival and employed the largest number of industrial workers.

In 1983, the signing of the General Agreement on Tariffs and Trade (GATT) told the world that Mexico, pressured by Washington, had resurrected the export-led model.[8] Mexico had unlocked its doors, and since the United States was the country's chief provider, it would decide the fate of the Mexican economy. In 1983, nearly all imports were subject to duties; less than a decade later, the number of import duties had dropped to just under a tenth of their total value.

When the curtain fell on the Soviet Union, the stage was set for globalization, a system anchored in Ricardo's geriatric doctrine of free trade. For Mexico, globalization was introduced via the North American Free Trade Agreement (NAFTA), a deal engineered by Carlos Salinas, president of Mexico (1988–94). Salinas was a technocrat who had been educated in the United States and who had never before held elective office; he dedicated himself to proselytizing emotionally and politically on behalf of the trade deal. A darling of American capitalists, Salinas, who learned his economics at the Massachusetts Institute of Technology, coveted Washington's blessings. A pied piper of the traditional school of economics, he is remembered for his boast that Mexico had become a "first-world country." NAFTA opened the gates to American multinational corporations and financial behemoths to Mexico. Dubbed "globalization" by economists, NAFTA eliminated trade barriers between Mexico and the United States and tied Mexico's economy more firmly to that of its powerful neighbor. With GATT and then NAFTA, Mexico had some of the lowest tariff rates in the entire world. At the same time, NAFTA shut the gates to Mexican labor; capital could cross borders, but workers could not. NAFTA also blunted environmental legislation and severely hampered the government's ability to regulate international corporations. With NAFTA, Salinas sought to ameliorate internal economic ills by expanding the foreign rather than the domestic market.[9] For Mexico, globalization brought a limited integration into the global economy: only some sectors of its economy were integrated; the rest, the poorest and most backward, stayed out.

Slogans abounded: "free enterprise," "private enterprise," and "no state interference," among others. All were sacred, and all were employed to justify the return to the past. The most popular was the ancient cry on behalf of "international competitiveness," counted on to spur development. Countries had to be ready to compete in the international marketplace and, by implication, at home too. This was a ruthless world where big and powerful corporations with access to the president and cabinet officers ran roughshod over small fry, reaping government largesse beneficial to them. Foreign investment, so crucial for peripheral countries such as Mexico, it was proclaimed again and again, depended on the rate of profit for the investor; a high rate of return dictated a high rate of investment, money needed for home development. The state, no longer the role fixer, had merely to ensure the well-being of the capitalist order.

II

Sympathetic pundits, especially in the United States, heaped praise upon Mexico for one of the fastest and most "successful divestitures of public assets anywhere" in the world.[10] The club of the rich nations hailed Mexico as a shining example of economic lessons learned. Salinas turned privatization into a holy crusade, selling off some of the country's biggest *paraestatales*, among them public television, the telephone system, airlines, and banks. Over 80 percent were sold or dissolved.[11] Under Salinas's successor, Ernesto Zedillo (1992–2000), another U.S.-trained technocrat, even the national railway system, the pride of the Porfiristas, felt the axe. By the mid-1990s, Mexico, in order to finance its operations, was borrowing almost 20 billion dollars a year.[12] Since its credit standing stood high in the financial capitals of the United States and Western Europe, loans and credit came easy. To woo foreigners, Salinas placed *tesobonos* on the stock exchange; these were highly speculative short-term bonds with high interest rates, redeemable at a moment's notice. For a while, the borrowing paid off; between 1990 and 1993, some 91 billion dollars entered Mexico, one-fifth of the flow of money from core countries to those on the periphery.[13] But much of it was speculative capital, ready to flee Mexico at the first sign of turbulence.

Meanwhile, monopolies, the age-old nemesis, survived. Open competition found no home in Mexico, despite calls from the World Bank, which believed monopolies put a brake on growth and hurt the consumer. But Mexican consumers, unlike their counterparts in other

Western countries, neither complained nor took steps to organize themselves. Telephone fees, for instance, were among the highest in Latin America, but users simply paid them.[14] Mexican industry, as always, was the story of monopolies, once again treated to old-style reverence, despite Article 28 of the Constitution, which had banned them. A handful of families in cahoots with foreign capitalists, reported the *Los Angeles Times,* controlled most of Mexico's beverage sales, cement, and even flour for tortillas. The telephone service, sold off to one of the richest men in the world, became Telmex, a national monopoly controlling most of the country's landline phone service as well as nearly three-fourths of the cell phone market. Televisa, a private company, controlled the nation's television. Cementos Mexicanos, shielded by high tariffs, had more than 80 percent of the cement market, though Mexicans controlled only a fraction of its stocks. Grupo Vitro ran the glass industry, Grupo Visa produced much of the beer made in Mexico, and Grupo Maseca produced most of the corn flour and tortillas. Bimbo, a company owned by one man, controlled 90 percent of national bread sales. Free to dictate prices, these monopolies drove up the cost of nearly everything.[15]

This was the golden age of transnational corporations that established production facilities in Mexico in order to retain old markets and win new ones. A goodly share of international trade arose from movements of raw materials and goods between these firms and their subsidiaries.[16] By 1996, Wal-Mart, the biggest of the big-box corporations, had scores of stores in Mexico, followed by Costco. Procter & Gamble and Anheuser-Busch were also doing business in Mexico, as was McDonald's, its hamburgers available in every town of any size. These were joined by seemingly every pizza franchise operating north of the border as well as Kentucky Fried Chicken ("para chuparse los dedos"), while Nestlé, another giant, sold almost all Mexican powdered milk and Carnation sold an equal percentage of condensed milk. General Motors, Volkswagen, Chrysler, and Nissan accounted for 80 percent of exports. It was cheap to assemble autos in Mexico and then ship parts and autos by truck or rail to the biggest market in the world.[17]

Hailed as a savior, neoliberalism proved niggardly, and for some it was a global nightmare. For a while, the Mexican economy headed for better times, largely because of low inflation rates, partly as a response to low wages, but growth soon bogged down. For the first twenty years, growth rates hovered at 0.32 percent, the lowest of the twentieth century.[18] Nor was Mexico's experience unique: sister Latin American republics that hewed rigorously to the neoliberal dogma also felt a sharp drop in macroeconomic indicators. Private ownership did not give birth to greater efficiency, more competition, or a better life for ordinary Mexicans; private owners turned out to be no better than the old bureaucrats. With privatization, sixty-five thousand Mexicans lost their railroad jobs; when Altos Hornos, the huge steel foundry in Monterrey, shut down, nearly twelve thousand more were lost. Privatization cost four hundred thousand Mexicans their jobs. Nor were the new owners more responsive to the public. The service of Teléfonos de México, once run at a profit by the government, did not change one bit: on any given day countless consumers had no service.

Nor did free trade reduce poverty or diminish the gap between the poor and the rich. On the contrary, the poor lost nearly half of their purchasing power, and unemployment ran rampant in the cities and countryside. In Latin America, only Ecuador, Costa Rica, and Honduras had lower per-capita incomes. Poor families somehow stayed alive with an income of less than twenty-six pesos a day. To pour salt on the wound, even subsidies on tortillas were thrown onto the trash heap. Less money was spent on education, health, and welfare; earlier, 24 percent of public funds had gone to them; less than a decade later, only 9.5 percent. Mexico, *Proceso* reported, spent less funds on social welfare than did Zambia, Bolivia, and Colombia, which had smaller and weaker economies.[19] To quote one facetious minister of hacienda, when asked about the state of the economy: "The economy is great, it is the people who are hurting."

III

Change, too, had come to Mexican society. The population, now over 100 million, had exploded: by the end of the century, Mexico was the eleventh most populous country in the world. Three out of four Mexicans had become urbanites, millions of them in Mexico City, one of the largest cities in the world. Middle-class families of physicians, lawyers, merchants, and managers, dwelling largely in the more dynamic northern and central states, made up nearly a fifth of the population. Birth rates had fallen in the cities, but not in the countryside. Aging Mexicans were plentiful, but only a minority had either pensions or old-age insurance. Thousands of Mexicans, unable to find decent jobs at home, fled to the United States. Each year during the 1960s, some twenty-seven thousand Mexicans had left; by 1999, that number had multiplied tenfold.[20] Unwilling to help their poor, Mexico's elite had chosen to rely on Uncle Sam to give the poor jobs and to feed them, and equally important, to avoid a potential social explosion of the restless.

Amiya Kumar Bagchi, writing about the capitalist classes in the peripheral world, chastised them for being "weak." They suffered from a "profound ignorance of their own economics," and he spoke of their "almost hereditary state of dependence" on the advanced capitalist countries, evidencing a tunnel vision that led them to "look at the potential for development . . . partly with an eye on their masters."[21] For Mexico's *empresarios,* that was surely true. For them, and for their allies in politics, nothing could be done without an influx of dollars, francs, or yen. So courting foreign capitalists became a religion of its own. To ensure that they came, policy was liberalized; no longer were foreigners barred from owning Mexican firms outright. In the 1990s, foreign investment, mostly American, exploded, rising to an average of nearly 11 billion dollars a year. The Mexican economy became increasingly dominated by United States capital, reverted to being more export-oriented, and became home to more and more transnational corporations, while the country's exports were increasingly controlled by American firms.[22] Earlier, most foreign investment had been in autos, petroleum, pharmaceuticals, and textiles; in the 1980s, investment moved to the export-processing industries, the *maquiladoras,* headquartered from Tijuana to Matamoros, responsible for the assembly of electronics, auto parts, clothing, furniture, sports equipment, and toys. Even in 1998, when foreigners owned only about 2.5 percent of Mexico's industrial firms, they produced nearly a third of its industrial exports.[23] While Mexico basked in the glow of the petroleum bonanza, Mexican auto assembly plants, geared largely to the U.S. market, had nevertheless sold some of their output in Mexico. When the economy collapsed, so did local sales. Not until ten years later did the industry return to its precollapse levels.[24]

These were turbulent decades. Beneath the glamour of the well-off, and although some claim it was a time of rising mobility, many Mexicans did not move up the economic ladder.[25] The middle class enjoyed better days, but nearly a fifth of Mexicans lived in conditions of extreme poverty, barely making it from one day to the next, even rationing the tortillas they ate. Alongside glittering shopping malls, bulging with upscale boutiques, were moats of open sewers and the putrid stench of rotting carcasses of dogs and cats. The rich, for all that, did well for themselves; they too had their problems, but of a different type altogether. During economic downturns, *empresarios* had rushed to sell off enterprises that had gone belly up: telecommunications, textiles, tourist havens, and hotels among others. The big *empresarios,* nonetheless, survived, joined together in Coparmex, Concanaco, and the Cámara Nacional de la Industria de la Transformación.

IV

Mexico, whatever the pundits of neoliberalism might allege, had one of the most lopsided distributions of income in the entire world, an unapologetic barrier between the blessed and the damned. Everything, apparently, favored the better-off, even school scholarships: the top 10 percent of society monopolized most of them. The tax structure was similar: the less favored carried the brunt of the fiscal burden; wage and salary workers, along with small shopkeepers, paid 62 percent of national taxes, while *empresarios* just 38 percent. To make up for tribute not collected, in 1980 the Congress passed the IVA, a regressive sales tax that included food and medicine. Everyone, poor and rich, paid it, but its weight fell on the backs of the less well-off.[26] No one, however, enforced the collection of the income tax; between 1921, when it was adopted, and 1977, only two persons had been jailed as tax evaders.[27]

Race, skin color, and physical profile rounded out this picture. Racial bigotry, as old as colonial times, reinforced a social and economic hierarchy: those with lighter skin who did not look "Indian" fared better.[28] A shameful correlation existed between class and color; the middle class, as expected, skewed to the lighter end of the racial spectrum, and the rich, most often than not, were white as white can be.[29] The psychiatrist Santiago Ramírez asserts that mestizos and criollo types equated Indians with weakness and passivity. I recall once having breakfast with Miguel de la Madrid and telling him that I thought it shameful that television anchors and reporters, as well as soap opera actors, were almost entirely fair and Spanish looking. He thought so too and promised to speak to Emilio Azcárraga, Televisa's owner, but since nothing has changed, I surmise that De la Madrid either failed to keep his word or that Azcárraga ignored his advice. In his memoir, Miguel de la Madrid, himself fair of skin, had this to say about the sorry plight of the poor in the heavily Indian states of southern Mexico: "Most likely [their] chronic underdevelopment" can be traced to "their racial composition." The population of Indian descent, he believed, had held back *mestizaje,* the blending of the Indian (the inferior race) and the Spaniard (the advanced race) and, by implication, progress.[30] Count Gobineau could not have said it better.

Where did the internal market fit into all of this? Not at the top of Mexico's priorities, especially if we take into account the buying power of workers. Between 1939, the last of the Cardenista years, and 1955, real wages had fallen, but not dramatically, but between 1982 and 1987, they plummeted.[31] Low wages hampered the growth of an internal market, although exports were spurred by lower production costs. By the year 2000, one-tenth of the labor force earned less than the minimum wage. Some estimates placed 40 percent of the working class in the "informal sector," the self-employed who earned a subsistence living bereft of benefits.[32] Less than a fifth of labor was unionized, but as Octavio Paz noted, unions, nearly always at the beck and call of Partido Revolucionario Institucional (PRI) officials, were but one more example of an institutional structure in which "form everywhere masquerades as substance."

Urban Mexico, moreover, had higher indexes of absolute poverty, and unlike earlier times, this was more so than the countryside. Campesinos had greater relative poverty, but more of the poor resided in cities. This rise in poverty was primarily urban. Women, in particular, felt the brunt of the rising poverty of the 1980s, the "lost decade," when neoliberal panaceas took hold.[33] More and more women went to work, nearly always in low-paying, unskilled jobs—if they could find them—to feed and clothe their children and not infrequently their own fathers and mothers. The employment of women had grown rapidly, but their wages had not; most earned less than men for doing the same job. They were also the first to be let go. The drive to export and "compete" became a drive to lower wages, for both men and women. In the poorest households, the need to buttress the man's labor fell on women, though children and teenagers also had to become wage earners. Households headed by women, perhaps as many as 5 million of them, were the most vulnerable, and so the chance of permanent poverty increased. In these homes, especially those headed by a woman, one tended to find undernourished children and higher levels of hunger. The more poverty, the higher the level of violence; women, whether wives or girlfriends, were the usual victims.[34] In some states, women had become the backbone of the subsistence economy because their menfolk had gone off to work in the United States.[35]

Agricultural policy, although not new, hammered more nails into the internal market's coffin. Under Salinas, changes in Article 27 made possible the sale of *ejidos* as well as the private ownership of as many as six thousand acres. Yet the largest percentage of the country's workers depended on agriculture for their livelihood. As Rodolfo Stavenhagen, a leading agronomist, said, instead of making campesinos the centerfold of their blueprint, the technocrats set out to favor a small elite of big landlords, to channel private investment into a commercially profitable agriculture.[36] Next came a dependence on imported corn and beans.[37] Mexico, once self-sufficient, had to import them and at the same time become the best customer of American dairy products. Included in this scheme was a cattle industry for export but also to supply meat for the tables of well-off Mexicans, prone to eating steaks, prime ribs, and pork. Yet over a third of the poor never ate meat.[38]

These changes were not entirely new; they had been on the drafting table since the days of Miguel Alemán, but they exacerbated the plight of campesinos. Denied federal aid, and faced with the advent of NAFTA, which opened the gates to imports of cheap corn and beans, campesinos, unable to compete, abandoned their plots to become sharecroppers or wage laborers. An untold number of villages and small towns, inhabited mainly by old men, women, and children, had to make do on money sent from the United States by the menfolk who had fled there. Armchair critics, who cannot tell the difference between a plow and a harrow, delight in putting the blame for this misfortune on the backs of campesinos. That is nonsense. As Lázaro Cárdenas knew, campesinos, given technical help, access to water, fertilizers, a bit of credit, and outlets to markets, turn out to be highly productive farmers. Until 1969, with less than a fifth of the federal aid distributed nationwide, campesinos had produced 38 percent of the Republic's harvests.[39] That was forgotten by Salinas and his technocrats. In the Laguna, where Cárdenas broke up the cotton haciendas, alfalfa and feed crops for the dairy industry now covered much of the land. *Ejidos* had become real estate developments, land for assembly plants, or golf courses. Many of the families who had lived off the cultivation and sale of cotton now labored in the assembly plants.

In the judgment of the sociologist Armando Bartra, the plight of corn under NAFTA was worse than was readily apparent. Bartra cites an old Mexican saying: "Sin maíz no hay país" (Without corn there is no country). Corn is culture; corn is identity. The traditional corn *milpa* of the campesino was abandoned to its fate, and thus the food sovereignty of Mexico was turned over to foreign transnationals, a move that was out of touch with native needs. Imported transgenic corn would contaminate Mexico's native varieties, to the ultimate harm of the country's culture. According to Bartra, "It appears that policy makers think it makes more sense to export Mexicans and import food than to support Mexicans who grow it." Why jettison the native corn of campesinos?" he asks. Beyond simple economic dogma, Bartra asserts, lies a racial prejudice. The welfare of native corn is cast aside because Mexican *burgueses* look down on the languages, cultures, and food of Mexico's pre-Columbian inhabitants. Only when a rebellion erupts do the rich and powerful share a concern for the hunger of the Indian, identified always with corn.

V

Salinas and his neoliberal cohorts, to the thunderous applause of Washington and the Mexican *burgueses,* were sailing along with the wind at their backs until January 1, 1994, when hundreds of lightly armed Indian campesinos captured San Cristóbal de las Casas, a small city, and three adjacent towns in the state of Chiapas. The uprising occurred with the signing of NAFTA that, along with the Salinistas' emasculation of Article 27, spelled disaster for the Indian. In Chiapas, 1 million Indians, the majority of the population, toiled on coffee plantations and cattle ranches, their trials and tribulations depicted in the novels of Rosario Castellanos, with hardly anyone to turn to but the Virgin of Guadalupe. Until a few years ago, it was said, Indians had to get off the sidewalks to allow criollos and mestizos to pass by. A poor state, Chiapas was nevertheless rich in natural resources. Its subsoil held vast quantities of petroleum and much of Mexico's drinkable water reserve, and the land sheltered forests, nurtured corn, and gave life to coffee trees. The state also produced over half of the country's hydroelectric power, but it ranked at the bottom of the totem pole in education. Corn flour, tortillas, and wood furniture constituted 40 percent of its industry.

The rebels demanded the overthrow of the Salinas regime. "We have nothing to lose, absolutely nothing," ran their communiqué, "no decent roof over our heads, no land, no work, poor health, no education, no right to chose our leaders freely . . . no independence from foreign interests, and no justice for ourselves and our children."[40] Bishop Samuel Ruiz, head of the local diocese and one of a handful of church prelates to take up the cause of the Indians, explained to an incredulous nation that the uprising "was caused by a society structured in such a way that the level of poverty . . . brings about an almost suicidal situation." How true! The per capita income of Indian campesinos stood at approximately 230 dollars a year—just over 19 dollars a month. In Chiapas, Mexico's leading coffee producer, some 60 percent of the farmers were Indians, but big landowners and rancheros monopolized the best lands, paid their workers poorly, and, with the cooperation of the PRI, ran local politics and corrupted justice. As the Salinistas, avid apostles of deregulation, dismantled safeguards and international coffee prices unexpectedly tumbled, the Indians rebelled. With the Chiapas uprising, the tattered remnants of miracles and boasts of first-world status by Salinas and his technocrats faded away. Salinas sent the army to quell the rebellion; the soldiers, mostly Indians themselves, killed nearly 150 of their compatriots.[41]

All the same, perennial headaches did not vanish. Despite a drop in the value of the peso, imports skyrocketed, but the value of exports rose by just 8 percent, and half of that from a temporary rise in oil prices. At the end of 1989, the trade deficit stood at 3.5 billion dollars, the highest it had been since 1981. For nearly a decade, Mexico's internal market had either stagnated or shrunk. At the same time, Western nations had erected barriers to shield their economies while, concomitantly, the peripheral world competed for a slice of the same pie. This led to a glutted world market and the lowest commodity prices in half a century.

Worse still, the bogeyman of perennial debt displayed prodigious staying power. The debt had not shrunk but, to the contrary, had ballooned, increased by the need to cover payments on interest and capital borrowed, thus serving as a self-perpetuating mechanism of poverty and a barrier to development. The rescue package of 1982 merely postponed Mexico's fall from grace. Debt renegotiations, for the same reason, became the watchword, and new agreements were signed in 1983, 1984, and 1985. Between 1981 and 1991, Mexico received thirteen structural and sectoral adjustment loans from the World Bank and endorsed six agreements with the IMF, all tied to demands to embrace free trade and open doors to foreign investors.[42] The debt stood at 102 billion dollars, and yearly payments ran from 12 billion to 16 billion dollars, down from 20 billion during the petroleum era. Mexico spent over half of its national budget to cover the interest. To no one's astonishment in the fall of 1988,

Mexico welcomed yet another 3.5 billion dollars from Washington, earmarked to pay interest on bank loans. At the behest of the IMF, spending on social services, already among the lowest in Latin America, felt the knife again. The goal was to right Mexico's balance of payments and reduce inflation. As the value of the peso fell, the rich sent their money out of Mexico, worsening its payment deficit. No less real were the skewed prices for food and clothing.

The blunder of 1994–95 dwarfed the earlier one. As the *New York Times* reported, one of the favorite Latin American success stories had been about a "closed economy thrown open by technocrats trained in the Ivy League, with investments pouring in, the inflation circus run out of town, and democracy taking root."[43] That fairy tale aside, the financial debacle of the 1990s, perhaps the biggest in the history of Latin America, occurred when real economic growth was a negative 6 percent, the worst since the Great Depression. News of the collapse broke in December, just as Ernesto Zedillo, picked by Salinas to succeed him, devalued the peso when he found his country bankrupt. The "peso crisis" shook Wall Street's faith "in Mexico's transition from a debt-ridden third world country to a prosperous free market economy." However, investors had already started to abandon the sinking ship. As this occurred, Mexico's store of foreign reserves shrank. Yet stories of the overvalued peso were hardly news; economists had been warning that Mexico's trade deficit would eventually compel a peso devaluation. Mexico had required, as the *New York Times* reported, "continuous injections of foreign money" ("tens of billions" of dollars). The money serviced the ballooning foreign debt and paid for the imports of the rich. Salinas, who thought of himself as something of an economist, had scoffed at worries of Mexico's financial health, but he had neglected to explain that the bulk of investments coming into Mexico came from speculators gambling on the Mexican stock market.[44] One of the worst decisions made by Salinas and his technocrats had been to offer foreign speculators, always on the lookout for easy profits, to invest in Mexico with *tesobonos,* short-term high-yield treasury notes. When the economic bubble burst in 1994 and speculators took their money out of Mexico, their appetite for easy profits from purely speculative investments turned the stock, currency, and real estate markets upside down, bringing on the Mexico peso crisis, as well as its Asian counterpart. Salinas's naiveté cost Mexico dearly. The peso's value dropped by half, interest rates went through the roof, and inflation jumped sky high. Bankruptcy weighed upon the nation like the plagues of ancient times. Countless small businesses closed their doors, and the jobless rolls nearly doubled. Hit hard by the peso's fall from grace was the middle class, its numbers decimated and its median income dropping by a whopping 40 percent. The debacle threatened the pocketbooks of American speculators and lenders, among them banks, mutual funds, and individuals who had purchased Mexican *tesobonos*.

Fearful that the crisis might spread and undermine the newly signed NAFTA, for which Americans had lobbied heavily, Wall Street and Washington had the IMF lend Mexico 50 billion dollars, 20 billion to stabilize the peso and put off a Mexican default.[45] It was essentially a bailout of American banks, which had lent billions to Mexico. Mexico had to hock its oil revenues, deposit them until the loan was paid off in the Federal Reserve of the United States, and allow American bankers to buy Mexican banks. And so petroleum, that national symbol of Mexican sovereignty, ended up in foreign hands. Once again, like a naughty child caught with its hands in the cookie jar, Mexico had to swear to cut out "wasteful public spending" and bless austerity. So ended the Salinas regime's dance with destiny.[46]

Zedillo, the last of the technocrats, not only accepted the loan but paid it off in the wink of an eye. He did this by slashing public spending on education, scientific and technical schools, and health. The burden of paying off the "rescue package" fell upon the shoulders of everyday Mexicans. Zedillo, however, behaved differently with the bankers, also caught up in the collapse of the economy. Previously nationalized by José López Portillo, the banks had been returned by Salinas to their former owners, who had foolishly lent money to their executives, stockholders, and to brothers, sisters, cousins, and friends and had doctored their books. Evidence surfaced of insider trading, self-lending by the bankers, and crony capitalism. Some 8 billion dollars of the so-called rescue package went to pay off loans that were highly irregular or just plain illegal. When the economy collapsed, so did the banks. Without consulting Congress, Zedillo bailed them out, using public funds, leaving Mexican taxpayers to foot the bill of 71 billion dollars. The bankers and speculators reaped a whirlwind of profits. By the end of the century, all but one bank had been sold to foreigner bankers, who used their expertise to market credit cards and auto loans, but proved niggardly with small businesses, the country's chief employers.[47]

This experience makes clear that peripheral states are rendered powerless by ensnaring themselves in debt adjustments and privatization schemes. Whatever financial clout they may have had goes out the window because of their indebtedness. With rising debts and depleted revenues, these countries have to turn, like beggars, to the World Bank, the IMF, or other satraps. Inevitably, they become trapped by the terms imposed by the lenders. By 1985, such was the condition of Mexico, one of the world's biggest debtors.

VI

In 1992, Roger Bartra published *La jaula de la melancolía: identidad y metamorfosis en el carácter del mexicano*, an examination of Mexican thought and culture. Bartra suggested that Mexicans, in their efforts to fit themselves into Western culture, were undergoing a traumatic passage. But it had to be made. The colonial years, independence, and the Revolution had only partially integrated Mexico. It was time to get beyond nationalistic nonsense in order to forge an identity based on multicultural norms. This interpretation essentially reflected that of urban Mexicans, particularly the better-off, the well traveled and educated. But Bartra, others could reply, suffered from what they described as the adulation of intellectuals of an underdeveloped country for the United States and Western Europe. Because this love affair distorted their perspectives, it became virtually impossible for them to come up with adequate answers to questions raised by their own country. This had not been so with early European intellectuals, who were unable to imitate more advanced countries. More likely, too, Bartra's views, whether consciously or not, reflected the bigotry of a society that prized blue-eyed *güeritos* (blonds).

Intellectuals may speak proudly of pre-Columbians, but they see contemporary Indians as a stone around the neck of modern Mexico.

The opinion of Bartra and his allies, unsettling echoes of the past, clashed with the duality of Mexico, one living in the present, and the other, in many ways, part of the past. That duality should have reminded them that culture and modes of thought change ever so slowly. How different, after all, were Bartra's conclusions from those of Francisco Bulnes and other Porfiristas? This rush to endorse the idea of a Mexico unrelated to its past seduced a host of writers, among them Carlos Fuentes, who, in the *La muerte de Artemio Cruz,* had laid bare the tragedy of the Revolution. Yet he came to praise the "economic reforms" of Carlos Salinas, who in his view had stabilized the economy, controlled inflation, set the state free from bloated responsibilities, and unlocked to world trade a formerly closed economy.[48] These intellectuals forgot that no newspaper in Mexico sold more than a hundred thousand copies, no weekly political journal more than eight thousand copies, and no monthly cultural magazine had twenty thousand readers.

Not all Mexican intellectuals worshiped at the neoliberal shrine. Critics had harsh words to say about current trends. Carlos Monsiváis reminded Mexicans that millions of their children still dropped out of school, that their parents viewed reading negatively, perhaps because of a Catholic belief that it corrupted the soul or that college-educated men and women took advantage of the poor. As long as poverty persisted, warned Monsiváis, more and more children would drop out of school. David Huerta, known as Mexico's Pablo Neruda, was a leftist who wrote with candor; his poetry of hope, battle, and despair exposed the brutality of capitalism. Elena Poniatowska, a writer and novelist, published a scathing account of the De la Madrid regime's callousness during the Mexico City earthquake of 1986, when the president and his aides did little to ameliorate suffering.

A barometer of these days was the Mexican film industry; its golden age had become history. No longer the beneficiaries of government largesse, directors and producers were left to fend for themselves and to scrounge for funds. The beloved dream of José Vasconcelos, secretary of public education in the 1920s, that the state must be a patron of the arts was tossed into the ashcan. The effects were catastrophic, especially because no tradition of private funding existed in Mexico. According to the country's Film Institute, once a hundred films were made yearly, but then just twenty-five. Most of the films that were made were of poor quality and dealt with sex, violence, and vulgarity. Critics said filmmakers lacked the money to make good films and decent movie houses to show them. Nor could Mexican filmmakers compete with Hollywood; they were the victims of changing tastes and government censorship.

Yet here and there, against the tide of mediocrity, filmmakers turned out remarkable dramas. One of them was Alejandro González's *Amores perros,* a story of a violent contemporary Mexico, which was nominated for a foreign-language Oscar. Guillermo del Toro made *The Devil's Backbone,* a horror story set against the drama of the Spanish Civil War, while Salvador Carrasco, in *The Other Conquest,* probed the tragedy of the Spanish conquest of ancient Tenochtitlán. *La Ley de Herodes,* a satire risking the ire of the government officials, takes place in a small village and explores the corruption of the PRI. *Como agua para chocolate,* produced by Alfonso Arau and based on the novel of the same name by his wife, Laura Esquivel, is set against the backdrop of the Revolution of 1910. Tina, the youngest of three daughters, is required by tradition to forgo marriage in order to care for her widowed, cold-hearted mother. Her lover, who wants to stay near her, agrees to marry the older sister in order to remain near the woman he loves. The title refers to that moment when water reaches the perfect temperature for melting chocolate. *Danzón,* a film by María Novaro, is a musical romance about the Caribbean-Mexican ballroom step and was one of the best women's films of 1991. The subject, played by the actress-politician María Rojo, is a woman trying to find herself. In *El crimen del Padre Amaro,* a young priest finds himself in a corrupt church bureaucracy that collaborates with local drug lords who rob villagers of their lands. Priests who dissent risk excommunication. Father Amaro, once a priest on a holy mission, ends up the portrait of a corrupt individual who sells himself so as to keep his job.

TEN NAFTA

I

Grand economic theories rarely last more than a few decades. Some, because they march in step with technological or political events, may make it to half a century. But only soldiers and guns can keep others alive.[1] Neoliberalism, replete with market idolatry and technocratic and technological determinism, had thirty years, but now, judging by its current rejection in South America, it agonizes on its deathbed.

Neoliberalism is dying everywhere, that is, but in Mexico, where the ruling oligarchy, those with commercial and financial ties to the United States especially, has for decades clutched the reins of power. Like the gnomish Ebenezer Scrooge of Charles Dickens's *Christmas Carol,* they hoard their gold, blind to what their southern cousins are doing, and dance blithely to the Western tune of neoliberal dogmas and with bulldog tenacity tightly clutch globalization, the new euphemism for Western imperialism. One truth is self-evident: long ago these Mexicans and their kin buried the aspirations of the Mexican Revolution of 1910, the summit of the national social conscience, transforming it from barefoot radical aspirations into a sleazy, hypocritical comic opera.[2] The last act of the upheaval of 1910, the glory of the historical chronicle, has turned into a travesty. Judged by its current blueprints, Mexico's oligarchy, those who dictate policy, are out of step with the needs of the country's majority. As Octavio Paz mused some years ago, one Mexico, the more developed, "imposes its model on the other, without noticing that the model fails to correspond to our historical, psychic and cultural reality, and is instead a . . . a degraded copy . . . of the North American archetype."[3] These revivalist architects forget that in poor countries it is ultimately the state that protects national resources from looters, provides a semblance of security for the poor, funds schools, and provides health care.[4]

Perhaps nothing better illustrates this neglect of the underdogs than the politics of Vicente Fox and Felipe Calderón, Panista (member of Partido Acción Nacional, or PAN) presidents who, along with Carlos Salinas and Ernesto Cedillo of the PRI, left their stamp on politics in the days of the North American Free Trade Agreement (NAFTA). Despite vociferous claims by both Salinas and Fox that Mexico boasted the eleventh-largest economy in the world, it had the peculiar and dubious honor, according to a United Nation report, of not standing alongside the fifty nations given credit for human development.[5] The prosperity of the elite and the welfare of the people were not one and the same.

By the same token, nothing reveals the nature of a society more than whom it entrusts with political power. Given the weak social conscience of these Mexican rulers, that does not speak well for society. Opinion polls bear this out. According to one, when Mexicans were asked if they had, either alone or with others, taken it upon themselves to resolve a community's dilemma, four out of five answered no. An overwhelming number replied that Mexicans preoccupied themselves only with their own selfish needs. The editors of *Proceso* asserted that we live in a society where a collective sense of responsibility is skimpy at best and politics are seen as a "contemptible activity."

This verdict has the ring of truth. Still, opinion polls tell us that four out of five Mexicans hunger for change. That said, the change they got from the PAN victory in 2000, which ended seventy years of virtual dictatorial rule by the Partido Revolucionario Institucional (PRI), falls short of their expectations. Vicente Fox, the victor, and his PAN allies left things more or less as they found them. The change they wrought conjures up what Mexicans call *gatopardismo:* things appear to change only to remain the same. That election, hailed as earthshaking because it led to the downfall of the despised PRI, made one lesson clear: increased political participation does not lead to a more equitable society. Between the PAN and the PRI, there was not a dime's worth of difference. Both danced to identical tunes; they were mouthpieces for the traditional lords of Mexico, and both were enamored of NAFTA. To quote Carlos Monsiváis, the perceptive critic, Fox, despite his cowboy boots and country slang, stepped out the mold of Salinas and Cedillo, the last of the *Priista* presidents, with his worship of neoliberalism, his kowtowing to *empresarios,* his ceaseless pursuit of foreign investments, and his subordination of the public interest to the private. Citing macroeconomic statistics, Fox hailed the Mexican economy, ignoring that millions of Mexicans live in poverty. As a Brazilian politico once said, no one lives in the macro economy, but apparently Fox did. Like his PRI predecessors, Fox, thinking like the Coca-Cola salesman he had been, put Mexico's fate in Washington's hands. Unfortunately for him, American leaders made clear that Mexico would not receive preferential treatment.

To keep politics and, most importantly, the economy safely neoliberal, Fox and his Panistas, in Machiavellian style, did what they could to rig the election of 2006. For this endeavor they had the enthusiastic backing of *empresarios,* Televisa, and *burgueses* from Tijuana to Tapachula in southern Chiapas. First, to disqualify Andrés Manuel López Obrador, the popular mayor of Mexico City and member of the left-of-center Partido de la Revolución Democrática, from seeking the presidency, Fox and his allies had a subservient Congress convict López Obrador of disobeying a court order, thus earning him a *desafuero* (removal of his immunity from prosecution and his right to run for office). Why this animosity? López Obrador, to boisterous public acclaim, had threatened to discard the neoliberal formula and wage a relentless battle against poverty and for social justice and jobs. To help small farmers he vowed to amend NAFTA. A huge public rally in Mexico City on his behalf put a halt to the diabolical *desafuero.* Felipe Calderón Hinojosa, the Panista candidate, no less Catholic and no less neoliberal than Fox, hailed NAFTA, promised to enhance public security, and at the last minute even talked of lifting the burden of poverty from the backs of the poor. After a nasty campaign, during which the *burguesía,* with *empresarios* in the lead, spent millions of pesos on dirty tricks to vilify López Obrador, the Panista won. In the opinion of many it was a fraudulent, hair-breadth victory. Public demands for a vote recount went unheeded. Things would stay the same. In office, Calderón put his antipoverty pledge on the back burner, dispatched the army to fight drug lords, and began speaking fondly of opening Pemex and the Comisión de Electricidad, a government monopoly, to private investment. With good reason, his critics suspected privatization. For their part, PRI politicians, their candidate defeated at the poles, clasped hands with victorious Panistas to hail neoliberal policies, as they had in the days of Salinas and Cedillo.

Why this blindness to public needs? The answer, or answers, are complex but not necessarily unknown. One Mexican psychiatrist draws a picture of an unruly land, a "dysfunctional" society, which operates badly and is impaired or abnormal.[6] To understand what this means, one must contrast it with the functions of a normal, healthy family, a unit with multiple roles, starting with the father, who rules, provides, begets, molds, and protects. The mother bears and cares, cherishes and succors; the offspring obeys and prepares to mate and to become a father or mother. At the top of the family pyramid stand the parents, watching out for the welfare of their offspring. That is exactly how it should be, but this is the opposite of how Mexican society operates. For the poor, survival is a rat race; the parents in this world of poverty may shelter and protect their offspring, but those above are indifferent to their welfare.

Most neglected is the Indian community, ancestral home of Mexico, ostracized and relegated to nonexistence in the minds of most Mexicans. Yet, because of a high birth rate and declining infant mortality, Mexico has more Indians now than it did when it gained independence. There are nearly 13 million Indians who belong to 62 ethnic groups and live in 871 municipalities, largely in Chiapas, Oaxaca, Guerrero, Veracruz, and Hidalgo. More than twenty-three hundred rural villages are primarily Indian. In Chiapas alone, nearly one out of four cannot read or write, while half never completed primary school. In Mexico City dwell half a million men and women who speak an Indian language, more than in any other locality in the Western hemisphere. To cite the anthropologist Eric Wolf, none of these Indian communities ever existed on a desert island but was always "part and parcel of the larger society."[7]

Why this hoary, unjust pyramid? Well, to start with, for centuries, class, race, and the color of one's skin determined where one stood in society. The exploitation of the poor is centuries old, but money, the essence of class in most societies, is only one factor. Money cements class status but only partly whitens the skin, and Indian "blood" rarely gains prestige. The scars on society date from the colonial years and are deepened by centuries of proximity to a powerful and rich neighbor always boastful of its European heritage.[8] Few wealthy Mexicans call attention to their Indian heritage, but they do take enormous pride in their Spanish ancestry. This gulf that separates certain Mexicans, criollo types, from others, mestizos or Indian by blood and physical features, has for centuries retarded the formation of a national culture and a united people.

In years past, American scholars were fond of writing about "many Mexicos," referring to racial, linguistic, and geographical divisions. That was surely exaggerated, but the idea had a grain of truth. One Mexico, if it has come to be, took a long time in coming. That, however, cannot paper over the gulf that separates the rich and well-off from the poor, a barrier as big as the ubiquitous mountain ranges. A testimony to this disparity are the popular *telenovelas* (soap operas), in which the virtuous and rich are light-skinned, the women are Western types, and the "bad" and wayward generally sport swarthy complexions and Indian profiles. Like most of the rich everywhere, the Mexican variety exhibit a weak social conscience and are indifferent to the fate of the downtrodden, while their representatives, as they fill workers' hearts with dreams, pick their pockets. So long as Dame Fortune smiles on them, they care not a whit what befalls the poor.

The cruelty and arrogance that have been inflicted on the poor since colonial days yield a bitter harvest of servility, but also one of anger and mistrust. *Lambiscones,* or sycophants, are found up and down the social ladder, especially among politicos, says Octavio Paz, but they can also be found in business, partly as a result of the cult of personalities rather than because of principles.[9] Mexicans, whatever their social and economic standing, but especially the downtrodden, are a cynical lot. They don't believe what is told them by those at the top, yet for centuries they passively accepted their condition, at times turning to the church for consolation. No wonder that, until recently, elections seldom drew much interest among the most exploited: in Guerrero, Oaxaca, and Chiapas, some of the poorest states in the Republic, 70 or 80 percent of eligible voters would stay home on election day.[10]

The nature and interests of the Mexican upper class date from centuries ago, to the final years of the colonial era. With independence, a criollo oligarchy of hacendados, mining moguls, and powerful merchants, all more or less dependent on exports, took over the reins of power. Names have changed, of course, but political and economic power rests with the old interests. Today's upper class, or classes, are generally an amalgam of the traditional ruling groups in land, commerce, banking, and industry. No evidence indicates that new groups have emerged that are ready to call into question the power of the traditional oligarchy. Industrialization, either during the Porfiriato or, more recently, in the years of "import substitution," left much of the old fabric untouched. Instead, argues Amiya Kumar Bagchi, the traditional ruling classes, "to the extent that this could be done," undertook new economic activities but held on tightly to their monopoly of land and government and added the few industrialists to their ranks. A notable characteristic, Bagchi continues, "is that from the last half of the nineteenth century economic life has been guided largely by the enterprise and requirements of the dominant capitalist country of the day, Britain up to 1914, and the United States since then."[11]

Proximity to the wealthy and powerful neighbor next door has left a legacy of servility, an exaggerated sense of dependency, a tourist industry, for instance, that caters to Americans but only marginally to

Mexicans, or reliance on foreign investment as a cure-all for what ails Mexico. NAFTA is a prime example of this psychology of dependency, emerging from the cockeyed belief that when all tariff barriers fall and foreigners rush to buy and sell, the Mexican economy will roar. Yet for the poor of Mexico, NAFTA has failed to deliver more jobs; half of the workforce is unemployed, underemployed, or in the informal sector, and to exacerbate matters, no country in the world has exported more manpower than Mexico. An average of 450,000 people a year are thought to have crossed into the United States during the early years of the twenty-first century. Some 2.5 million workers had left their families for jobs in the United States, more than sixteen times the rate for the 1960s, when only thirty thousand Mexicans per year had fled northward. Clearly, social programs have not been working.

The Mexican *empresario* emerged in an era when outsiders controlled nearly all profitable opportunities. It is small wonder, consequently, that there was born a subordination of the native elite before metropolitan capitalists. That is the story of the Mexican oligarchy, always ready to bend a knee before their foreign masters. So, after a brief whiff of economic independence, the oligarchy quickly renewed its ties with American capital, a logical step, since the new *burguesía* arose from the ranks of the old hacendado and merchant families, who had wielded their power in association with American capitalists as well. The "revolutionaries" described by Carlos Fuentes in *La muerte de Artemio Cruz,* rushed to join the "new boys on the lot." Much of the middle class fell in step, overwhelmed by a barrage of Hollywood films with happy endings, Movietone newsreels heralded American accomplishments, beauty contests featured tall blondes, and sales pitches from American radio and television hawked the shiny autos that were rolling off Detroit's assembly lines. Before long, the well-off, to cite José López Portillo, were imitating American ways of doing things, wearing clothes made in the "USA," glibly paying homage to globalization, shopping at malls, dancing to rock 'n' roll, and identifying their self-interest with that of the foreigners.[12] Carlos Monsiváis, the literary sage, referred sarcastically to them as the "first generations of North Americans born in Mexico."

One fact stares one in the face. The well-off hate paying taxes, and Mexico has one of the lowest tax rates in the world. Less than half of 1 percent of Mexico's local budgets are collected from property taxes, and much the same can be said of *empresarios*, who, relying on an old fairy tale, claim that taxing them discourages investment in productive enterprises. When oil revenues are set aside, Mexican rulers raise the equivalent of just 9 percent of the gross national product (GNP) from taxes, roughly equivalent to the rate of taxation in Haiti, the poorest country in Latin America. To make up for this disparity, Pemex, the Mexican petroleum monopoly, turns over 40 percent of its profits to the federal government. Lacking funds for reinvestment, Pemex is seldom at the cutting edge of modern operations.[13] Revenues also come from taxes paid by middle-class consumers and from duties on foreign commerce. When Luis Echeverría, then president of Mexico, attempted to reform the tax base in the 1970s, he ran into a stone wall of opposition from *empresarios* and their allies. "I couldn't do it," he told me. Mexico, let it be said, has earned a reputation in financial circles for being one huge "tax-free enterprise zone for the rich." To quote one Mexican *empresario*, "We have a saying here: 'If you pay taxes in Mexico, then you don't have a good accountant.'"[14] Some might argue that the future lies with the middle class. But to visualize the middle class as the harbinger of some kind of economic independence overlooks that it was sired by the old, dependent *burguesía.* In 1940, the middle class constituted only 4.5 percent of the national population, and 75 percent were urban; by 1980 the middle class included 33 percent of Mexicans, but just 19.5 percent of households.[15] It is an intermediate class, standing between the poor, the huge majority, and the rich: in the 1980s three out of four middle-class Mexicans dwelt in cities of over a hundred thousand inhabitants. Some two-thirds of the heads of middle-class households were salaried employees; the rest were small business owners, all susceptible to the ups and downs of the economy. The crisis of 1994, which brought a sharp decline in middle-class income, decimated it, leaving just one-fifth of the population in its ranks. Through good times and poor ones, most members of the middle class struggle to imitate the lifestyles of the rich, parroting their views and voting for the PAN. Many heed the preaching of the conservative Catholic hierarchy, which has been more politically outspoken since Carlos Salinas, who possessed a Promethean view of his talents, renewed Mexico's ties with the Vatican. From the ranks of this class come lifelong practicing Catholics, who uphold the right to life, vehemently oppose all abortions, and decry the use of contraceptives, including condoms. None of the church's 132 bishops is an Indian. No wonder, therefore, that the PAN administration of Vicente Fox, which was heavily supported by the middle class, left untouched the hallowed principles of the past, seeking above all else to improve Mexico's image abroad so as to encourage foreign investment.

Historical evidence tells us that the Western nations did not always embrace the economic practices they now seek to foist upon peripheral countries. At one time they all fought tooth and nail to protect their infant industries, erecting tariff walls and using subsidies or discriminatory shipping rules. Most certainly those were the practices of the United States and Great Britain, which now hypocritically call for a ban on all barriers to capital. Laissez-faire, a dogma only partly embraced by the West, may have once yielded results, but today the state must play an active role if resources are to be used to produce items that will meet basic needs, rather than to manufacture commodities for export under unequal exchange terms. A proper balance is needed between state regulation and the rule of the market; a centralized authority must raise capital and draw up an economic blueprint, given the nature and magnitude of the development challenge, made all the more difficult by an international economic system that has historically relegated peripheral countries to the role of suppliers of raw materials.[16]

The economist Albert Fishlow points out that state supervision of the Mexican economy led to sustained growth; the failure of this approach should not be an argument for a return to laissez-faire but rather for a correction of errors.[17] Whatever its drawbacks, the state during the days of the corrupt Miguel Alemán regime paved the way for industrialization, and under Lázaro Cárdenas Mexico witnessed agrarian reform and took steps to lessen the terrible inequities in the distribution of income and wealth. State intervention had been a fact of life since the days of Porfirio Díaz, when the state, albeit belatedly, started to play a central role. In a society as diverse, skewed, and complex as Mexico's, the state is the one unifying force. The challenge was not whether to weaken it, but how to make it more democratic. It should not be shrunk into oblivion. To do so cripples the economy and places the majority of Mexicans at the mercy of a rapacious *burguesía* that has yet to demonstrate that its leadership will benefit everyone.

Reliance on exports, the perennial economic sin, is a two-edged sword. As the political economist Joan Robinson understood, a government resolved to eliminate mass poverty and unemployment may garner much help from export earnings, which can be used to improve the productivity of agriculture and increase the capacity to produce vital consumer goods. But, she continued, an increase in profits from foreign trade in itself cannot be relied upon to bring about a better life for the majority of the population. Profits may simply exacerbate economic disparities and heighten social tensions.[18] There was a time when Western economies hungered for raw materials, but not today. The global economy relies more and more on high-tech manufactures and, above all, sophisticated services. The old strengths of the peripheral world, abundant raw materials and cheap labor, are every day less important. According to the World Bank, raw material prices, already below those of the Great Depression, will decline further.[19] Campesinos in Chiapas, for example, recently left their coffee crops unpicked because the price of coffee on the international market was too low. Recent studies show that even the prices of textiles, clothing, wood products, and chemicals produced by Latin American, Asian, and African countries of the periphery have fallen since 1970. Mexican goods sold abroad are still largely primary products or manufactures of minimal technological content, both unable to compete with exports from China, South Korea, Malaysia, Singapore, Hong Kong, or Taiwan.[20] The income derived from such exports will not create jobs or satisfy the needs of the burgeoning population. Due to international competition, export-led growth keeps wages low. Low wages, in turn, weaken domestic consumption, stunt the development of an internal market, and generate destructive regional competition. Additionally, Mexico has a new problem: China has become the chief exporter, in dollar terms, to the United States, Mexico's principal export market.[21] Worse still, in the not too distant future Mexico could well become a net importer of oil, which for over sixty years has supplied a goodly share of government expenses. The last two decades have witnessed a decline in oil production, while proven oil resources have declined.

Mexico is a capitalist country, but its capitalism is one of underdevelopment, making it excessively vulnerable to the ups and downs of financial markets. Old traditions and the framework of an advanced economy exist side by side; ancient forms of economic and social organization share the national stage with globalization. It is a dependent capitalism; Mexican welfare rests essentially on the United States. In Mexico, recovery cycles, on the heels of recessions, do not restore jobs to the same degree they do in industrialized nations. Poverty, unemployment, and small farmers in distress characterize Mexican capitalism. In urban areas, settlements consisting of flimsy hand-built shacks without running water, toilets, or even windows, once thought temporary, have become a permanent fixture. Poverty, formerly identified with campesinos, is becoming increasingly urban; millions of the poor dwell in close proximity to wealth and opulence.

Other ills confront Mexico. We must not forget that over half of Mexico's land surface is either arid or semiarid; it is a parched, empty landscape with obstacles as huge as the surrounding mountains. Regular rainfall covers just over 7 percent of the land. Water scarcity is a growing national problem. Mexico has less drinking water per capita than it did half a century ago, and much of it is contaminated, presenting a danger to public health. Over 100 million Mexicans share this water, if not always equally; by 2050, some 130 million will be dependent on it. Even now, over 12 million Mexicans do not have running water in their homes.[22] The poor and the wealthy alike share contaminated cities crowded with too many people and too many autos. Mexico City, home to over 20 million Mexicans, has some of the most polluted air in the world; taxi drivers, street vendors, and residents complain of hacking coughs, watery eyes, and headaches. Yet not until 1995 did Mexican authorities declare its air unhealthy.

The Panista leadership shows little inclination to make the internal market the national engine. Mexico is one of the fifteen leading export-oriented countries in the world, with nearly all of its sales ending up in the United States. In one month alone, what Mexico sells on that market equals its yearly commerce with all the nations of the European Union. Nothing has been done to rescue small and medium-sized industries, which have been left to fend for themselves. These enterprises, the hardest hit by NAFTA, employ 80 percent of the labor force, turning out huaraches, western saddles, belts, candies, cheese, and so forth. Unemployment soars to heights not seen for decades. No week goes by without news of small businesses closing and jobs being lost. More than 4.5 million Mexicans, one-tenth of the workforce, are unemployed. Wages, furthermore, stagnate; for an economy relying on the open market, wage control is a powerful tool for achieving the much-heralded ideal of "competitiveness."

Over the last decades, economic growth has stalled at about 2.3 percent.[23] But according to INEGI, the government's office of statistics (often accused of sugarcoating bad news), by 2008, the year of the Great Recession in the United States, that figure stood at 1.6 percent, the lowest growth rate since 2004. Even worse, the Banco de México predicted that the economy would grow at a measly 0.5 percent during 2009.[24] The underground economy, estimated at about 25.5 million people, fuels the country's primary job engine.[25] Wages, calculated in real terms, had fallen to 25 percent of their equivalent in 1976. Mexican capitalism, it must be told, bestows benefits on the top 15 to 20 percent of population but fails to meet the basic physical and emotional needs of the great majority. That is Mexico, where the country's architects wave the anti-inflation flag and demand "competitiveness" of one and all, thus creating a dog-eat-dog world in the face of surging poverty and unemployment.

Globalization is a blueprint for economic growth that integrates peripheral countries into the Western economy. The subservient classes of the peripheral countries embrace globalization, which resurrects the old reliance on exports. But this integration benefits mostly the well-off, perhaps one-fifth of the population. The idea of "one world" is a myth, propagated by those who want you to believe in a "one-world economy," which in reality is neocolonialism.[26] Globalization, the current Western drive to tear down international barriers to capital, represents nothing more than the search for profitable investment opportunities abroad, its architects multinational corporations and the powerful states that speak for them. What NAFTA peddles is little more than the right of these corporations to exploit the resources and markets of Mexico. But, then, this is how it has always been. To quote Thucydides, the venerated historian, "The strong do as they can, and the weak suffer as they must." This drive endangers what is left of national industry and the jobs of those not members of the global elite. Globalization purports to reduce differences between core and peripheral countries, but the world evolves in the opposite direction, accentuating them.

Meanwhile, corruption, that old nemesis, haunts Mexico. The poor economy leaves an opening for it. According to one estimate, nearly one-tenth of the GNP is lost to it. Corruption finds fertile soil among all classes, the rich and the poor, whether politicos, *empresarios,* merchants, or guardians of the public order. Mexico, if truth be told, is one of the most corrupt countries in the Western hemisphere, and as the journal *Proceso* writes, the situation can only go from bad to worse. *Proceso* estimates that some 60 percent of politicos either accept bribes or have criminal backgrounds. Asked to find a incorruptible politico *(honrado),* even Diogenes the cynic, with his long beard and lamp, would have thrown up his hands in despair. Corruption eats at the heart of Mexico, rendering moot the trust between people and their leaders. It springs forth from the unholy marriage of political and economic power; money buys influence, and power attracts money. All the same, millions of Mexicans, particularly the less well-off, are as honest as the day is long.

Corruption, in Mexico apparently a kind of aphrodisiac, makes a mockery of politics. Until the election of 2000, the PRI machine, in an alliance with *empresarios,* television moguls, and the wealthy, relied on the purchase of votes, threats, and the military to rid itself of rivals. To quote Carlos Hank González, a *Priista* oligarch, "a politico without money is an incompetent politico." The courts, and justice itself, look the other way. Unhappy politicos and businessmen might speak ill of the president behind his back, but in public, like good *lambiscones,* they heed his beck and call. Fear of angering *el Presidente* leaves no one willing to speak up. The political apparatus has been so well oiled that during the presidential elections of 1988, when early returns favored the opposition candidate, PRI politicos in Mexico City shut down the computers and the next morning proclaimed their candidate the victor. To quote a Mexican saying: "Our elections are burdened with the dubious prestige of a whorehouse: they work but are they virtuous?

The drug traffic exacerbates corruption. When huge sums of dollars are at stake, police, soldiers, public officials, and even *empresarios* dig their fingers into the drug pie. *Proceso* estimates that half of the agents of the Procuraduría General de la República, the Justice Department, receive money from drug lords. Poverty, too, plays a role, for one must eat, and, if one has a wife and children, take care of them, and the drug trade pays well. According to one estimate, nearly half a million Mexicans have links to drug trafficking. In the early years of the nefarious trade, it was thought that the drug gangs were merely ferrying cocaine, heroin, and marijuana through Mexico to markets across the border. That myth has gone up in smoke. In 1993 only 8 percent of Mexicans had used drugs; by the turn of the century nearly one out of five Mexicans were either users or had tried drugs. Cocaine, not marijuana, became the drug of choice. The largest number of drug users lived in the northern states, the most prosperous. One reason for the growth in drug use is that peddlers, unable to transport drugs across the border, sell them on the local market. That, plus deteriorating social conditions, rampant inequality, the lack of jobs, and recurrent economic crises help explain ballooning drug use.

Rival drug cartels in cities such as Tijuana and Ciudad Juárez, havens of the unruly, have turned their cities into shooting galleries where police and drug mafiosos kill each other. The corruption of soldiers asked to clean up the drug mess goes on unabated. During 2002, in Guamúchil, Sinaloa, some six hundred soldiers of the Sixty-fifth Battalion were detained on suspicion of having helped local drug dealers escape detection. That same year, two generals were tried for their ties to the

Juárez drug fiefdom. Not long ago, the country's top drug enforcer, a general, was sent to jail after it was learned that he had ties to one of the drug cartels. Yet no other agency has done more to stem the drug trade than the military. When the government tries to eradicate marijuana and heroin poppies, the campesinos who cultivate them complain. As José López Portillo tells it, when his soldiers uprooted marijuana and heroin poppies in Sinaloa, a hotbed of the nefarious business, campesinos asked, "¿Entonces que vamos a sembrar para comer?" ("What are we going to grow so that we can eat?")[27]

A macabre irony of the odious business is that it became a national calamity with the victory of the PAN in the election of 2000, which was hailed as a hallmark of Mexico's democratic maturity. Until then, the PRI political machine had, in its own tenebrous ways, kept the drug business under wraps; that is, it was merely a problem but not a major national worry. Governors, mayors of towns and cities, and their underlings, some undoubtedly with ties to the drug peddlers, were left to make whatever arrangements suited them with their nefarious neighbors. Though Vicente Fox, whose election toppled the PRI, left this scene more or less undisturbed, Felipe Calderón, his successor in the national palace, made the drug trade his chief concern. Calderón believed that taking on the traffickers was good politics, and he feared that unless the drug business was stopped, it would in time turn Mexico into a facsimile of the Republic of Colombia, a notorious pariah. By openly repudiating the PRI's policy of accommodation, declaring a "war on drugs," and calling more and more on soldiers to hunt down the culprits, Calderón unwittingly unleashed a Republic-wide wave of terror. The army, with some help from unreliable police agencies, on occasion caught a major drug mafioso, but in so doing they brought on a bloody aftermath, as the mafioso's underlings killed each other to determine who would succeed him, while rival gangs then fought over control of territories. As the number of murders, increasingly of local police and innocent bystanders, escalated, the weakness of the federal apparatus to put a stop to the butchery became obvious. The president of Mexico had been defrocked, shorn of the power to dictate events, a power long attributed to him by Mexicans and a legion of pundits and scholars. Before long, inhabitants of Ciudad Juárez and Tijuana, where violence became endemic, refused to venture out at night, and the tourist trade in much of the Republic, a mainstay of the federal budget, tottered as fewer Americans and Europeans, fearful for their safety, came to visit.

II

With the signing of NAFTA, by which giant American corporations gobbled up the small, Salinas and his cohorts, and later Fox and Calderón, made clear that more than ever the fate and welfare of Mexico's economy rested on Uncle Sam's shoulders. To cite a Mexican critic, one began to discern a certain resemblance between contemporary Mexico and the country of Porfirio Díaz, when foreign investors had the run of the country. Certainly, foreign investment can be helpful, but capitalists, we have to remind ourselves, do not come to Mexico to develop national industries; they come to operate businesses of their own, largely to take advantage of cheap labor costs. The investment of capital takes second place to the extraction of profits, and most of the reinvestment, says Bagchi, goes "to other advanced capitalist countries."[28] Capital flows in the form of investments from core countries to peripheral ones tend to generate debt and currency crisis as a result of excessive borrowing by the client as well as the repatriation of profits.

And Mexico, we must not forget, has accumulated debts. In 1964, it owed just 2.3 billion dollars to private and government lenders; by 1972, that sum had jumped to 7 billion dollars, and in 1982 it was 87 billion dollars, with the government in hock for 70 percent of it and the private sector for the rest. By 2003, the debt had reached the astronomical figure of 97 billion dollars, a sum equivalent to 43.7 percent of the GNP. The debt included the 1980s bailouts of Mexico and that of 1994–95. Some 70 percent of the federal budget in 2003 was earmarked for payment on the national debt and FOBAPROA, the bank bailout. A debt of $1,317 dollars hangs over every Mexican.[29] Only Brazil had a bigger debt among the impecunious countries. The International Monetary Fund, moreover, wanted borrowers to pay promptly.[30]

NAFTA, besides, has reinforced social inequality. This is what Andrés Manuel López Obrador had to say after a tour of every municipality in the country: "We must not forget that the current economic model has created tiny islands of progress in a sea of poverty."[31] Or to cite the newspaper *La Jornada:* "In our country there coexists a way of life at levels of those of Italy, side by side with regions of poverty comparable to those of the poorest of the African nations.[32] No one who knows Mexico can dispute that. Mexico is a land of extremes, where the rich wallow in the lap of luxury next door to the miserably poor. Distribution of income is so uneven that the poorest fifth of the population has an income comparable to that of the poorest fifth of Sri Lanka. The polarization is worse where industry has a toehold. In the Colonia Álvaro Obregón of Mexico City, a manufacturing hub, families live in caves. According to the March 2007 issue of *Forbes* magazine, ten of the world's billionaires were from Mexico, among them the telecommunications magnate Carlos Slim, mentioned earlier. Their total value added up to 6 percent of the GNP. None, significantly, was an industrialist, unless one includes the making of cement, but Lorenzo Zambrano, head of Cemex, owns only a quarter of its stock, the rest of which rests largely in the hands of Americans. To cite Carlos Monsiváis, when these pampered families are worth billions of dollars, the news transcends the ordinary and becomes a moral scandal. In a country where some 20 million people live in extreme poverty and another 35 million are considered poor, the wealth of these individuals equals Mexico's budgets. Social inequality is as Mexican as the tortilla; it has been a hallmark of the country since the arrival of the Spaniards, but not as it is today, to cite a common opinion among many Mexicans.

That assessment rings true. For example, in March 2007, *Proceso* published a story about the inhabitants of El Nayar, a municipality in Nayarit with thirty thousand inhabitants, most of them Cora or Huichol Indians. In Los Encinos, one of the villages in the municipality, a doctor comes only once or twice a month. The sick have to walk miles to the nearest clinic; some die on the way. One child, one of many, survived just fifteen months, dying from malnutrition, a daily affliction of El Nayar. So poorly fed was the child that he could not sit up; he breathed with difficulty and sobbed day and night. One day, his paternal grandfather, worried that the child was dying, walked for an hour to find a *curandero* (healer) in a nearby village, only to learn that the healer could not come until later that day. When the *curandero* arrived, the child was dead. Taking the child to the nearest hospital would have cost six hundred pesos, a sum beyond the grandfather's ability to pay. When a scorpion bit two-year-old Martha Griselda, Martha's mother took her to a nearby clinic but found it closed. When the attendant arrived some two hours later, he gave Martha an injection, but it was too late. The child died, as had her two older brothers, one five and the other one, also from scorpion bites. The father, a campesino, lacked the money required to take them to a clinic.

Los Encinos, whose inhabitants are corn farmers, have no electricity, sewers, or running water. Their sole modern convenience is a school with sixty-seven students; their teacher tells a reporter from *Proceso* that some of his students have only a tortilla to eat at lunchtime. "That tells me," says the teacher, "that they eat sparsely at home and are hungry all of the time," so "when we can we give them crackers to eat." Hungry children, he adds, are notoriously poor students: "They seldom pay attention, reveal scant interest in learning, and spend their time dwelling on food."[33] El Nayar is part of the Mexico where Slim and his companions enjoy their billions.

The origins of today's scandalous inequality go back to the ballyhooed miracle years of Miguel Alemán, who, along with his gang of rapacious *empresarios*, politicos, and landlords, enriched himself as few Mexicans had done before. As Carlos Fuentes wrote eloquently in *La muerte de Artemio Cruz*, the revolutionary elite married into the old Porfirista families and laid the basis for a new oligarchy of wealth. For these *empresarios*, landlords, bankers, and politicos, modernity, which they claimed to have brought to Mexico, meant an opulent home in Mexico City or Cuernavaca, wealthy friends, nightclubs in Acapulco, with mistresses, fiestas, and being part of the international jet set. Their only worry was that one of their grandchildren might marry a swarthy Mexican. Modernity meant costly autos, fancy coming-out parties for their daughters, sumptuous weddings, women in high heels, a cigarette in their mouth, and dining on prime rib at the San Angel Inn.

What passed for moral outrage was tempered by an urban society that enjoyed the fashionable notion of getting rich quickly and mysteriously. This was the world of the super rich, replete with the racist and classist attitudes toward the poor. Unholy alliances with the kingpins of politics and monopoly magnates were common among them. Carlos Slim, for example, purchased the nation's telephone network from Carlos Salinas at a bargain price; his monopoly nonetheless, according to Guillermo Prieto, head of the Mexico's Central Bank, charges some of the world's highest phone rates. Emilio Azcárraga, the major stockholder of Televisa, the country's television channel, banked millions from his alliance with PRI politicos. These wealthy men shared close ties to presidents, were party to juicy federal contracts, were privy to insider knowledge of the stock market, enjoyed scandalously low prices for *paraestatales,* failed to pay taxes, and maintained incestuous ties with foreign capital.

As they always do, some pundits will tell you that inequities are inevitable, that eventually the gap between the rich and the poor will disappear or at least diminish considerably. That is humbug. As the political theorist Immanuel M. Wallerstein argues, the gap, which day by day grows bigger, is "not an anomaly but a continuing basic mechanism of the operation of the world economy."[34] In previous eras, core and periphery were such that the development of laggard countries appeared possible, but not today. So the discourse of development has gone by the wayside, replaced by talk of "adjustment." Macroeconomic growth helps, but as in the case of Mexico, it does not provide solutions. The course pursued by Mexico amply illustrates this truth: macroeconomic growth rates come at the cost of social neglect and economic inequality. According to the World Bank, in 2002 Mexico had the ninth-largest economy in the world but ranked sixty-ninth in per capita income, and it had one of the least equitable income distributions in Latin America. The top 10 percent of Mexicans had 42 percent of the national income, but the bottom 10 percent had a mere 1 percent.[35] The gap between the haves and the have-nots has widened since 1982. Mexico is the eleventh most populated country in the world, and the poor are far more numerous than before. Nor is poverty simply a rural problem; city folk are poor too, often plagued by malnutrition, alcoholism, and prostitution. Poverty and misery dictate life spans: seventy-five years on average for the better-off; just forty for the rural poor. About 15 million people purchase much of what they want; the others simply try to provide food, clothing, and shelter for themselves and their families and pray that illness or some unforeseen catastrophe does not befall them.

III

Even Carlos Slim, the richest of the richest, admits the problem in Mexico is "neoliberalism gone wild." With that dogma, he goes on to say, Washington denies Mexico any chance for internal growth. His verdict certainly applies to NAFTA. Or, to cite the opinion of Ricardo Pascoe, a diplomatic figure of note, NAFTA traps Mexico into the position of servant to the United States. The elimination of tariffs on American goods and the failure of Mexico to support its own industries weakens the country. The rush to join the global economy opens channels only for groups of select Mexicans and excludes many others, polarizing society because it offers opportunity for just a few. No one pushed Mexico to join NAFTA, declares Victor Flores Olea, a diplomat and intellectual. Mexican leaders did so on their own, "subordinating national interests to those of the United States." *Empresarios* and technocrats fell in step with American claims that, by dropping trade barriers and opening Mexico to their investments, Mexico would bloom. Superficial benefits came, but mostly to members of a domestic elite willing to cooperate so long as there was something in it for them. NAFTA conferred on foreign investors a special bonanza; between 1995 and 2001, foreign investments rose dramatically. Most Mexicans' standard of living, however, declined, and Mexico ranked fifty-fourth in the development chain.

Since the signing of NAFTA, economic growth has been a meager 1 percent. For the majority of Mexicans, the medicine offered is not going to make the patient better. Trade ministers, *La Jornada* reminds us, do not speak for the majority but for an elite that benefits from joint ventures with transnationals. Some of NAFTA's advantages to Mexico have fallen by the wayside. Mexico's proximity to the United States no longer carries the weight it once did, because air and sea transportation are faster and cheaper than ever, while trade barriers have fallen around the world. In the last three years, Mexico lost almost half a million manufacturing jobs to countries as diverse as China and tiny Honduras. Those jobs have been replaced by the informal sector, what economists refer to as off-the-books employment, and poor Mexicans, more sanguine, do "what one does in order to keep body and soul together." By one estimate, over 62 percent of Mexicans with "jobs" survive in the informal economy.[36] Foreign investment, meanwhile, has dropped to its lowest level in a decade. NAFTA, while enhancing Mexico's ability to supply manufacturing firms from the United States with low-cost parts, declared the *New York Times,* has not transformed Mexico into an independently productive economy. With NAFTA, to cite *La Jornada,* "we rely on our exports . . . but our national industry has virtually disappeared."[37] Contraband textiles supplied over half of Mexico's needs, lamented *La Jornada,* despite it being an industry that dates from the early years of independence.

IV

What about NAFTA and the Mexican farmer? One of the oddities of the Mexican picture is that, although city dwellers outnumber campesinos, today more Mexicans till the land for a living than at the time of the Revolution of 1910. According to *La Jornada,* at least three out of four of them live in dire poverty.[38] Fox, the PAN president of Mexico, liked to boast that under his leadership rural poverty had declined slightly. If true that was not due to Fox's policies but to the huge volume of remittances sent home by Mexicans in the United States. In just one year, Mexicans working in the United States send home some $20 billion. However, as stated before, campesinos simply cannot compete with big

American commercial farms. One statistic tells volumes about the magnitude of this disparity. On American farms there are 1.6 tractors for each farm laborer; in Mexico, there are just two tractors for every hundred. As Octavio Paz recognized years ago, "Our rural population, poorly clothed, illiterate and underfed, has paid for the development of that other Mexico."[39]

NAFTA, which already threatens the welfare of campesinos, is about to jettison all tariff barriers. In 2009 all tariffs fell by the wayside. By the terms of the agreement, Mexico has opened its grain market, as well as dry beans, apples, meat, and dairy products, while Washington has accepted Mexican vegetables, cotton, and sugar. Mexico's comparative advantages are few: cheap and abundant labor, some land and, here and there, water. The principal beneficiaries have been the vegetable growers, large-scale exporters, of the Yaqui and Mayo river valleys of Sonora and the Fuerte River region of neighboring Sinaloa. Experts predicted that trade asymmetries would likely grow under free trade unless dramatic growth occurred in the Mexican agricultural export sector. Failing that, NAFTA would most likely weaken Mexico's farm sector.

That is precisely what has occurred. The big farms, feasting on irrigated land, thrived. They exported vegetables and fruits, gaining an advantage over their American rivals because of longer seasons of sunshine and cheaper labor. These farms supplied over 80 percent of the fresh vegetables purchased by the United States, while exports of products made by large Mexican and transnational food-processing corporations jumped upward dramatically. Just the same, in 1996, just months after the signing of NAFTA, Mexican imports of basic staples from American farms, corn, beans, and wheat among them, were three times those of preceding years and represented nearly half of Mexico's consumption. The worst was yet to come. By 2007, imports of American corn had risen from less than l million metric tons in 1993 to nearly ten times that amount, at the expense of millions of campesinos, whose corn and beans made up the diet of the poor. Among the winners, reported the *New York Times*, were the Grupo Bimbo, Mexico's largest food company, reaping profits from cheap grain imports; Maseca, the world's biggest producer of cornmeal and tortillas; and Sigma, the importer of cheap pork and poultry.[40] Other beneficiaries included the upper class and elements of the middle class, which purchased most processed foods. By 2002, Mexicans imported half of the food they ate; cheap cornmeal from the United States went into the making of one out every three tortillas. Yet, as Joan Robinson wrote, raising your own food is an effective form of import-saving investment. Consequently, when a country borrows money to buy its food, it is "borrowing in order to eat."[41]

NAFTA along with the dismantling of the *ejido* system, which includes some 70 percent of Mexico's farmers, will drive an estimated 15 million campesinos off their lands in the next twenty years. When asked how he felt about their plight, Fox, the former Coca-Cola salesman and ardent free trader, replied callously that "a farmer who cannot survive in the 21st century is simply going to have to find another job." Unbelievably, in the inner circles of government suggestions surface from time to time for special programs to teach campesinos and workers fleeing Mexico the rudiments of gardening and of home care for the elderly, skills supposedly required for jobs in the United States. Fox was so much of a free trader that when his Congress passed a 20 percent tax on soft drink bottlers who used high fructose corn sweeteners from the United States, he vetoed it, but the Mexican Supreme Court overruled him. The tax shielded Mexico's sugar industry from low-cost American imports. However, Fox won, because the World Trade Organization sided with the United States and ruled the tax a restraint of trade.

Is there a lesson for us in the plight of Mexican small farmers? Trade deals such as NAFTA offer no solutions. Governments of the peripheral countries cannot simply stand by but must take an active role in the transformation of their farm sector, not just to ensure sound environmental techniques, but more to the point, to allow large numbers of campesinos to remain on the land. Until industry can muster up the requisite number of jobs in the cities, agriculture must support the campesinos. Keeping them on their lands and subsidizing the production of the basic food staples is a prerequisite for alleviating poverty and hunger. Yet, in the face of cheap corn imports from the United States, Calderón, like Fox before him, turns a deaf ear to small farmers pleading that Mexico renegotiate NAFTA.

What about industry in the days of NAFTA? One term, coined by *La Jornada,* comes to mind: *desindustrialización.* The number of large industries declines, but since their focus is the export market, their importance rises, as smaller establishments fall by the wayside, left to find customers on the internal market, weakened by low urban wages and, in the countryside, by the inability of campesinos to compete with cheap imports of corns and beans from American farmers. Ironically, as exports grow, so do imports, more so than sales abroad, and the result is a deficit in balance of payments.[42] More and more industry is the story of *maquiladoras,* assembly plants of foreign corporations.[43] NAFTA, boasts the *Los Angeles Times,* turned Mexico into "an exporting power house," but it is the saga of the *maquiladoras.* By 2001, the *maquiladora* sector of the economy accounted for half of all trade between Mexico and the United States. It was estimated that 40 percent of American exports to Mexico returned in the guise of finished goods. This, said some observers, was not trade but the rental by American corporations of cheap Mexican labor; as Guillermo Bonfil Batalla lamented, "we sell our labor so that others can profit from it."

V

Current life on the Mexican side of the borderlands rarely conjures up that of the 1920s. For those of us who knew the latter, the dissimilarity is striking. The arrival of *maquiladoras* has dramatically altered the contours of the region. Old tourist spots recede into memory as urbanization takes hold, transforming hamlets into big cities; Tijuana and Ciudad Juárez, plant kingpins, shelter hordes of inhabitants, teeming with the social ills that are typical of chaotic, unplanned growth. Migrants from every corner of the Republic flock north, lured by the dreams of jobs in industry. Yet globalization, what *maquiladoras* exemplify, merely shuffles the outlines of the asymmetrical relationship. Mindful of their consequences, critics in Ciudad Juárez have dubbed the society of *maquiladoras* "Maquilamex," a term that grudgingly acknowledges the weighty role that assembly plants play from Tijuana to Matamoros and captures the ambivalence of a people troubled by what they witness.

Workers in *maquiladoras* assemble articles of sundry nature from components of foreign manufacture, parts that stay in Mexico just long enough to emerge as computers, television sets, auto parts, and textiles. One apt description is that the plants, on orders from outsiders, perform production tasks for others. These articles are sold abroad, mainly in the United States, where most of the components originate. Their sales abroad represent a hefty slice of Mexico's industrial exports.[44] Mexicans contribute their labor, as well as the water and the land on which the *maquilas* stand. These plants are offshoots of a global economy that has reshaped the role of the peripheral world, changing it from simply a supplier of raw materials to a purveyor of cheap labor. That change relegates certain kinds of jobs to a rubbish heap in countries such as the United States and transfers them to places where women and children labor for a pittance. As Pat Buchanan put it, capitalists "anxious to offload their American workers on the junk heap of the global economy" make the peripheral world a mecca for transnationals.

The Mexican border once housed over two thousand *maquiladoras.* Until their recent decline, their numbers multiplied almost daily, transforming dusty tourist towns, once havens for whorehouses and saloons catering to American tourists, into cities that were home to Fortune 500 companies but also to shantytowns bereft of running water, sewers, paved streets, and schools. Workers in the *maquilas* dwell in hovels in the slums of Tijuana, Ciudad Juárez, Mexicali, Nuevo Laredo, and Matamoros. Ciudad Juárez, baptized the "queen of the *maquilas,*" has over 1 million inhabitants; less than half of its roads are paved, while discarded cardboard makes up the walls of some its homes. The *New York Times* reports that in Ciudad Acuña, just across the border from Del Rio, Texas, *maquila* workers earn "miserable wages and American companies pay . . . minimal taxes"; its "schools are a shambles, its hospital crumbling, its trash collection slapdash," and "half of its 150,000 thousand residents" used backyard latrines.[45] What was said of Ciudad Juárez and Ciudad Acuña applies more or less to the other cities along the border.

Yet *maquilas* drive the local economy and are the Republic's chief source of industrial jobs.[46] They employ more than a million Mexicans. At first they hired predominantly young single women between the ages of eighteen and twenty-six, and they account for over one-third of the Republic's labor force. Today the ratio of men to women is about even, though men have the better jobs. *Maquila* jobs entail hardship. Wages are kept low, kept there by plant decision, Mexican government policy, and unforeseen events, such as devaluation of the peso; the cheap labor makes for windfall profits for management. Workers theoretically earn the federally mandated minimum wage, but their take-home pay is less than one-fifth the minimum wage of the United States, because they live in a border community where rent and food cost dollars. Job security and health and disability benefits hang by a thread, and hope of advancement is a dream. Work conditions, though better now, are often poor. But for young women from southern Mexico, what the *maquila* represents is a job, especially for those struggling to survive at the bottom of the economic and social scale. A female officer in the Beta corps, Mexico's border patrol, tells a young woman looking for a job in the *maquila:* "They don't pay all that well, but at least you can live. . . . You'll have to limit how much meat or chicken you buy. You'll get to eat it but not every day." Low wages, like those paid to *maquila* workers, limit the growth of an internal market.

The coming of NAFTA has also cost jobs. Reforms that required the privatization of *paraestatales,* railroads, and airlines have led to layoffs. In Mexico, NAFTA is referred to by the initials TLC (Tratado de Libre Comercio), but workers say that TLC really stands for "Todos a la calle," everyone out on the street. According to the Carnegie Endowment for International Peace, during NAFTA's first eight years Mexico lost 1.3 million jobs and wages fell to one-seventh or one-eighth of those paid in the United States. Even by government statistics, after NAFTA took effect, manufacturing wages dropped, showing a decline in real wages of 21 percent between 1994 and 2000. About 25 percent of Mexico's workers earned the minimum wage, the equivalent of four dollars a day; half of the workforce made less than eight dollars. These wages have been estimated to have lost half of their purchasing power since the advent of NAFTA; according to Mexican officials, the income of over half of the population failed to cover the cost of food, clothing, health care, public transportation, and schooling. Low wages throttle the purchasing power of millions of Mexico and consequently do little to build up an internal market.

The *maquila* phenomenon began as a temporary expedient, an attempt to capitalize on U.S. tariffs that allowed offshore subsidiaries of American transnational corporations to assemble products from American components for resale in the United States. Tariff duties were imposed only on the "value added," that is, the cost of foreign labor. The cheaper the labor, the lower the value added and the bigger the profits. The plan was to entice American corporations to build plants along the border by allowing them duty-free access to imports of necessary machinery, equipment, and raw materials, including components to be assembled. Mexican legislation that set limits on foreign ownership and management did not apply to *maquiladoras*. When legislation barred the transnationals from owning land along the border, Mexican politicians rewrote it quickly to permit full use for up to thirty years. In 1972, legislation threw open the whole Republic to them, with the exception of Mexico City, Guadalajara and Monterrey, industrial citadels. Now Aguascalientes, Puebla, and Yucatán house many of them.

Foreign investment is the lifeblood of the *maquiladoras*, an industry beholden to foreign decisions and events. The absence of linkages to Mexican industry ensures the survival of the *maquilas* as enclave operations, which in turn guarantees continued dependence on the United States. The border is an industrial enclave of *maquilas* that employ cheap labor and whose corporate offices are usually in the United States. Assembled goods wend their way north, but these exports do not represent trade in the conventional sense. Even so, they muddle the significance of trade statistics for both Mexico and the United States, a point emphasized by the economist Victor Urquidi, who talks of "hyperbolic figures given out by authorities and accepted by not a few of his fellow tradesmen." Urquidi had the facts on his side. More than four-fifths of these exports represent United States companies trading with themselves.[47]

That asymmetrical relationship spells disaster. Since the market for the *maquilas'* output lies largely north of the border, every crisis there strikes the industry with sledgehammer blows. When American consumers stop buying, *maquilas* shut down, their workers go jobless, and local merchants find themselves with shelves of unsold goods. Moreover, since the year 2000, for a variety of reasons, lower-paying jobs for one, Mexico's *maquilas* have lost ground to those in Central America and China; the American market is no longer sacred territory for them.[48] China now controls it. Equally important, if not more so, once the cost of the imported components *(insumos)* is subtracted from the sale price, profits to Mexico are minimal.[49] Maquilas offer no way out of the morass of Mexico's underdevelopment.

Yet, thanks to the *maquila,* a growing middle class prospers, and the rich and the well-off are numerous, dwell in comfortable houses, send their children to private schools, and raise prosperous and happy families. Numerous employees of federal, state, and municipal governments are hardly reliant for their livelihood on their Yankee neighbor. Professionals, among them physicians, lawyers, architects, and engineers, sell their services to Mexicans and are seldom indebted to tourists. They make up part of what Mexican scholars refer to as a national *burguesía.*

But the transformation may be more mirage than reality. Economic growth continues to be an offshoot of American capitalism. Mexicans, even the *burguesía nacional,* rely for their daily bread on economic ties with Uncle Sam. This relationship, regardless of what is beneficial about it, spells dependency. The northern side of the border, with its far larger capital resources and its gigantic market, controls the dynamics of the southern side. The availability of cheap labor is still the principal reason for border *maquilas.* At the same time, their reliance on the U.S. market makes them highly vulnerable to the ups and downs of its economy. During the economic crisis of the mid-1970s, as many as thirty-two thousand *maquila* jobs along the border vanished. Nearly half of the workers in the *maquilas* of Ciudad Juárez lost their jobs. This unpredictable employment picture is hardly the cement for an internal market, nor does the border represent a dynamic binational economy. There can be no equality between two societies as long as one, the more powerful and rich, gets the better of the other. Unless a miracle occurs, the Mexican side will always be the tail of the dog.

Maquiladoras are merely one aspect of this dependent relationship. Mexico's export economy relies mainly on American customers. Most Mexican exports end up in the U.S. marketplace. Most of what Mexico buys also comes from north of the border, one more sign of Mexico's precarious dependency. Mexico's trade with sister Latin America nations is minuscule. Mexico's trade with Brazil, the biggest of the South American countries, is less than 1 percent; the entire Mercosur bloc—Argentina, Brazil, Paraguay, and Uruguay—absorbs just 1 percent of Mexico's trade.[50] As an editorial in *La Jornada* argued, reliance on traditional exports to spur the economy makes no sense for Mexican industry, nor does it expand the domestic market. Stagnation, or worse, shrinkage, of the U.S. market would bring about a decline in real wages, a spike in unemployment, and more poverty.[51]

VI

One would think that conservatives who welcome change only if it occurs slowly would support public education, lest the pent-up anger of the dispossessed boil over. But not in Mexico, where until recently just 3 percent of the federal budget went to schools, one of the lowest percentages in Latin America. Today teachers are better paid, but little else has changed. A recent study by the World Economic Forum paints a grim picture: Ghana, Kenya, Uganda, and Zimbabwe—African countries hardly at the forefront of modernity—rank above Mexico in the quality of their education. To cite a report by the United Nations Educational, Scientific, and Cultural Organization, many Mexican students do poorly when it comes to comprehending what they read, and they cannot solve simple mathematical equations. In the classroom, teachers, who too often behave as autocrats, dictate but seldom encourage open discussions: "Obey the teacher and do not question"; that is the rule. As one observer put it, Mexican schools suffer from a *pedagogía memorista* (a pedagogy of memorization). In 2006, Mexico had 32 million Mexicans older than fifteen who had not completed *la educación básica completa*, primary school.[52]

The state of public education in Mexico, most observers agree, is deplorable. To make matters worse, the country lacks a teacher corps sufficiently prepared to undertake the necessary changes. Teachers are poorly trained and are beholden to the corrupt *charros* (bosses) who run the biggest labor union in Latin America. Those *charros* have the power to appoint teachers, name school heads, supervisors, and even state educational authorities. Students attend schools with broken windows, leaky roofs, and faulty toilets, when they have them at all, and they are beset by a dearth of schools supplies, including textbooks. Rural schools are the worst off. One out of every five students in the primary schools abandons them before the fifth grade. Called upon to help support their family, students, particularly in the countryside and in urban ghettoes, miss classes; absenteeism is a major problem.[53] Almost half of Mexico's population has not completed grade school. In the Indian communities, just one out of five students finishes grade school. At the secondary level, nearly one out of every two students does not graduate because they must work. Among older Mexicans, between the ages of fifty-five and sixty-five, just one out of ten finished high school. Illiteracy, the old nemesis, hangs on and is as high as 70 percent in regions of Guerrero and Oaxaca. Over 6 million Mexicans ages fifteen and older cannot read or write. One reason for this illiteracy is that large numbers of students drop out of school before they have mastered basic reading and writing.[54]

No better is the state of higher education, though Mexico spends sixteen times as much per university student as it does for those in primary school. Yet Mexico is not competitive in most high-tech industries that require substantial research or advanced skills. Only a tiny percentage of the GNP is devoted to industrial research.[55] In most Western nations, the federal government is primarily responsible for the funding of basic research, especially at the university level, but Mexicans depend largely on the scientific and technological advances of other nations. Research scientists, asserted a former rector of the National University, have to make due with *migajas* (crumbs), since neither federal authorities nor the private sector display any inclination to support them.[56] Mexicans become "managers of what others invest, build, and sell to them."[57]

VII

But change has come. The dominant culture of the United States recasts the daily lives of Mexicans through television, radio, and film, imperiling the local culture, to quote Carlos Fuentes. Some admire the United States so much that they endeavor to superimpose its way of life on Mexico.[58] With that attitude comes a contempt for everything Mexican. As the artist Daniel Manrique says, Mexicans prefer to be the *nalgas* (ass end) of North America rather than the leaders of Latin America. That, according to a Mexican scholar, stems from the desire of the middle and upper classes to "develop" Mexico, even if it costs "our self identity." Whatever the validity of these views, the truth is that the presence of American culture is overwhelming. American films, rock 'n' roll, artists, writers, and even cuisine—the popularity of hamburgers attests to that—are now part of Mexican daily life.

NAFTA spurred that transition, modifying key aspects of Mexican culture. Even the young acknowledge it, as Barbie dolls, toy jeeps, miniature motorcycles, and toy guns made in American factories replace the traditional wooden toys. Especially susceptible to American ways are the middle and upper classes, who, because of travel, Hollywood films, and television, know more about the life and aspirations of Americans than they do of their country's Indians. It is becoming virtually impossible for Mexican heroes to compete with Superman. Young Mexicans, neither sadder nor wiser, rarely read the giants of Mexican literature, the novels of Juan Rulfo or José Rubén Romero; listen to the music of Juventino Rosas or Blas Galindo; know the heroes of Mexican history, Melchor Ocampo and Lázaro Cárdenas; or prize the monumental art of José Clemente Orozco and Diego Rivera. That, to a large extent, may be because heroes of the past have been used to justify all sorts of shenanigans on behalf of a false patriotism that eulogizes dead heroes who can no longer endanger the privileges of the ruling classes.

A few decades ago, Octavio Paz labeled Mexicans *malinchistas* (Uncle Toms). That holds true even more today. The admiration for Americans and Western Europeans, how they look and dress and think, is more alive than ever. The color of one's skin frequently, if not always, opens or closes employment doors; the lighter one's skin, the brighter the future. What you have, as Raúl Béjar and Héctor Rosales say, is a "racismo a la mexicana."[59] The love affair with globalization, say Mexican students of the national psyche, implies a sense of defeat: Mexicans have given up trying to forge their own destiny. Yet, to call up a celebrated dictum, a belief that a just society is just around the corner, if it is to prevail, requires that you believe in it with all your heart. Yet Mexicans cannot hide behind others, nor can they simply imitate what works for others. Mexico is not the United States, and Mexicans are not Americans.

Epilogue

So, what can we conclude? Why is Mexico underdeveloped? Surely, the question is thorny and labyrinthine: there is no simple answer. But no matter how we frame the inquiry, time is all-important: the historical background looms elephantine. As Marx, in one of his most eloquent moments, wrote, "The tradition of all dead generations weighs like a nightmare on the brains of the living." The ills of underdevelopment took centuries to arise; they did not appear overnight. The gargantuan cracks in the social and economic edifice are old and deep. True, many are manmade, one being the decades-long absence of law and order in the new Republic. Anthropologists and sociologists point an accusatory finger at hurdles to social mobility, a tyrannical nuclear family, religious dogmas, and so on, but upon closer examination, these turn out to be consequences of a peculiar historical legacy. The secrets of yesterday are rarely singular but are complex phenomena concealed from view by evanescent centuries. Nor can all faults be laid at Mexico's door. Despite the Cornucopia fable, Mexico has neither a plentiful supply of water nor abundant fertile soil for farming. The terrain, mountainous and cavernous, made national unity nearly impossible. Not until the coming of the iron horse, nearly four centuries after the Conquest, did Mexico set out on the road to territorial unification. Exploitation by foreign powers, first Great Britain and then the United States, has played a pivotal role.

Whatever may be said, the colonial centuries weigh heavily on today's Mexico. One must turn back the clock to begin to understand what went wrong. We must examine the causes, not just the effects, of the malady. The question, if results are the culprits, is how did they come about? We must acknowledge that the cultural mix of Spaniard and pre-Columbians was an uneasy one; for the natives it was a psychological trauma. Not long ago, the denial of a "Black Legend" of an evil Spanish conquest was virtually automatic. But the Spaniards were not just bad apples individually: injustices were not just the work of a small band of heartless Europeans but rather of the social system implanted in the New World. Had the conqueror attempted a conciliatory approach, perhaps a matter of wishful thinking, the results might not have been irreconcilable. Even then it would have taken years, perhaps a century or two, before a blend of the two cultures might have formed a perfect union, one synchronizing values and practices. What occurred instead, was the unraveling of the indigenous universe, including, surely, the chronic stress that arose out from a deep sense of helplessness and an inability to take charge of one's life. Poverty, it is said, traps its victims in a kind of eternal adolescence, where psychologically it becomes comfortable to stay put rather than risk new adventures. Belief in mobility can require a terrifying act of faith. For this tragic drama, the entire cast of Spaniards, except for a few missionaries and priests, shares responsibility for what befell the Indians. The arrogant and often undisciplined Spaniard simply rode roughshod over them, a largely passive people; whether willing or not, they were driven to accept the Spaniards' dictates, which left behind a dysfunctional society.

After three centuries of colonial rule, two societies emerged: that of the Spaniard and his progeny, the criollo and light-skinned mestizos, the better-off, and, at the bottom of the social scale, Indians and dark-skinned mestizos, the majority of the Mexican people. Spaniards and criollos could dream of a better world for themselves and their families; Indians and most mestizos learned early to accept their status as God-given. After all, as the church lectured them, the almighty had a special place in heaven for the poor and downtrodden.

Sadly for the future of Mexico, the Spaniard, from the start, was hardly a man of rectitude. Corruption and incompetence had a special place in colonial government, whether at the viceroy's table or that of his underlings. No wonder, therefore, that official corruption and ineptitude fostered a public attitude of distrust and contempt toward state and public bureaucracy. For Spaniards and criollos, and later their progeny in the new Republic, state and bureaucracy became avenues for upward mobility, the door to personal enrichment. The idea that the state might serve a social function, that it might speak for the common man, took centuries to gain ground; it did not do so until years after independence was achieved. Even now, most Mexicans rarely look upon the state and its bureaucracy as allies in the daily struggle for survival.

But above all, the nature of the economy blocked progress. The Spanish lust for gold and silver gave form and shape to Mexico's dependent society. For three hundred long years, New Spain's economy rested on the export of silver bullion to European buyers. Whether they paid well or not, their market set the tone for New Spain's economy. Nearly everything rested on the sale of silver and, to a far lesser extent, on exports of cochineal and diverse agricultural products. Over the centuries, New Spain put together an export economy of primary goods, using profits to buy what goods the well-off in society purchased. Local industry consisted mostly of primitive *obrajes* that turned out cheap cotton cloth for the poor. The "curse," as some refer to it, and what splendidly epitomizes what befell New Spain, sets forth how exports of natural resources of pecuniary value turn into the major source of revenue and block domestic economic growth. It is a paradox of plenty that encourages the conspicuous consumption of imported goods, a system that magnifies inequality. Worse still, the rise in exchange rates, the result of an accumulation during boom eras, spurs "de-industrialization" as the factory and farming sectors become less competitive on the global and domestic markets.

Independence in 1821 did not put an end to this deadly dance with outsiders. Until the 1880s, the main export was still silver, and after that industrial metals, particularly copper. Then, with the discovery of petroleum deposits in the subsoil, exports of the black gold kept the wheels of the economy turning. Only briefly, first under the Cardenista regime of the 1930s and then during the years of import substitution, did Mexico attempt to break the old dependency. The Cardenista expropriation of Standard Oil and Royal Dutch Shell earmarked natural resources for national development instead of foreign exchange, an article of belief in industrialization by way of import substitution. By the late 1970s, however, it was back to the old ways of dependency on the exports of petroleum. Mexicans, once again, had mortgaged their future to foreign capitalists.

The reliance on exports of primary goods has blocked any possibility of fundamental economic and social change. Exports of petroleum finance nearly half of the government's operating costs. The international trading system largely determines Mexico's "backwardness," the result of a belief in free trade doctrines as old as the fairy tales concocted by Adam Smith and David Ricardo. Trade, after all, is not always beneficial; it can be, as it has been for much of Mexico's history, a vehicle for exploitation. The "equal terms of trade" ideal is more myth than truth. Exporters of primary goods, whether of the agricultural variety, metals, or petroleum, seldom sit in the driver's seat, a place reserved for the buyers, the powerful industrialized nations of the West, and now Japan.

The consequences of this unequal relationship are enormous. Not only is the export sector of the economy dependent on outsiders, but so is the nation. Decisions in government rest largely on what occurs in the dependent economy. Foreigners control the good and bad times and, by implication, the ups and downs of the everyday lives of millions of Mexicans. Whether you can purchase daily essentials depends largely on whether outsiders are buying what your country exports; today that is petroleum, a commodity with a short life expectancy. Some thirty or forty years from now, Mexico will run out of its deposits of the black gold. Then what? In this scenario, national industry takes a backseat. *Empresarios,* the local lords of what passes for a national industry, seldom command much respect, because the public looks upon them as imitators, not, as in the industrial West, as innovators. They copy what outsiders do much better at cheaper prices. It is no wonder, therefore, that the Mexican middle class hungers for American-made goods.

Mexicans have created for themselves a semicolonial economy. Like a beggar asking for alms, they rely on foreign investment and exports to generate growth. Exports alone account for almost a third of the country's gross domestic product; 90 percent of them are exported to markets on the other side of the border. NAFTA perpetuates this asymmetrical relationship. When American consumers stop buying, the market for assembled television sets, auto parts, and winter fruits and vegetables vanishes. A pall then descends on Mexico.

If the pitfalls of this lamentable dependency needed further proof, it came in the wake of the Great Recession of 2009, one of the most spectacular man-made financial calamity in modern experience, which set Mexico adrift on a sea of troubles. Coming out of Wall Street, the financial citadel of the United States, the recession was the result of a banking debacle, a stock market slump, and a housing bust, exacerbated by greedy speculators and chicanery of all sorts. The shock in Mexico was felt at once. The peso's value dropped, spurring capital flight, inflation, and speculation, as well as a sharp rise in the price of imports, dealing hammer blows to Mexican consumers as well as businesses that relied on foreign goods. Exports fell, dropping precipitously for auto assembly and auto parts, with plants in over half of the Republic's states. Even Volkswagen, the German giant, laid off workers, while industrial production and retail sales plummeted. *Maquiladoras* shut down or cut workers in Baja California Norte, Sonora, Chihuahua, Nuevo León, Tamaulipas, and Coahuila, once the most prosperous region of the Republic. For some economists, to quote a disgruntled Jesuit priest, a spokesman for the Centro de Reflexión y Acción Laboral, a labor body, what was obvious was "the bankruptcy of a model that merely exports, that relies on foreign capital and worships it." Even orthodox economists, once bell ringers for Mexican neoliberal policies, an austerity formula that reduced the national debt and tamed inflation, had second thoughts: their sage advice had not saved the country from the pain of the global recession, especially when investors pulled dollars from Mexico's "emerging market." Out the window went a cockeyed claim, that when the U.S. economy catches a cold, Mexico's gets pneumonia. Now the new assumption was that it was the other way around.

On the political front, a Quisling class, the handmaiden of the rich and powerful, was as always ready to join hands with the traditional exporters. Once hacendados and foreign mining moguls, and now *empresarios* and big farmers, their fortunes, especially with NAFTA, were tied to foreign corporations. This Quisling class ostensibly sets policy. The political reforms of recent years, giving huge amounts of money to political parties supposedly to make them independent, have merely made politicos more interested in remaining in office rather than in seeking ways to curb economic and political ills. One party, the PAN, apparently cares not a whit about the awful predicament of the poor, while the PNR splits between a faction that does and others who want simply to feed at the public trough. The PRI, a cynical lot, always scheming to return to power, shifts gears with the prevailing political winds. At another level, what you have on the part of sundry bureaucrats is a callous indifference *(desprecio)* toward the plight of the poor, as the following story, told to me by a friend from Tijuana, illustrates. My friend, accompanied by the state secretary of education, drove to the outskirts of the border city, where the shacks were made of tarpaper and discarded plywood. Upon seeing that the local school was in no better condition than the hovels around it, my friend asked why was this so. Should not the school have been a worthy model for local residents? The responsibility lay with the teacher, replied the bureaucrat, not his office. He was not at all troubled that the teacher, probably young and poorly paid, was woefully unprepared to get local parents, most likely penniless, to build a better school. Corruption in politics goes on as before, to the scorn of a cynical public. At this juncture, the PRI no longer wields dictatorial power, but this democratic change, oddly enough, makes the appearance of a reformer such as the Lázaro Cárdenas of the 1930s virtually impossible. With the political reforms, it behooves politicians, whatever their so-called ideological leanings, to keep the public trough full. Why alter the system when you have money in the bank?

The effects of this historical drama on Mexican society are devastating, as *Rudo y Cursi,* a film by Carlos Cuarón, tells us. That Mexicans are daily victims of corruption is now accepted as commonplace, inevitable. Things are as they are because that is the way they are in Mexico. For one to climb the stairs of society requires either big or small acts of corruption. The exception would be if things were not that way. No one is shocked anymore by the breakup of the Mexican family, nor by the rise of drug addiction. Single women with families abound, and no one takes notice. In *Rudo y Cursi,* one female head of a household is a single mother of eight, each by a different man. In this society where *machismo* dictates, the woman, more vulnerable now, simply goes from one man to another. When one leaves, she finds someone else. Yet the Mexican man, asserts Cuarón, never stops dreaming; even when trampled underfoot, he dreams of when he will be well enough so that he can get drunk.

Many Mexicans ask, where does the responsibility for our *atraso* (backwardness) lie? Is it in ourselves or in the outside world that exploits us? A good question. The answer is that both share blame. The United States, the colossus next door, has not always been a friend, taking half of Mexico's territory by force in 1847, and twice more invading its neighbor in the next century. Today, some 90 percent of Mexican exports travel north to American markets, while Mexicans buy from their neighbors an equivalent amount. The *maquila* industry of the northern border, from Tijuana on the Pacific Ocean to Matamoros on the Gulf, is simply an adjunct of American industry. Were a miracle to occur and Mexicans attempt basic structural reforms that endangered American interests, they would surely face a hostile colossus. And yet, what would Mexico be without access to the giant market and capital next door? As things stand, that marriage, for better worse, is a fact of life.

The Mexican dependency on and admiration for the colossus next door hardly help turn things around. Self-denigration, say some, is one result. Mexicans are only too ready to condemn themselves, to admire Western Europe and the United States. Too often, like their *empresarios,* they become imitators and not innovators. Copycats they are, particularly the well-off with economic ties to American capital. That NAFTA virtually wiped out small and medium-sized local industry matters little to them. So long as Americans buy avocados and vegetables from giant farms, import copper and other industrial metals, establish assembly plants for autos in Mexico, and come as tourists, Mexicans are a contented lot. Even Mexican artists, writers, and filmmakers, once on the hunt for the authentic, imitate their colleagues across the border and in Western Europe. The upshot of this economic, political, and social morass, say observers, is a culture of dependency. All of the above helps to explain why Mexico is underdeveloped.

Notes

PREFACE

1. Oscar Wilde, *The Artist as Critic: Writings of Oscar Wilde* (Chicago: University of Chicago Press, 1982), p. 359.

ONE. RAMBLINGS ON MEXICAN UNDERDEVELOPMENT

1. José López Portillo, *Mis tiempos: Biografía y testimonio político* (Mexico, 1988), vol. 1, p. 329.

2. Julio Boltvinik Kalinda, *Pobreza y estratificación social en México* (Mexico, 1994), pp. 82–83.

3. Jorge Zepeda Patterson, ed., *Los amos de México* (Mexico, 2007), pp. 16–17.

4. Quoted in Fernando Paz Sánchez, ed., *Vida y pensamiento de Narciso Bassols* (Mexico, 1986), p. 18.

5. López Portillo, *Mis tiempos*, vol. 1, p. 376.

6. Rudolph H. Strahm and Ursula Oswald Spring, *Por esto somos tan pobres* (Mexico, 1990), p. 37.

7. Manning Nash, ed., "Essays on Economic Development and Cultural Change in Honor of Bert F. Hoselitz," *Economic Development and Cultural Change* 25, supplement (Chicago, 1977): 316–17.

8. *Monthly Review,* July–August 2007, pp. 136–37.

9. Andre Gunder Frank, *Latin America: Underdevelopment or Revolution* (New York, 1967), p. 4.

10. Héctor Guillén Romo, *La contrarrevolución neoliberal* (Mexico, 1997), p. 157.

11. Alfonso Aguilar Monteverde, *Dialéctica de la economía mexicana* (Mexico, 1972), p. 19.

12. Paul Baran, *The Political Economy of Growth* (New York, 1957), p. 163.

13. Fernand Braudel, *Afterthoughts on Material Civilization and Capitalism* (Baltimore and London, 1977), p. 69.

14. David Landes, *The Wealth and Poverty of Nations: Why Some Are So Rich and Some So Poor* (New York, 1998), pp. 186, 190, 214, 238.

15. Robert Claiborne, *Climate, Man, and History* (New York, 1970), p. 365.

16. Kenneth Pomeranz, *The Great Divergence: Europe, China, and the Making of the Modern World Economy* (Princeton, NJ, 2000), pp. 61, 68, 283.

17. Landes, *Wealth and Poverty of Nations,* 187.

18. Cited in *Monthly Review,* May 5, 2006, p. 6. On the importance of the discovery of the Americas, see also Derek H. Aldcroft and Ross E. Catterall, eds., *Rich Nations—Poor Nations: The Long-Run Perspective* (Brookfield, VT, 1996), p. 5; Pomeranz, *Great Divergence,* pp. 113, 241, 263, 270, 367; and Eric Williams, *Capitalism and Slavery* (New York, 1944), p. 102.

19. Immanuel M. Wallerstein, *The Modern World System II: Mercantilism and the Consolidation of the European World Economy, 1600–1750* (New York, 1980), p. 142.

20. *Monthly Review,* November 2004, p. 1.

21. Frank, *Underdevelopment or Revolution,* p. 9; cited in Wallerstein, *Modern World System II,* p. 92.

22. Braudel, *Afterthoughts on Material Civilization,* p. 92.

23. López Portillo, *Mis tiempos,* vol. 1, p. 376.

24. Octavio Paz, *The Labyrinth of Solitude* (New York, 1985), p. 146.

25. Ibid.

26. Moses Abramovitz, *Thinking about Growth: And Other Essays on Economic Growth and Welfare* (Cambridge, 1989), p. 4.

27. Landes, *Wealth and Poverty of Nations,* p. 286.

28. Cited in Amiya Kumar Bagchi, *The Political Economy of Underdevelopment* (Cambridge, 1990), p. 17.

29. Edward G. Stockwell and Karen Laidlaw, *A Third World Development Problem and Prospects* (Chicago, 1990), p. 72.

30. Ibid., p. 102.

31. Landes, *Wealth and Poverty of Nations*, p. 174; Frank, *Underdevelopment or Revolution*, p. 67.

32. Landes, *Wealth and Poverty of Nations*, p. 174; Stockwell and Laidlaw, *Third World Development Problem*, p. 141.

33. Cited in Landes, *Wealth and Poverty of Nations*, p. 176.

34. Braudel, *Afterthoughts on Material Civilization*, pp. 66–67.

35. Frank, *Underdevelopment or Revolution*, pp. 36–37.

36. Stockwell and Laidlaw, *Third World Development Problem*, p. 114.

37. Jorge Carrión, *Mito y magia del mexicano y un ensayo de autocrítica* (Mexico, 1952), pp. 63, 111–12.

38. Nash, "Essays on Economic Development," p. 101; Claiborne, *Climate, Man, and History*, p. 318.

39. Nash, "Essays on Economic Development," p. 6; Aldcroft and Catterall, *Rich Nations*, p. 1.

40. Jesús Silva Herzog, *El pensamiento económico, social y político de México, 1810–1964* (Mexico, 1967).

41. Samuel Ramos, *Profile of Man and Culture in Mexico* (New York, 1962), pp. 57, 154.

42. Paz, *Labyrinth of Solitude*, p. 192.

43. Silva Herzog, *Pensamiento económico*, p. 605.

44. Carrión, *Mito y magia*, p. 35.

45. Paz, *Labyrinth of Solitude*, p. 217.

46. Stockwell and Laidlaw, *Third World Development Problem*, p. 35.

47. Joan Robinson, *Aspects of Development and Underdevelopment* (Cambridge, 1979), p. 51.

48. Claudio Véliz, *Obstacles to Change in Latin America* (New York, 1965), 1.

49. Paz, *Labyrinth of Solitude*, p. 11.

50. Ibid.

51. Ramos, *Profile of Man and Culture*, p. 57.

52. Carrión, *Mito y magia*, p. 63.

TWO. EL MEXICANO

1. Miguel León-Portilla, *The Broken Spears: The Aztec Account of the Conquest of Mexico* (Boston, 1990), p. xxxiii.

2. Sergio Zermeño, *La desmodernidad Mexicana y las alternativas a la violencia y a exclusión en nuestros días* (Mexico, 2005), p. 29.

3. Samir Amin, *Unequal Development: An Essay on the Social Formation of Peripheral Capitalism* (New York, 1976), pp. 19, 57.

4. Robert Claiborne, *Climate, Man, and History* (New York, 1970), p. 234.

5. *New York Times*, July 7, 2001; Jared Diamond, *Guns, Germs, and Steel: The Fate of Human Societies* (New York, 1997), p. 222.

6. León-Portilla, *Broken Spears*, p. xxiv.

7. Ibid.; June 6, July 6, 2003; Colegio de México, *Nueva historia mínima de México* (Mexico, 2004), 38; L. Don Lambert, "The Role of Climate in the Economic Development of Nations," *Land Economics* 47, 1948.

8. León-Portilla, *Broken Spears*, p. xxxii.

9. Ibid., p. 22.

10. Ibid., p. 23.

11. Michael Harner, "The Ecological Basis for Aztec Sacrifice," *American Ethnologist* 4 (February 1977), pp. 117–18, 128; Eric R. Wolf, *Sons of the Shaking Earth: The People of Mexico and Guatemala—Their Land and Culture* (Chicago, 1959), p. 197.

12. Harner, "Ecological Basis," p. 197.

13. Ibid., p. 120.

14. Ibid., p. 127.

15. *Harper's Magazine*, September 2003, pp. 44–45, 48, 50.

16. Jaime Vicens Vives, *An Economic History of Spain* (Princeton, NJ, 1969), p. 293.

17. Ibid., p. 296.

18. Ibid., p. 417.

19. Manning Nash, ed., "Essays on Economic Development," *Economic Development and Cultural Change*, p. 327.

20. Vicens Vives, *Economic History*, p. 505.

21. Ibid., pp. 454 and 476.

22. Ibid., p. 495.

23. Ibid., p. 492.

24. Ramón Eduardo Ruiz, *Triumphs and Tragedy: A History of the Mexican People* (New York, 1992), p. 33.

25. Ibid., p. 36.

26. *Harper's Magazine*, September 9, 2003, p. 52.

27. Bartolomé Bennassar and others, *Orígenes del atraso español* (Barcelona, 1985), p. 177.

28. Immanuel M. Wallerstein, *The Capitalist World Economy* (New York, 1979), p. 38.

29. Vicens Vives, *Economic History*, p. 412.

30. Ibid., p. 428.

31. Kenneth Pomeranz, *The Great Divergence: Europe, China, and the Making of the Modern World Economy* (Princeton, NJ, 2000), p. 42.

32. David Landes, *The Wealth and Poverty of Nations: Why Some Are So Rich and Some So Poor* (New York, 1998), p. 172.

THREE. THE LEGACY

1. Eric Williams, *Capitalism and Slavery* (New York, 1944), p. 51.
2. Guillermo Bonfil Batalla, *México profundo: Una civilización negada* (Mexico, 1987), p. 103.
3. *Harper's Magazine*, April 2007, pp. 28–29.
4. Miguel León-Portilla, *The Broken Spears: The Aztec Account of the Conquest of Mexico* (Boston, 1990), p. xxvi.
5. Robert Claiborne, *Climate, Man, and History* (New York, 1970), p. 236.
6. Quoted in Paul Harrison, *Inside the Third World: The Anatomy of Poverty* (Brighton, England, 1980), p. 42.
7. Quoted in Ramón Eduardo Ruiz, *Triumphs and Tragedy: A History of the Mexican People* (New York, 1992), p. 55.
8. Samuel Ramos, *Profile of Man and Culture in Mexico* (New York, 1962), p. 31.
9. Santiago Ramírez, *El mexicano: Psicología de sus motivaciones* (Mexico, 1961), p. 40.
10. Ibid., p. 53.
11. Stanley J. Stein and Barbara H. Stein, *The Colonial Heritage of Latin America: Essays on Economic Dependence in Perspective* (New York, 1970), p. 87.
12. León-Portilla, *Broken Spears*, p. 51.
13. Andre Gunder Frank, *Lumpenbourgeoisie, Lumpendevelopment: Dependence, Class, and Politics in Latin America* (New York, 1972), p. 19.
14. Kenneth Pomeranz, *The Great Divergence: Europe, China, and the Making of the Modern World Economy* (Princeton, NJ, 2000), p. 273.
15. Alfonso Aguilar Monteverde, *Dialéctica de la economía mexicana* (Mexico, 1972), p. 40; Stein and Stein, *Colonial Heritage*, pp. 32, 45–46.
16. Eric R. Wolf, *Sons of the Shaking Earth: The People of Mexico and Guatemala—Their Land and Culture* (Chicago, 1959), p. 177.
17. Leopoldo Solis, *La realidad mexicana: Retroversión y perspectiva* (Mexico, 1979), p. 17.
18. John H. Coatsworth, *Los orígenes del atraso mexicano: Nueve ensayos de historia económica de México en los siglos XVIII y XIX* (Mexico, 1990), p. 75; Enrique Florescano, *Precios del maíz y crisis agrícola en México (1708–1810)* (Mexico, 1969), pp. 150–51 and 155; Aguilar Monteverde, *Dialéctica*, p. 51.
19. Quoted in Andre Gunder Frank, *Latin America: Underdevelopment or Revolution* (New York, 1969), pp. 235–36.

20. Florescano, *Precios del maíz,* p. 188.

21. Francois Chevalier, *Land and Society in Colonial Mexico* (Berkeley, CA, 1963), p. 297.

22. Ibid., p. 164.

23. Aguilar Monteverde, *Dialéctica,* p. 48.

24. Florescano, *Precios del maíz,* p. 129.

25. Alejandro de Humboldt, *Ensayo político sobre el reino de la Nueva España* (Mexico, 1966), pp. 284, 293, and 503; Wolf, *Sons of the Shaking Earth,* pp. 179 and 181; Frank, *Lumpenbourgoisie, Lumpendevelopment,* p. 28.

26. Florescano, *Precios del maíz,* p. 93; Ruiz, *Triumphs and Tragedy,* p. 126.

27. Coatsworth, *Los orígenes del atraso mexicano,* p. 32; Florescano, *Precios del maíz,* p. 190; Aguilar Monteverde, *Dialéctica,* p. 33.

28. Solis, *La realidad mexicana,* p. 15; Wolf, *Sons of the Shaking Earth,* p. 204.

29. Alan Knight, *Mexico: The Colonial Era* (Cambridge, 2003), p. 223.

30. Coatsworth, *Los orígenes del atraso mexicano,* pp. 53 and 98; Mariano Otero, *Obras,* 2 vols. (Mexico, 1967), vol. 1, p. 134.

31. Solis, *La realidad mexicana,* p. 26; Aguilar Monteverde, *Dialéctica,* p. 106.

32. Aguilar Monteverde, *Dialéctica,* p. 106.

33. Stein and Stein, *Colonial Heritage,* p. 68.

34. Ibid., p. 124.

35. Gustavo Esteva, *The Struggle for Rural Mexico* (South Hadley, MA, 1983), p. 5.

36. Ramírez, *El mexicano,* p. 60.

37. Frantz Fanon, *The Wretched of the Earth* (New York, 1963), p. 7.

38. Ruiz, *Triumphs and Tragedy,* p. 65.

39. Jaime Vicens Vives, *An Economic History of Spain* (Princeton, NJ, 1969), p. 391; Wolf, *Sons of the Shaking Earth,* p. 207.

40. Chevalier, *Land and Society,* pp. 263 and 285.

41. Vicens Vives, *Economic History of Spain,* p. 397; Knight, *The Colonial Era,* p. 79.

42. Stephen H. Haber, *Industry and Underdevelopment: The Industrialization of Mexico, 1890–1940* (Stanford, CA, 1989), p. 54; Solis, *La realidad mexicana,* p. 12.

43. Humboldt, *Ensayo político,* pp. 47 and 449; Wolf, *Sons of the Shaking Earth,* p. 185.

44. Aguilar Monteverde, *Dialéctica,* p. 52; Frank, *Lumpenbourgoisie, Lumpendevelopment,* p. 25; Knight, *The Colonial Era,* p. 27.

45. Stein and Stein, *Colonial Heritage,* p. 134; Harrison, *Inside the Third World,* p. 42.

46. Knight, *The Colonial Era,* p. 165.

47. Stein and Stein, *Colonial Heritage,* p. 71.

48. Vicens Vives, *Economic History of Spain,* p. 316.

49. Aguilar Monteverde, *Dialéctica,* p. 50.

50. William B. Taylor, *Magistrates of the Sacred: Priests and Parishioners in Eighteenth-Century Mexico* (Stanford, CA, 1996), p. 61.

51. Ibid., pp. 48 and 50.

52. Ibid., p. 60.

53. Stein and Stein, *Colonial Heritage,* pp. 57–58.

54. Julio Jiménez Rueda, *Historia de la literatura mexicana* (Mexico, 1946), p. 160.

55. Francisco González Pinedo, *El mexicano: Psicología de su destructividad* (Mexico, 1965), pp. 33 and 102; Ramos, *Profile of Man and Culture,* p. 64.

56. Octavio Paz, *Labyrinth of Solitude* (New York, 1985), pp. 22, 40, 70; González Pinedo, *El mexicano,* p. 29.

FOUR. FREE TRADERS AND CAPITALISTS

1. John H. Coatsworth, *Los orígenes del atraso mexicano: Nueve ensayos de historia económica de México en los siglos XVIII y XIX* (Mexico, 1990), p. 56.

2. Andre Gunder Frank, *Lumpenbourgeoisie, Lumpendevelopment: Dependence, Class, and Politics in Latin America* (New York, 1972), p. 29.

3. Eric Van Young, *The Other Rebellion: Popular Violence, Ideology, and the Mexican Struggle for Independence,* 1810–1821 (Stanford, CA, 2001), pp. 70–71.

4. Manuel López Gallo, *Economía política en la historia de México* (Mexico, 1965), p. 50.

5. Ramón Eduardo Ruiz, *Triumphs and Tragedy: A History of the Mexican People* (New York, 1992), p. 153.

6. López Gallo, *Economía política,* pp. 76 and 79.

7. Amiya Kumar Bagchi, *The Political Economy of Underdevelopment* (Cambridge, 1990), p. 50; Paul Harrison, *Inside the Third World: The Anatomy of Poverty* (Brighton, England, 1980), pp. 52–53.

8. Octavio Paz, *Labyrinth of Solitude* (New York, 1985), p. 120.

9. Andre Gunder Frank, *Latin America: Underdevelopment or Revolution in Latin America* (New York, 1969), p. 376.

10. Quoted in Brian Hamnett, *Juárez* (New York, 1994), p. 8.

11. Claudio Véliz, *Obstacles to Change in Latin America* (New York, 1965), p. 235.

12. Mariano Otero, *Obras,* 2 vols. (Mexico, 1967), vol. 1, p. 127.

13. Enrique Cárdenas Sánchez, *Cuando se originó el atraso económico mexicano: La economía en el largo siglo XIX, 1780–1920* (Mexico, 2003), pp. 51–52.

14. Ibid., p. 73.

15. Ibid., p. 71.

16. Samuel Ramos, *Profile of Man and Culture in Mexico* (New York, 1962), p. 21.

17. López Gallo, *Economía política,* p. 66.

18. Quoted in López Gallo, *Economía política,* p. 172.

19. Enrique Serna, *El seductor de la patria: D. Antonio López de Santa Ana* (Mexico, 1999), p. 111.

20. Walter L. Berneker, *De agiotistas y empresarios: En torno de la temprana industrialización mexicana (siglo XIX)* (Mexico, 1992).

21. Otero, *Obras,* vol. 1, p. 28.

22. Julio Jiménez Rueda, *Historia de la literatura mexicana* (Mexico, 1946), pp. 168–69.

23. Ramos, *Profile of Man and Culture,* pp. 9 and 18.

24. Lorenzo de Zavala, *Obras: Viaje a los Estados Unidos de América* (Mexico, 1976), p. 180.

25. Francisco González Pineda, *El mexicano: Su dinámica psicosocial* (Mexico, 1961), p. 133.

26. José Joaquín Fernández de Lizardi, *The Mangy Parrot: The Life and Times of Periquillo Sarniento* (Cambridge, 2004), p. 307.

27. Serna, *El seductor de la patria,* p. 253.

28. José María Luis Mora, *México y sus revoluciones,* 3 vols. (Mexico, 1950), vol. 1, pp. 33 and 56; Jesús Reyes Heroles, *El liberalismo mexicano,* 3 vols. (Mexico, 1961), vol. 3, p. 435.

29. Otero, *Obras,* vol. 1, p. 113.

30. Mora, *Revoluciones,* vol. 1, p. 78.

31. Eric R. Wolf, *Sons of the Shaking Earth: The People of Mexico and Guatemala—Their Land and Culture* (Chicago, 1959), p. 235.

32. Justo Sierra, *The Political Evolution of the Mexican People* (Austin, TX, 1969), p. 191.

33. Ruiz, *Triumphs and Tragedy,* p. 197.

34. Otero, *Obras,* vol. 1, pp. 101 and 130.

35. Mora, *Revoluciones,* vol. 1, p. 90.

36. Fernández de Lizardi, *Mangy Parrot,* pp. 45–46.

37. Mora, *Revoluciones,* vol. 1, pp. 45–46.

38. Reyes Heroles, *El liberalismo mexicano,* vol. 3, p. 463.

39. Mora, *Revoluciones,* vol. 1, p. 65.

40. Enrique Krauze, *Mexico: Biography of Power* (New York, 1997), p. 29.

41. Mora, *Revoluciones,* vol. 1, p. 57.

42. Arturo Arnáiz y Freg, *Lucas Alamán: Semblanza e ideario* (Mexico, 1939), p. xiii.

43. Stanley J. Stein and Barbara H. Stein, *The Colonial Heritage of Latin America: Essays on Economic Dependence in Perspective* (New York, 1970), p. 134.

44. Berneker, *De agiotistas y empresarios*, p. 124.

45. Ibid., p. 130.

46. Ibid., p. 90.

47. Ibid., p. 67.

48. Paz, *Labyrinth of Solitude*, p. 124.

49. Secretaría de Industria y Comercio, ed., *La economía mexicana en la época de Juárez* (Mexico, 1972), p. 113.

50. Cárdenas Sánchez, *El atraso económico mexicano*, p. 134.

51. E. J. Hobsbawm, *The Age of Capital, 1848–1875* (New York, 1975), p. 78.

52. Mike Davis, *Late Victorian Holocausts: El Niño Famines and the Making of the Third World* (New York, 2001), pp. 62–63.

53. Alfonso Aguilar Monteverde, *Dialéctica de la economía mexicana* (Mexico, 1972), p. 179.

54. Ruiz, *Triumphs and Tragedy*, p. 234.

55. Ibid.

56. Francisco Xavier Guerra, *México: Del antiguo régimen a la Revolución*, 2 vols. (Mexico, 1988), vol. 1, p. 49; Hamnett, *Juárez*, p. 23.

57. Comisión Nacional para la Conmemoración del fallecimiento de Don Benito Juárez, *Testimonio de Don Melchor Ocampo* (Mexico, 1972), p. 25.

58. Raúl Arreola Cortés, *Melchor Ocampo: Textos políticos* (Mexico, 1975), p. 45.

59. Ibid., p. 46.

60. Ibid., p. 10.

61. Ibid., p. 52.

62. Ibid., p. 55.

63. Ibid., p. 149.

64. Hamnett, *Juárez*, p. 27.

65. Ibid., p. 42; Raymond Vernon, *The Dilemma of Mexico's Development: The Role of the Private and Public Sectors* (Cambridge, MA, 1965), p. 29.

66. Vernon, *Dilemma of Mexico's Development*, pp. 35–36; Jesús Silva Herzog, *El pensamiento económico, social y político de México, 1810–1946* (Mexico, 1967), p. 189.

67. Julio Jiménez Rueda, *Antología de la prosa en México* (Mexico, 1946), p. 259.

68. Secretaría de Industria y Comercio, *La economía mexicana*, p. 53.

69. Quoted in Jiménez Rueda, *Antología*, p. 259.

70. Herzog, *El pensamiento económico*, p. 231.

71. Ibid., pp. 196–97.

72. Ruiz, *Triumphs and Tragedy*, p. 258.

73. Mariano Azuela, *Cien años de novela mexicana* (Mexico, 1947), p. 116.

74. Ibid., p. 130.

75. Leopoldo Solis, *La realidad mexicana: Retrovisión y perspectiva* (Mexico, 1979), p. 30.

76. Ruiz, *Triumphs and Tragedy,* p. 172.

77. Coatsworth, *Los orígenes del atraso mexicano,* p. 153.

78. Ruiz, *Triumphs and Tragedy,* p. 232.

79. Ibid., p. 230.

80. Aguilar Monteverde, *Dialéctica,* p. 152; Ruiz, *Triumphs and Tragedy,* pp. 230–31.

81. Marcelo Carmagnani, *El estado y el mercado: La economía pública del liberalismo mexicano, 1850–1911* (Mexico, 1994), p. 35; Secretaría de Industria y Comercio, *La economía mexicana,* p. 100.

82. Secretaría de Industria y Comercio, *La economía mexicana,* p. 101.

83. Daniel Cosío Villegas, ed., *Historia moderna de México: El Porfiriato,* vols. 2, 7, and 8 (Mexico, 1959), vol. 2, p. 713.

84. Joan Robinson, *Aspects of Development and Underdevelopment* (Cambridge, 1979), p. 61.

85. Aguilar Monteverde, *Dialéctica,* p. 158.

86. Cosío Villegas, *Historia moderna de México,* vol. 2, p. 82.

87. Secretaría de Industria y Comercio, *La economía mexicana,* p. 52.

88. Ibid., p. 52.

89. López Gallo, *Economía política,* p. 131.

90. Ibid., p. 127.

91. Krauze, *Biography of Power,* p. 29.

92. Ibid.

93. Ibid., p. 225.

94. Aguilar Monteverde, *Dialéctica,* p. 148.

95. Andre Gunder Frank, *Capitalism and Underdevelopment in Latin America* (New York, 1967), p. 376.

FIVE. COLONIALISM'S THUMB

1. E. J. Hobsbawm, *The Age of Capital, 1848–1875* (New York, 1975), p. 235.

2. Ibid., pp. 135 and 267; Federico Gamboa, *Santa* (Mexico, 1992), pp. 90 and 173.

3. Mike Davis, *Late Victorian Holocausts: El Niño Famines and the Making of the Third World* (New York, 2001), p. 83.

4. Gamboa, *Santa,* p. 173.

5. Gregorio López y Fuentes, *Tierra* (Boston, 1949), p. 58.

6. Manuel López Gallo, *Economía política en la historia de México* (Mexico, 1965), p. 261; Guillermo Bonfil Batalla, *México profundo: Una civilización negada* (Mexico, 1987), p. 158.

7. Ramón Eduardo Ruiz, *Triumphs and Tragedy: A History of the Mexican People* (New York, 1992), p. 272.

8. Ibid., p. 275.

9. Octavio Paz, *Labyrinth of Solitude* (New York, 1985), pp. 129–30.

10. John H. Coatsworth, *Los orígenes del atraso mexicano: Nueve ensayos de historia económica de México de los siglos XVIII y XIX* (Mexico, 1990), pp. 145 and 137; Alicia Hernández Chávez, *México: Breve historia contemporánea* (Mexico, 2000), p. 265; Claudio Véliz, *Obstacles to Change in Latin America* (New York, 1965), p. 18; Raymond Vernon, *The Dilemma of Mexico's Development: The Role of the Private and Public Sectors* (Cambridge, MA, 1965), pp. 42 and 57.

11. Stephen H. Haber, *Industry and Underdevelopment: The Industrialization of Mexico, 1890–1940* (Stanford, CA, 1989), p. 207; John Mason Hart, *Empire and Revolution: The Americans in Mexico since the Civil War* (Berkeley, CA, 2002), p. 33; Jesús Silva Herzog, *El pensamiento económico, social y político de México, 1810–1964* (Mexico, 1967), p. 248.

12. José Ives Limantour, *Apuntes sobre mi vida pública* (Mexico, 1965), pp. 39, 54, 55; Manuel Calero, *Un decenio de política mexicana* (New York, 1920), p. 19; Silva Herzog, *El pensamiento económico*, pp. 229 and 331.

13. Mariano Azuela, *Cien años de novela mexicana* (Mexico, 1947), p. 75.

14. Samuel Ramos, *Profile of Man and Culture in Mexico* (New York, 1962), p. 95; Daniel Cosío Villegas, ed., *Historia moderna de México: El Porfiriato*, vols. 2, 7, and 8 (Mexico, 1959), vol. 7, p. 317.

15. Paz, *Labyrinth of Solitude*, p. 131; Ramos, *Profile of Man and Culture*, pp. 51 and 53.

16. Ramos, *Profile of Man and Culture*, p. 53.

17. Julio Jiménez Rueda, *Historia de la literatura mexicana* (Mexico, 1946), p. 311; Silva Herzog, *El pensamiento económico*, p. 366.

18. Francisco Bulnes, *El porvenir de las naciones Latinoamericanas ante las recientes conquistas de Europa y Norteamérica* (Mexico, 1889), pp. 10–11.

19. Enrique Ochoa, *Feeding Mexico: The Political Uses of Food since 1910* (Wilmington, DE, 2000), p. 25.

20. Jiménez Rueda, *Historia*, p. 282.

21. Azuela, *Cien años*, p. 193; Jiménez Rueda, *Historia*, p. 305.

22. Jiménez Rueda, *Historia*, p. 156.

23. Cosío Villegas, *Historia moderna de México*, vol. 7, pp. 643 and 1171.

24. Hart, *Empire and Revolution*, p. 152; Cosío Villegas, *Historia moderna de México*, vol. 7, p. 241; Earl Shorris, *The Life and Times of Mexico* (New York, 2004), pp. 198 and 210; Silva Herzog, *El pensamiento económico*, p. 251.

25. López Gallo, *Economía política,* p. 276; Leopoldo Solis, *La realidad mexicana: Retrovisión y perspectiva* (Mexico, 1979), p. 48.

26. Richard J. Salvucci, "The Origins and Progress of U.S. Mexican Trade, 1825–1948: Hoc opus hic est," *Hispanic American Historical Review* 1973 (December 1991), p. 723; Stanley J. Stein and Barbara H. Stein, *The Colonial Heritage of Latin America: Essays on Economic Dependence in Perspective* (New York, 1970), p. 140.

27. Enrique Florescano, *Ensayos sobre el desarrollo económico de México y América Latina, 1500–1976* (Mexico, 1979), p. 186.

28. Quoted in Hart, *Empire and Revolution,* p. 790.

29. Quoted in Hart, *Empire and Revolution,* p. 123.

30. Ibid., p. 163; Ramón Eduardo Ruiz, *The People of Sonora and Yankee Capitalists* (Tucson, AZ, 1988), p. 114.

31. Ruiz, *Triumphs and Tragedy,* p. 278.

32. Cosío Villegas, *Historia moderna de México,* vol. 7, p. 384.

33. Haber, *Industry and Underdevelopment,* p. 38.

34. Ibid.

35. Ibid., p. 280.

36. Cosío Villegas, *Historia moderna de México,* vol. 7, p. 463.

37. Stephen H. Haber, ed., *How Latin America Fell Behind: Essays on the Economic Histories of Brazil and Mexico, 1800–1914* (Stanford, CA, 1997), p. 211.

38. Cosío Villegas, *Historia moderna de México,* vol. 7, p. 476.

39. Haber, *Industry and Underdevelopment,* p. 193.

40. Haber, *How Latin America Fell Behind,* p. 157.

41. Francois Xavier Guerra, *México: Del antiguo régimen a la Revolución,* 2 vols. (Mexico, 1988), vol. 1, p. 330; Haber, *Industry and Underdevelopment,* p. 64.

42. Quoted in Cosío Villegas, *Historia moderna de México,* vol. 7, p. 330.

43. Ruiz, *Triumphs and Tragedy,* p. 292.

44. Cosío Villegas, *Historia moderna de México,* vol. 7, p. 348.

45. Silva Herzog, *El pensamiento económico,* p. 259.

46. Joseph Conrad, *"Heart of Darkness" and "The Secret Sharer"* (New York, 2004), p. 100.

47. López Gallo, *Economía política,* p. 299.

48. Stephen H. Haber, Armando Razo, and Noel Maurer, *The Politics of Property Rights: Political Stability, Credible Commitments, and Economic Growth in Mexico, 1876–1929* (New York, 2003), p. 285.

49. Stein and Stein, *Colonial Heritage,* p. 143.

50. Enrique Krauze, *Mexico: Biography of Power* (New York, 1997), p. 219.

51. Vernon, *Dilemma of Mexico's Development,* p. 50.

52. Tom Barry, *Zapata's Revenge: Free Trade and the Farm Crisis in Mexico* (Boston, 1995), p. 16.

53. Viviane Brachet-Marquez, *The Dynamics of Domination: State, Class, and Social Reform in Mexico, 1910–1990* (Pittsburgh and London, 1994), p. 5.

54. Shorris, *Life and Times of Mexico,* p. 196.

55. Krauze, *Biography of Power,* p. 38.

56. Azuela, *Cien años,* p. 6.

SIX. LOST OPPORTUNITY

1. Ramón Eduardo Ruiz, *The Great Rebellion: Mexico 1905–1924* (New York, 1980), p. 73. See this study for a full discussion of the upheaval of 1919, known as the *Revolución* in Mexico.

2. Ruiz, *Great Rebellion,* p. 73.

3. Ibid., p. 79.

4. Mike Davis, *Late Victorian Holocausts: El Niño Famines and the Making of the Third World* (New York, 2001), p. 261.

5. Davis, *Late Victorian Holocausts,* p. 63.

6. Francois Xavier Guerra, *México: Del antiguo régimen a la Revolución,* 2 vols. (Mexico, 1988), vol. 2, p. 236.

7. Ibid., vol. 2, p. 252.

8. Ruiz, *Great Rebellion,* p. 124; Guerra, *México,* vol. 2, pp. 237 and 235.

9. *Ruiz, Great Rebellion,* p. 110.

10. José Ives Limantour, *Apuntes sobre mi vida pública* (Mexico, 1965), pp. 101, 196–97, 199.

11. Guillermo Bonfil Batalla, *México profundo: Una civilización negada* (Mexico, 1987), p. 165; Alfonso Aguilar Monteverde, *Dialéctica de la economía mexicana* (Mexico, 1972), p. 210.

12. Andre Gunder Frank, *Lumpenbourgeoisie, Lumpendevelopment: Dependence, Class, and Politics in Latin America* (New York, 1972), p. 134.

13. Alberto J. Pani, *Apuntes autobiográficos,* 2 vols. (Mexico, 1950), vol. 1, p. 196, and vol. 2, p. 211; Colegio de México, *Nueva historia mínima de México* (Mexico, 2004), p. 233.

14. Jesús Silva Herzog, *El pensamiento económico, social y político de México, 1810–1964* (Mexico, 1967), p. 437.

15. Ruiz, *Great Rebellion,* pp. 158–59.

16. Silva Herzog, *El pensamiento económico,* p. 539.

17. Ruiz, *Great Rebellion,* p. 160.

18. Silva Herzog, *El pensamiento económico,* p. 386.

19. Ibid., p. 517.

20. Comisión Nacional, *Diario de los debates del Congreso Constituyente, 1916–1917,* 2 vols. (Mexico, 1960), vol. 2, p. 499.

21. Tom Barry, *Zapata's Revenge: Free Trade and the Farm Crisis in Mexico* (Boston, 1995), p. 1995.

22. Raymond Vernon, *The Dilemma of Mexico's Development: The Role of the Private and Public Sectors* (Cambridge, MA, 1965), p. 79.

23. Stephen H. Haber, Armando Razo, and Noel Maurer, *The Politics of Property Rights: Political Stability, Credible Commitments, and Economic Growth in Mexico, 1876–1929* (New York, 2003), p. 346; Leopoldo Solis, *La realidad mexicana: Retrovisión y perspectiva* (Mexico, 1979), p. 95.

24. Alberto J. Pani, *El problema supremo de México: Ensayo de crítica constructiva de la política financiera* (Mexico, 1955), p. 60; Silva Herzog, *El pensamiento económico*, p. 504.

25. Martín Guzmán, *El águila y la serpiente* (Mexico, 1941), p. 78.

26. Heberto Castillo, *Desde la trinchera* (Mexico, 1986), p. 186.

27. Ruiz, *Great Rebellion*, p. 384.

28. Manuel López Gallo, *Economía política en la historia de México* (Mexico, 1965), p. 426.

29. Ruiz, *Great Rebellion*, p. 402.

30. Stephen H. Haber, *Industry and Underdevelopment: The Industrialization of Mexico, 1890–1940* (Stanford, CA, 1989), p. 124; Judith Adler Hellman, *Mexico in Crisis* (1985), p. 15.

31. Pani, *Problema supremo*, pp. 56–57; Albert J. Pani, *Mi contribución al nuevo régimen* (Mexico, 1936), pp. 242–43.

32. Pani, *Apuntes autobiográficos*, vol. 2, p. 216.

SEVEN. INTERNAL MARKET

1. Alberto Pani, *Mi contribución al nuevo régimen* (Mexico, 1936), p. 332; Enrique Cárdenas Sanchez, ed., *Historia económica de México* (Mexico, 1994), p. 143; Colegio de México, *Nueva historia mínima de México* (Mexico, 2004), p. 263; Stephen H. Haber, *Industry and Underdevelopment: The Industrialization of Mexico, 1890–1940* (Stanford, CA, 1989), p. 151; Stanley J. Stein and Barbara H. Stein, *The Colonial Heritage of Latin America: Essays on Economic Dependence in Perspective* (New York, 1970), p. 191.

2. Ramón Eduardo Ruiz, *Triumphs and Tragedy: A History of the Mexican People* (New York, 1992), pp. 386–87.

3. Ibid., p. 387.

4. Derek H. Aldcroft and Ross E. Catterall, eds., *Rich Nations—Poor Nations: The Long-Run Perspective* (Brookfield, VT, 1996), p. 49; Claudio Véliz, *Obstacles to Change in Latin America* (New York, 1965), p. 78; Andre Gunder Frank, *Lumpenbourgeoisie, Lumpendevelopment: Dependence, Class, and Politics in Latin America*

(New York, 1972), p. 130; Raymond Vernon, *The Dilemma of Mexico's Development: The Role of the Private and Public Sectors* (Cambridge, MA, 1965), p. 84.

5. Adolfo Gilly, *El Cardenismo: Una utopía mexicana* (Mexico, 1994), p. 148.

6. Alicia Hernández Chávez, *México: Breve historia contemporánea* (Mexico, 2000), pp. 385 and 388.

7. Tom Barry, *Zapata's Revenge: Free Trade and the Farm Crisis in Mexico* (Boston, 1995), p. 24; Judith Adler Hellman, *Mexico in Crisis* (New York, 1985), p. 36; Ruiz, *Triumphs and Tragedy*, pp. 392–93.

8. Ruiz, *Triumphs and Tragedy*, p. 398.

9. Ibid.

10. Amiya Kumar Bagchi, *The Political Economy of Underdevelopment* (Cambridge, 1990), p. 161.

11. Ruiz, *Triumphs and Tragedy*, pp. 401–2.

12. Ibid., p. 401.

13. Hernández Chávez, *México*, p. 402; Véliz, *Obstacles to Change*, p. 16.

14. Fernando Paz Sánchez, *Vida y pensamiento de Narciso Bassols* (Mexico, 1986), pp. 56, 61, 70, 167; Jesús Silva Herzog, *El pensamiento económico, social y político de México, 1810–1964* (Mexico, 1967), p. 563.

15. Gilly, *El Cardenismo*, p. 37; Cárdenas Sánchez, *Historia económica de México*, p. 332; Hellman, *Mexico in Crisis*, p. 36.

16. Viviane Brachet-Marquez, *The Dynamics of Domination: State, Class, and Social Reform in Mexico, 1910–1990* (Pittsburgh and London, 1994), p. 77; Cárdenas Sánchez, *Historia económica de México*, p. 313; Haber, *Industry and Underdevelopment*, p. 171; Vernon, *Dilemma of Mexico's Development*, p. 84.

17. Héctor Guillén Romo, *La contrarrevolución neoliberal* (Mexico, 1997), p. 114.

18. Rafael Izquierdo, "Proteccionismo en México," in Raymond Vernon, ed., *Public Policy and Private Enterprise in Mexico* (Cambridge, 1964), p. 283; Ruiz, *Triumphs and Tragedy*, p. 395.

19. José López Portillo, *Mis tiempos: Biografía y testimonio político*, 2 vols. (Mexico, 1988), vol. 1, pp. 148–49.

20. Roger Simon, *Gramsci's Political Thought: An Introduction* (London, 1991), p. 91.

21. Alastair Davidson, *Antonio Gramsci: The Man, His Ideas* (Sydney, Australia, 1967–1968), pp. 44–47.

22. Guillermo Bonfil Batalla, *México profundo: Una civilización negada* (Mexico, 1987), p. 90.

23. Ibid., p. 167.

24. Ruiz, *Triumphs and Tragedy*, p. 365.

25. Ibid., pp. 367–70.

26. Ibid., pp. 375–76.

27. Ibid., p. 377.

28. Samuel Ramos, *Profile of Man and Culture in Mexico* (New York, 1962), p. 155.

EIGHT. FALSE MIRACLE

1. Joan Robinson, *Aspects of Development and Underdevelopment* (Cambridge, 1979), p. 129; Alicia Hernández Chávez, *México: Breve historia contemporánea* (Mexico, 2000), p. 431.

2. José Agustín, *Tragicomedia mexicana: La vida en México de 1940 a 1970*, 2 vols. (Mexico, 1990), vol. 1, p. 263.

3. Ibid., vol. 1, pp. 22, 27, 43, 49.

4. Ibid., vol. 1, pp. 107, 113.

5. Heberto Castillo, *Desde la trinchera* (Mexico, 1986), p. 45.

6. Ibid., pp. 31–33.

7. Quoted in Earl Shorris, *The Life and Times of Mexico* (New York, 2004), p. 322.

8. Agustín, *Tragicomedia mexicana*, vol. 1, p. 116.

9. José López Portillo, *Mis tiempos: Biografía y testimonio político*, 2 vols. (Mexico, 1988), vol. 1, pp. 457–58; Raymond Vernon, *The Dilemma of Mexico's Development: The Role of the Private and Public Sectors* (Cambridge, MA, 1965), p. 116.

10. Agustín, *Tragicomedia mexicana*, vol. 1, p. 58.

11. Edward G. Stockwell and Karen Laidlaw, *A Third World Development: Problems and Prospects* (Chicago, 1981), p. 215.

12. Claudio Véliz, *Obstacles to Change in Latin America* (New York, 1965), p. 5.

13. Ramón Eduardo Ruiz, *Triumphs and Tragedy: A History of the Mexican People* (New York, 1992), p. 411; Hernández Chávez, *México*, p. 397.

14. Guillermo Bonfil Batalla, *México profundo: Una civilización negada* (Mexico, 1987), p. 177.

15. Kenneth Pomeranz, *The Great Divergence: Europe, China, and the Making of the Modern World Economy* (Princeton, NJ, 2000), p. 243.

16. López Portillo, *Mis tiempos*, vol. 1, p. 378; Octavio Paz, *Labyrinth of Solitude* (New York, 1985), p. 255.

17. López Portillo, *Mis tiempos*, vol. 1, p. 375.

18. Stephen H. Haber, *Industry and Underdevelopment: The Industrialization of Mexico, 1890–1940* (Stanford, CA, 1989), p. 2; Dennis Gilbert, *Mexico's Middle Class in the Neoliberal Era* (Tucson, AZ, 2007), pp. 2–3.

19. Amiya Kumar Bagchi, *The Political Economy of Underdevelopment* (Cambridge, 1990), p. 205; Stockwell and Laidlaw, *Third World Development*, p. 280; Ansley J. Coale and Edgar M. Hoover, *Population Growth and Economic Development in Low-Income Countries: A Case Study of India's Prospects* (Princeton, NJ, 1958), p. 331.

20. *New York Times*, July 8, 1999.

21. Stockwell and Laidlaw, *Third World Development*, p. 286.

22. Bonfil Batalla, *México profundo*, p. 178; Stockwell and Laidlaw, *Third World Development*, p. 86.

23. Derek H. Aldcroft and Ross E. Catterall, eds., *Rich Nations—Poor Nations: The Long-Run Perspective* (Brookfield, VT, 1996), p. 9.

24. Haber, *Industry and Underdevelopment*, p. 2; Bagchi, *Political Economy of Underdevelopment*, pp. 242 and 245; Samir Amin, *Unequal Development: An Essay on the Social Formation of Peripheral Capitalism* (New York, 1976), p. 210.

25. Judith Adler Hellman, *Mexico in Crisis* (New York, 1985), pp. 68–69.

26. Ibid., pp. 210–11.

27. Agustín, *Tragicomedia mexicana*, vol. 1, p. 247.

28. Castillo, *Desde la trinchera*, p. 231; Manuel Camacho Solis, *Cambio sin ruptura* (Mexico, 1994), p. 53; Rodolfo H. Strahm and Ursula Oswald Spring, *Por esto somos tan pobres* (Mexico, 1990), p. 111.

29. Paul Baran, *The Political Economy of Growth* (New York, 1957), p. 77.

30. López Portillo, *Mis tiempos*, vol. 1, 366–67, 377, 430; Francisco González Pineda, *El mexicano: Psicología de su destructividad* (Mexico, 1965), pp. 218–19.

31. Shorris, *Life and Times*, p. 521; Castillo, *Desde la trinchera*, p. 93.

32. López Portillo, *Mis tiempos*, vol. 1, 452.

33. Agustín, *Tragicomedia mexicana*, vol. 2, p. 234.

34. Ibid., vol. 2, p. 232; Castillo, *Desde la trinchera*, p. 92.

35. Véliz, *Obstacles to Change*, p. 26; González Pineda, *El mexicano*, p. 224; Castillo, *Desde la trinchera*, p. 189.

36. Manning Nash, ed., "Essays on Economic Development and Cultural Change in Honor of Bert F. Hoselitz," *Economic Development and Cultural Change* 25, supplement (Chicago, 1997): 255.

37. Vernon, *Dilemma of Mexico's Development*, pp. 95 and 227; Nash, "Essays on Economic Development," p. 393.

38. Robinson, *Aspects of Development*, p. 107.

39. Vernon, *Dilemma of Mexico's Development*, p. 101.

40. Aldcroft and Catterall, *Rich Nations*, p. 52; Agustín, *Tragicomedia mexicana*, vol. 1, p. 175.

41. Vernon, *Dilemma of Mexico's Development*, p. 103.

42. Héctor Guillén Romo, *El sexenio de crecimiento cero: Contra los defensores de las finanzas* (Mexico, 1990), p. 50.

43. González Pineda, *El mexicano,* p. 244; Castillo, *Desde la trinchera,* p. 39.

44. Hellman, *Mexico in Crisis,* pp. 65–66.

45. Ibid., pp. 224–25; Ruiz, *Triumphs and Tragedy,* p. 416.

46. Ruiz, *Triumphs and Tragedy,* p. 451.

47. Agustín, *Tragicomedia mexicana,* vol. 2, p. 234.

48. Guillén Romo, *El sexenio de crecimiento cero,* p. 11.

49. Ruiz, *Triumphs and Tragedy,* p. 456.

50. Ibid., pp. 460–61.

51. Baran, *Political Economy of Growth,* p. 174.

52. Immanuel M. Wallerstein, *The Capitalist World Economy* (New York, 1979), p. 85.

53. David Barkin, *Un desarrollo distorsionado: La integración de México a la economía mundial* (Mexico, 1991), pp. 127 and 141.

54. Véliz, *Obstacles to Change,* pp. 79–80; Baran, *Political Economy of Growth,* p. 175; Bagchi, *Political Economy of Underdevelopment,* p. 132.

55. Agustín, *Tragicomedia mexicana,* p. 49.

56. Leopoldo Solis, *La realidad mexicana: Retrovisión y perspectiva* (Mexico, 1979), p. 32.

57. Andre Gunder Frank, *Lumpenbourgeoisie, Lumpendevelopment: Dependence, Class, and Politics in Latin America* (New York, 1972), p. 43.

58. Castillo, *Desde la trinchera,* p. 152.

59. Hellman, *Mexico in Crisis,* p. 95; Barkin, *Un desarrollo distorsionado,* pp. 39 and 127.

60. Agustín, *Tragicomedia mexicana,* vol. 1, p. 196; *Proceso,* October 6, 2002; *Los Angeles Times,* November 28, 2001; *New York Times,* October 1, 2001.

61. Paz, *Labyrinth of Solitude,* p. 290.

62. Gustavo Esteva, *The Struggle for Rural Mexico* (South Hadley, MA, 1983), pp. 65–66.

63. Nash, "Essays on Economic Development," p. 391.

64. Tom Barry, *Zapata's Revenge: Free Trade and the Farm Crisis in Mexico* (Boston, 1995), p. 29.

65. Bagchi, *Political Economy of Underdevelopment,* p. 156.

66. Paul Harrison, *Inside the Third World: The Anatomy of Poverty* (Brighton, England, 1980), pp. 93–94; Barry, *Zapata's Revenge,* p. 101.

67. Barry, *Zapata's Revenge,* p. 31.

68. Agustín, *Tragicomedia mexicana,* vol. 1, p. 149.

69. Ibid., vol. 1, pp. 207 and 221.

70. Ibid., vol. 1, p. 27.

71. Bonfil Batalla, *México profundo,* p. 93.

72. López Portillo, *Mis tiempos,* vol. 1, p. 448; Agustín, *Tragicomedia mexicana,* vol. 1, p. 211.

73. Agustín, *Tragicomedia mexicana,* vol. 1, p. 138.

74. Carlos Fuentes, *The Death of Artemio Cruz* (New York, 1964), pp. 28, 46, 117, 130, 186, 256, and 268.

75. Agustín, *Tragicomedia mexicana,* vol. 1, p. 221.

76. Ibid., vol. 1, p. 101.

77. Ibid., vol. 1, p. 73.

78. Samuel Schmidt, *El deterioro del presidencialismo mexicano: Los años de Luis Echeverría* (Mexico, 1986), p. 61.

NINE. DEATH OF A DREAM

1. Héctor Guillén Romo, *La contrarrevolución neoliberal* (Mexico, 1997), pp. 101–3.

2. Amiya Kumar Bagchi, *The Political Economy of Underdevelopment* (Cambridge, 1990), p. 143.

3. Héctor Guillén Romo, *El sexenio de crecimiento cero: Contra los defensores de las finanzas* (Mexico, 1990), p. 112.

4. Joan Robinson, *Aspects of Development and Underdevelopment* (Cambridge, 1979), p. 130.

5. Bagchi, *Political Economy of Underdevelopment,* p. 146.

6. Quoted in Claudio Véliz, *Obstacles to Change in Latin America* (New York, 1965), p. 109.

7. Arturo Escobar, *Encountering Development: The Making and Unmaking of the Third World* (Princeton, NJ, 1995), p. 213.

8. Colegio de México, *Nueva historia mínima de México* (Mexico, 2004), p. 294; Rodolfo H. Strahm and Ursula Oswald Spring, *Por esto somos tan pobres* (Mexico, 1990), p. 159; Guillén Romo, *La contrarrevolución neoliberal,* p. 107.

9. Andre Gunder Frank, *Lumpenbourgeoisie, Lumpendevelopment: Dependence, Class, and Politics in Latin America* (New York, 1972), p. 133.

10. Tom Barry, *Zapata's Revenge: Free Trade and the Farm Crisis in Mexico* (Boston, 1995).

11. Earl Shorris, *The Life and Times of Mexico* (New York, 2004), p. 594; Alicia Hernández Chávez, *México: Breve historia contemporánea* (Mexico, 2000), p. 484.

12. *Los Angeles Times,* January 12,1994. p. A1.

13. Oswaldo de Rivero B., *The Myth of Development: Nonviable Economies of the 21st Century* (London, 2001), p. 85.

14. Jorge Zepeda Patterson, ed., *Los amos de México* (Mexico, 2007), p. 30.

15. Ibid., p. 242.

16. Bagchi, *Political Economy of Underdevelopment*, pp. 194–95.

17. *New York Times*, July 21, 2006, p. C1.

18. *La Jornada*, March 21, 2002.

19. *Proceso*, September 12, 1999, pp. 43–44.

20. *New York Times*, June 9, 1999, p. A3.

21. Bagchi, *Political Economy of Underdevelopment*, p. 141.

22. Leslie Sklair, *The Transnational Capitalist Class* (Malden, MA, 2001), p. 69; Narciso Bassols Batalla, *La revolución mexicana cuesta abajo* (Mexico, 1960), p. 207.

23. Sklair, *Transnational Capitalist Class*, p. 69.

24. Gabriel Székely, ed., *Manufacturing across Borders and Oceans: Japan, United States, and Mexico* (La Jolla, CA, 1991), p. 15.

25. Dennis Gilbert, *Mexico's Middle Class in the Neoliberal Era* (Tucson, AZ, 2007), pp. 11, 27, 29, and 63.

26. José Agustín, *Tragicomedia mexicana: La vida en México de 1940 a 1970*, 2 vols. (Mexico, 1990), vol. 2, p. 226.

27. *Los Angeles Times*, April 3, 1997, p. A1.

28. Guillermo Bonfil Batalla, *México profundo: Una civilización negada* (Mexico, 1987), p. 92; Gilbert, *Mexico's Middle Class*, p. 12.

29. Santiago Ramírez, *El mexicano: Psicología de sus motivaciones* (Mexico, 1961), pp. 66–67.

30. *Proceso*, March 7, 2004, pp. 32–34.

31. Stephen H. Haber, *Industry and Underdevelopment: The Industrialization of Mexico, 1890–1949* (Stanford, CA, 1989), p. 1.

32. *La Jornada*, August 8, 2001, p. 4.

33. Mercedes González de la Rocha and Barbara B. Gant, "The Urban Family and Poverty in Latin America," *Latin American Perspectives* 22 (1995): 12–25.

34. Mercedes González de la Rocha, *The Resources of Poverty: Women and Survival in a Mexican City* (Oxford, 1994), pp. 31, 33, 41.

35. Barry, *Zapata's Revenge*, p. 188.

36. Guillén Romo, *La contrarrevolución neoliberal*, p. 122.

37. Barry, *Zapata's Revenge*, p. 103; David Barkin, *Un desarrollo distorsionado: La integración de México a la economía mundial* (Mexico, 1991), pp. 40 and 61; Barry, *Zapata's Revenge*, p. 103.

38. Escobar, *Encountering Development*, p. 104; James H. McDonald, "NAFTA and the Milking of Dairy Farmers in Central Mexico," *Culture and Agriculture* 51–52 (1995).

39. Strahm and Spring, *Por esto somos tan pobres*, p. 55.

40. Barry, *Zapata's Revenge*, p. 153.

41. *Los Angeles Times*, January 25, 1994, p. A10.

42. Barry, *Zapata's Revenge*, p. 43.

43. *New York Times,* December 23, 1994, p. A1.

44. *Los Angeles Times,* December 29, 1994, p. A3.

45. David Landes, *The Wealth and Poverty of Nations: Why Some Are So Rich and Some So Poor* (New York, 1998), p. 494; Shorris, *Life and Times,* p. 588.

46. Samuel Schmidt, *El deterioro del presidencialismo mexicano: Los años de Luis Echeverría* (Mexico, 1986), p. 126; Guillén Romo, *La contrarrevolución neoliberal,* p. 198.

47. *New York Times,* July 9, 1999, p. A3.

48. Guillén Romo, *La contrarrevolución neoliberal,* p. 186.

TEN. NAFTA

1. *Harper's,* March 3, 2004, p. 33.

2. Gabriela Coronado and Bob Hodge, *El hipertexto multicultural en México posmoderno: Paradojas e incertidumbres* (Mexico, 2004), p. 178.

3. Octavio Paz, *Labyrinth of Solitude* (New York, 1985), p. 285.

4. Edward G. Stockwell and Karen Laidlaw, *A Third World Development: Problems and Prospects* (Chicago, 1981), pp. 251 and 261.

5. *Proceso,* January 4, 2009, p. 29.

6. Santiago Ramírez, *El mexicano: Psicología de sus motivaciones* (Mexico, 1961), pp. 95–96.

7. Eric R. Wolf, *Sons of the Shaking Earth: The People of Mexico and Guatemala—Their Land and Culture* (Chicago, 1959), p. 114; Guillermo Bonfil Batalla, *México profundo: Una civilización negada* (Mexico, 1987), p. 88.

8. Jorge Carrión, *Mito y magia del mexicano y un ensayo de autocrítica* (Mexico, 1952), p. 122.

9. Paz, *Labyrinth of Solitude,* p. 78.

10. *Siglo Veintiuno,* February 24, 1993.

11. Samir Amin, *Unequal Development: An Essay on the Social Formation of Peripheral Capitalism* (New York, 1976), pp. 196 and 298; Amiya Kumar Bagchi, *The Political Economy of Underdevelopment* (Cambridge, 1990), pp. 68–189.

12. José López Portillo, *Mis tiempos: Biografía y testimonio político,* 2 vols. (Mexico, 1988), vol. 1, pp. 456–57.

13. Earl Shorris, *The Life and Times of Mexico* (New York, 2004), pp. 706–7.

14. *Los Angeles Times,* May 5, 24, 2006; Paul Baran, *The Political Economy of Growth* (New York, 1957), p. 216; David Barkin, *Un desarrollo distorsionado: La integración de México a la economía mundial* (Mexico, 1991).

15. Dennis Gilbert, *Mexico's Middle Class in the Neoliberal Era* (Tucson, AZ, 2007), pp. 1, 2, 4, 9, 14.

16. Stockwell and Laidlaw, *Third World Development*, p. 256.

17. Quoted in Héctor Guillén Romo, *La contrarrevolución neoliberal* (Mexico, 1997), p. 207.

18. Joan Robinson, *Aspects of Development and Underdevelopment* (Cambridge, 1979), pp. 67 and 80.

19. Oswaldo de Rivero B., *The Myth of Development: Nonviable Economies of the 21st Century* (London, 2001), p. 119.

20. Paul Harrison, *Inside the Third World: The Anatomy of Poverty* (Brighton, England, 1980), p. 363; Rivero B., *Myth of Development*, p. 7.

21. Shorris, *Life and Times*, pp. 706–7, 709.

22. *La Jornada*, May 22, 2003, p. 18.

23. *New York Times*, January 7, 8, 2004, pp. A1 and A2.

24. *Proceso*, November 30, 2008, pp. 26–28.

25. *Los Angeles Times*, July 28, 2005, p. A6.

26. Rodolfo H. Strahm and Ursula Oswald Spring, *Por esto somos tan pobres* (Mexico, 1990), p. 244.

27. López Portillo, *Mis tiempos*, vol. 1, p. 639.

28. Bagchi, *Political Economy of Underdevelopment*, p. 36.

29. John Mason Hart, *Empire and Revolution: The Americans in Mexico since the Civil War* (Berkeley, CA, 2002), p. 433; Strahm and Spring, *Por esto somos tan pobres*, p. 125.

30. Bonfil Batalla, *México profundo*, p. 220.

31. *La Jornada*, March 10, 2009, p. 2.

32. *La Jornada*, July 13, 2005.

33. *Proceso*, March 18, 2007, pp. 36–39.

34. Immanuel M. Wallerstein, *The Capitalist World Economy* (New York, 1979), pp. 49 and 73.

35. Shorris, *Life and Times*, p. 471.

36. Sergio Zermeño, *La desmodernidad Mexicana y las alternativas a la violencia y a la exclusión en nuestros días* (Mexico, 2005), p. 29.

37. *La Jornada*, January 29, 2004, p. 25.

38. *La Jornada*, September 9, 1998; Tom Barry, *Zapata's Revenge: Free Trade and the Farm Crisis in Mexico* (Boston, 1995), p. 129.

39. *La Jornada*, September 9, 1998; Paz, *Labyrinth of Solitude*, p. 271.

40. *New York Times*, December 19, 2002, p. A3.

41. Robinson, *Aspects of Development*, p. 132.

42. Enrique de la Garza and Carlos Salas, eds., *Nafta y Mercosur: Proceso de apertura económica y trabajo* (Mexico, 2003), pp. 95, 105.

43. For the *maquila* industry, see Ramon Eduardo Ruiz, *On the Rim of Mexico: Encounters of the Rich and Poor* (Boulder, CO, 2000), chap. 4.

44. Zermeño, *La desmodernidad Mexicana*, p. 70.

45. *New York Times,* February 15, 2001, p. A16.

46. Enrique de la Garza and Carlos Salas, eds., *La situación del trabajo en México, 2006* (Mexico, 2006), p. 26.

47. Ruiz, *On the Rim of Mexico,* p. 67.

48. Enrique de la Garza Toledo, "The Crisis of the Maquiladora Model in Mexico," *Work and Occupations* (New York, 2007), vol. 34, pp. 399–429.

49. Ibid., p. 38.

50. *New York Times,* July 16, 2002, p. W1.

51. *La Jornada,* April 5, 2003, p. 25.

52. Rafael Ricardo, *Los socios de Elba Esther* (Mexico, 2007), pp. 318–19.

53. Guillén Romo, *La contrarrevolución neoliberal,* p. 167.

54. Stockwell and Laidlaw, *Third World Development,* pp. 243–44.

55. Claudio Véliz, *Obstacles to Change in Latin America* (New York, 1965), p. 102.

56. *La Jornada,* January 20, 2004, p. 15.

57. Shorris, *Life and Times,* p. 523.

58. Coronado and Hodge, *El hipertexto multicultural,* p. 13.

59. Raúl Béjar and Héctor Rosales, eds., *La identidad mexicana como problema político y cultural* (Mexico, 1999), p. 130.

Bibliography

NEWSPAPERS AND JOURNALS

Mexico

Excelsior
El Financiero
El Imparcial
La Jornada
El Mexicano
Siglo Veintiuno
El Universal

United States

American Ethnologist
American Historical Review
Barrons
Christian Science Monitor
Forbes
Harper's Magazine
Hispanic American Historical Review

In These Times
Land Economics
Los Angeles Times
Monthly Review
The Nation
The New Yorker
New York Times
San Diego Union-Tribune
Siempre

BOOKS

Abramovitz, Moses. *Thinking about Growth: And Other Essays on Economic Growth and Welfare.* Cambridge, 1989.

Aguilar Monteverde, Alfonso. *Dialéctica de la economía mexicana.* Mexico, 1972.

Aguilar Mora, Jorge. *Una muerte sencilla, justa, eterna: Cultura y guerra durante la Revolución Mexicana.* Mexico, 1990.

Agustín, José. *Tragicomedia mexicana: La vida en México de 1940 a 1970.* 2 vols. Mexico, 1990.

Alamán, Lucas. *Obras de D. Lucas Alamán: Historia de México.* 10 vols. Mexico, 1969.

Aldcroft, Derek H., and Ross E. Catterall, eds. *Rich Nations—Poor Nations: The Long-Run Perspective.* Brookfield, VT, 1996.

Amin, Samir. *Unequal Development: An Essay on the Social Formation of Peripheral Capitalism.* New York, 1976.

Arnáiz y Freg, Arturo, ed. *Lucas Alamán: Semblanza e ideario.* Mexico, 1939.

Arnaut, Alberto. *Historia de una profesión. Los maestros de educación premaria en México (1887–1994).* Mexico, 1998.

Arreola Cortés, Raúl. *Melchor Ocampo: Textos políticos.* Mexico, 1975.

Azuela, Mariano. *Cien años de novela mexicana.* Mexico, 1947.

———. *Los de abajo.* Mexico, 1925.

Bagchi, Amiya Kumar. *The Political Economy of Underdevelopment.* Cambridge, 1990.

Baran, Paul. *The Political Economy of Growth.* New York, 1957.

Barkin, David. *Un desarrollo distorsionado: La integración de México a la economía mundial.* Mexico, 1991.

Barry, Tom. *Zapata's Revenge: Free Trade and the Farm Crisis in Mexico.* Boston, 1995.

Bartra, Roger. *La jaula de la melancolía: Identidad y metamorfosis en el carácter mexicano.* Mexico, 1992.

Bassols Batalla, Narciso. *La revolución mexicana cuesta abajo.* Mexico, 1960.
Béjar, Raúl, and Héctor Rosales, eds. *La identidad nacional mexicana como problema político y cultural.* Mexico, 1999.
Bennassar, Bartolomé, and others. *Orígenes del atraso español.* Barcelona, 1985.
Berneker, Walter L. *De agiotistas y empresarios: En torno de la temprana industrialización mexicana (siglo XIX).* Mexico, 1992.
Bernstein, Marvin D. *The Mexican Mining Industry, 1890–1950.* New York, 1964.
Blackhawk, Ned. *Violence over the Lands: Indians and Empires in the Early American West.* Cambridge, 2006.
Boatz, Jeffrey L., and Stephen Haber, eds. *The Mexican Economy, 1870–1930: Essays on the Economic History of Institutions, Revolution and Growth.* Stanford, CA, 2002.
Boltvinik Kalinda, Julio. *Pobreza y estratificación social en México.* Mexico, 1994.
Bonfil Batalla, Guillermo. *México profundo: Una civilización negada.* Mexico, 1987.
Brachet-Marquez, Viviane. *The Dynamics of Domination: State, Class, and Social Reform in Mexico, 1910–1990.* Pittsburgh and London, 1994.
Braudel, Fernand. *Afterthoughts on Material Civilization and Capitalism.* Baltimore and London, 1977.
Bulmer-Thomas, Victor, John Coatsworth, and Roberto Cortés Conde, eds. *The Cambridge Economic History of Latin America.* Vol. 2. Cambridge, 2006.
Bulnes, Francisco. *El porvenir de las naciones Latinoamericanas ante las recientes conquistas de Europa y Norteamérica.* Mexico, 1899.
———. *El verdadero Díaz y la revolución.* Mexico, 1967.
Cabrera, Luis. *Obras completas.* 5 vols. Mexico, 1975.
Calero, Manuel. *Un decenio de política mexicana.* New York, 1920.
Camacho Solis, Manuel. *Cambio sin ruptura.* Mexico, 1994.
Cárdenas, Lázaro. *Obras.* Mexico, 1972.
Cárdenas Sánchez, Enrique. *Cuando se originó el atraso económico mexicano: La economía en el largo siglo XIX, 1780–1920.* Mexico, 2003.
———, ed. *Historia económica de México.* Mexico, 1994.
Carmagnani, Marcelo. *El estado y mercado: La economía pública del liberalismo mexicano, 1850–1911.* Mexico, 1994.
Carrión, Jorge. *Mito y magia del mexicano y un ensayo de autocrítica.* Mexico, 1952.
Casas Gragea, Angel María, ed. *La teoría de la dependencia.* Madrid, 2006.
Castillo, Heberto. *Desde la trinchera.* Mexico, 1986.
Chevalier, Francois. *Land and Society in Colonial Mexico.* Berkeley, CA, 1963.
Claiborne, Robert. *Climate, Man, and History.* New York, 1970.
Coale, Ansley J., and Edgar M. Hoover, *Population Growth and Economic Development in Low-Income Countries: A Case Study of India's Prospects.* Princeton, NJ, 1958.

Coatsworth, John H. *Los orígenes del atraso mexicano: Nueve ensayos de historia económica de México en los siglos XVIII y XIX.* Mexico, 1990.

Colegio de México. *Nueva historia mínima de México.* Mexico, 2004.

Comisión Nacional. *Diario de los debates del Congreso Constituyente, 1916–1917.* 2 vols. Mexico, 1960.

Comisión Nacional para la Conmemoración del fallecimiento de Don Benito Juárez, *Testimonio de Don Melchor Ocampo.* Mexico, 1972.

Conrad, Joseph. *"Heart of Darkness" and "The Secret Sharer."* New York, 2004.

Coronado, Gabriela, and Bob Hodge. *El hipertexto multicultural en México posmoderno: Paradojas e incertidumbres.* Mexico, 2004.

Cosío Villegas, Daniel, ed. *Historia moderna de México: El Porfiriato.* Vols. 2, 7, and 8. Mexico, 1959.

Davidson, Alastair. *Antonio Gramsci: The Man, His Ideas.* Sydney, Australia, 1967–1968.

Davis, Mike. *Late Victorian Holocausts: El Niño Famines and the Making of the Third World.* New York, 2001.

De la Garza, Enrique, and Carlos Salas, eds. *Nafta y Mercosur: Proceso de apertura económica y trabajo.* Mexico, 2003.

———, eds. *La situación del trabajo en México, 2006.* Mexico, 2006.

Diamond, Jared. *Guns, Germs, and Steel: The Fate of Human Societies.* New York, 1997.

Díaz del Castillo, Bernal. *Historia verdadera de la conquista de la Nueva España.* Mexico, 2005.

Díaz Dufoo, Carlos. *México y los capitales extranjeros.* Mexico, 1918.

Escobar, Arturo. *Encountering Development: The Making and Unmaking of the Third World.* Princeton, NJ, 1995.

Esteva, Gustavo. *The Struggle for Rural Mexico.* South Hadley, MA, 1983.

Fanon, Frantz. *The Wretched of the Earth.* New York, 1963.

Fernández de Lizardi, José Joaquín. *The Mangy Parrot: The Life and Times of Periquillo Sarniento.* Cambridge, 2004.

Florescano, Enrique. *Ensayos sobre el desarrollo económico de México y América Latina, 1500–1976.* Mexico, 1979.

———. *Precios del maíz y crisis agrícola en México (1708–1810).* Mexico, 1969.

Frank, Andre Gunder. *Capitalism and Underdevelopment in Latin America.* New York, 1967.

———. *Latin America: Underdevelopment or Revolution.* New York, 1969.

———. *Lumpenbourgeoisie, Lumpendevelopment: Dependence, Class, and Politics in Latin America.* New York, 1972.

Fuentes, Carlos. *La muerte de Artemio Cruz.* Mexico, 1962.

———. *La región más transparente.* Mexico, 1958.

Gamboa, Federico. *Santa.* Mexico, 1992.
Gilbert, Dennis. *Mexico's Middle Class in the Neoliberal Era.* Tucson, AZ, 2007.
Gilly, Adolfo. *El Cardenismo: Una utopía mexicana.* Mexico, 1994.
González Pineda, Francisco. *El mexicano: Psicología de su destructividad.* Mexico, 1965.
———. *El mexicano. Su dinámica psicosocial.* Mexico, 1961.
González Roa, Fernando, and José Covarrubias. *El problema rural de México.* Mexico, 1917.
Guerra, Francois Xavier. *México: Del antiguo régimen a la Revolución.* 2 vols. Mexico, 1988.
Guillén, Arturo. *Problemas de la economía mexicana; tendencias y problemas.* Mexico, 1986.
Guillén Romo, Héctor. *La contrarrevolución neoliberal.* Mexico, 1997.
———. *El sexenio de crecimiento cero: Contra los defensores de las finanzas.* Mexico, 1990.
Guzmán, Martin Luis. *El águila y la serpiente.* Mexico, 1941.
Haber, Stephen H. *Crony Capitalism and Economic Growth in Latin America.* Stanford, CA, 2002.
———, ed. *How Latin America Fell Behind: Essays on the Economic Histories of Brazil and Mexico, 1800–1914.* Stanford, CA, 1997.
———. *Industry and Underdevelopment: The Industrialization of Mexico, 1890–1940.* Stanford, CA, 1989.
Haber, Stephen H., Armando Razo, and Noel Maurer. *The Politics of Property Rights: Political Stability, Credible Commitments, and Economic Growth in Mexico, 1876–1929.* New York, 2003.
Hamnett, Brian. *Juárez.* New York, 1994.
Harrison, Paul. *Inside the Third World: The Anatomy of Poverty.* Brighton, England, 1980.
Hart, John Mason. *Empire and Revolution: The Americans in Mexico since the Civil War.* Berkeley, CA, 2002.
Hart, Paul. *Bitter Harvest: The Social Transformation of Morelos, Mexico, and the Origins of the Zapatista Revolution, 1840–1910.* Albuquerque, NM, 2005.
Hellman, Judith Adler. *Mexico in Crisis.* New York, 1985.
Hernández Chávez, Alicia. *México: Breve historia contemporánea.* Mexico, 2000.
Hernández Medina, Alberto, and Luis Narro Rodríguez. *Como somos los mexicanos.* Mexico, 1987.
Hirschman, Albert O. *A Bias for Hope.* Boulder, CO, and London, 1985.
Hobsbawm, E.J. *The Age of Capital, 1848–1875.* New York, 1975.
Humboldt, Alejandro de. *Ensayo político sobre el Reino de la Nueva España.* Mexico, 1966.

Ibargüengoitia, Jorge. *Los relámpagos de agosto.* Madrid, 2002.
Jenkins, Arthur Hugh. *Adam Smith Today: An Inquiry into the Nature and Causes of the Wealth of Nations.* Port Washington, NY, 1948.
Jiménez Rueda, Julio. *Antología de la prosa en México.* Mexico, 1946.
———. *Historia de la literatura mexicana.* Mexico, 1960.
Knight, Alan. *Mexico: The Colonial Era.* Cambridge, 2002.
Krauze, Enrique. *Mexico: Biography of Power.* New York, 1997.
Landes, David. *The Wealth and Poverty of Nations: Why Some Are So Rich and Some So Poor.* New York, 1998.
León-Portilla, Miguel. *The Broken Spears: The Aztec Account of the Conquest of Mexico.* Boston, 1990.
Limantour, José Ives. *Apuntes sobre mi vida pública.* Mexico, 1965.
López Cámara, Francisco. *La estructura económica y social de México en la época de la Reforma.* Mexico, 1967.
López Gallo, Manuel. *Economía política en la historia de México.* Mexico, 1965.
López Obrador, Andrés Manuel. *Un proyecto alternativo de nación.* Mexico, 2004.
López Portillo, José. *Mis tiempos: Biografía y testimonio político.* 2 vols. Mexico, 1988.
López Sánchez, Fernando, ed. *Vida y pensamiento de Narcisco Bassols.* Mexico, 1986.
López y Fuentes, Gregorio. *Campamento.* Mexico, 1938.
———. *El Indio.* Mexico, 1937.
———. *Tierra.* Boston, 1949.
Molina Enríquez, Andrés. *Los grandes problemas nacionales.* Mexico, 1909.
Mora, José María Luis. *México y sus revoluciones.* 3 vols. Mexico, 1950.
Nash, Manning, ed. "Essays on Economic Development and Cultural Change in Honor of Bert F. Hoselitz." *Economic Development and Cultural Change* 25, supplement (Chicago, 1977).
Ochoa, Enrique. *Feeding Mexico: The Political Uses of Food since 1910.* Wilmington, DE, 2000.
Otero, Mariano. *Obras.* 2 vols. Mexico, 1967.
———. *La política hacendaría de la Revolución.* Mexico, 1926.
Pani, Alberto J. *Apuntes autobiográficos.* 2 vols. Mexico, 1950.
———. *Mi contribución al nuevo régimen.* Mexico, 1936.
———. *El problema supremo de México: Ensayo de crítica constructiva de la política financiera.* Mexico, 1955.
Paz, Octavio. *Labyrinth of Solitude.* New York, 1985.
Paz Sánchez, Fernando. *Vida y pensamiento de Narciso Bassols.* Mexico, 1986.
Pomeranz, Kenneth. *The Great Divergence: Europe, China, and the Making of the Modern World Economy.* Princeton, NJ, 2000.

Pozas A., Ricardo. *Juan Pérez Jolote*. Mexico, 1952.
Prieto, Guillermo. *Memorias de mis tiempos (1856–1875)*. Mexico, 1971.
Rafael, Ricardo. *Los socios de Elba Esther*. Mexico, 2007.
Ramírez, Santiago. *El mexicano: Psicología de sus motivaciones*. Mexico, 1961.
Ramos, Samuel. *Profile of Man and Culture in Mexico*. New York, 1962.
Rangel, Carlos. *Third World Ideology and Western Reality: Manufacturing Political Myths*. New Brunswick, NJ, 1986.
Reyes Heroles, Jesús. *El liberalismo mexicano*. 3 vols. Mexico, 1961.
Riding, Alan. *Distant Neighbors: A Portrait of the Mexican*. New York, 1984.
Rivero B., Oswaldo de. *The Myth of Development: Nonviable Economies of the 21st Century*. London, 2001.
Robinson, Joan. *Aspects of Development and Underdevelopment*. Cambridge, 1979.
Romero, J. Rubén. *Una vez fuí rico*. Mexico, 1937.
Rueda, Julio Jiménez. *Historia de la literatura mexicana*. Mexico, 1946.
Ruiz, Ramón Eduardo. *The Great Rebellion: Mexico, 1905–1924*. New York, 1980.
———. *On the Rim of Mexico: Encounters of the Rich and Poor*. Boulder, CO, 1998.
———. *The People of Sonora and Yankee Capitalists*. Tucson, AZ, 1988.
———. *Triumphs and Tragedy: A History of the Mexican People*. New York, 1992.
Schmidt, Samuel. *El deterioro del presidencialismo mexicano: Los años de Luis Echeverría*. Mexico, 1986.
Secretaría de Industria y Comercio, ed. *La economía mexicana en la época de Juárez*. Mexico, 1972.
Serna, Enrique. *El seductor de la patria: D. Antonio López de Santa Ana*. Mexico, 1999.
Sesto, Julio. *El México de Porfirio Díaz (hombres y cosas)*. Valencia, Spain, 1910.
Shorris, Earl. *The Life and Times of Mexico*. New York, 2004.
Showstack Sassoon, Anne. *Approaches to Gramsci*. London, 1982.
Sierra, Justo. *Juárez: Su obra y su tiempo*. Mexico, 1905–6.
———. *The Political Evolution of the Mexican People*. Austin, TX, 1969.
Silva Herzog, Jesús. *El pensamiento económico, social y político de México, 1810–1964*. Mexico, 1967.
Simon, Roger. *Gramsci's Political Thought: An Introduction*. London, 1991.
Sklair, Leslie. *The Transnational Capitalist Class*. Malden, MA, 2001.
Solis, Leopoldo. *La realidad mexicana: Retrovisión y perspectiva*. Mexico, 1979.
Stein, Stanley J., and Barbara H. Stein. *The Colonial Heritage of Latin America: Essays on Economic Dependence in Perspective*. New York, 1970.
Stockwell, Edward G., and Karen Laidlaw. *A Third World Development: Problems and Prospects*. Chicago, 1981.
Strahm, Rodolfo H., and Ursula Oswald Spring. *Por esto somos tan pobres*. Mexico, 1990.

Székely, Gabriel. *Manufacturing across Borders and Oceans: Japan, United States, and Mexico.* La Jolla, CA, 1991.

Taylor, William B. *Magistrates of the Sacred: Priests and Parishioners in Eighteenth-Century Mexico.* Stanford, CA, 1996.

Thorp, Rosemary. *Progress, Poverty, and Exclusion: An Economic History of Latin America in the 20th Century.* Washington, DC, 1998.

United Nations. Economic Commission for Latin America. *The Economic Development of Latin America in the Post-War Period.* New York, 1964.

Van Young, Eric. *The Other Rebellion: Popular Violence, Ideology, and the Mexican Struggle for Independence, 1810–1821.* Stanford, CA, 2001.

Véliz, Claudio. *Obstacles to Change in Latin America.* New York, 1965.

Vernon, Raymond. *The Dilemma of Mexico's Development: The Role of the Private and Public Sectors.* Cambridge, MA, 1965.

Vicens Vives, Jaime. *An Economic History of Spain.* Princeton, NJ, 1969.

Villarreal, René. *El desequilibrio externo en la industrialización de México (1929–1975), un enfoque estructuralista.* Mexico, 1976.

Wallerstein, Immanuel M. *The Capitalist World Economy.* New York, 1979.

———. *The Modern World System II: Mercantilism and the Consolidation of the European World Economy, 1600–1750.* New York, 1980.

Williams, Eric. *Capitalism and Slavery.* New York, 1944.

Wionzcek, Miguel S. *El nacionalismo mexicano y la inversión extranjera.* Mexico, 1967.

Wolf, Eric R. *Sons of the Shaking Earth: The People of Mexico and Guatemala—Their Land and Culture.* Chicago, 1959.

Zavala, Lorenzo de. *Obras: Viaje a los Estados Unidos de América.* Mexico, 1976.

Zepeda Patterson, Jorge, ed. *Los amos de México.* Mexico, 2007.

Zermeño, Sergio. *La desmodernidad Mexicana y las alternativas a la violencia y a la exclusión en nuestros días.* Mexico, 2005.

ARTICLES

French, William E. "The New Cultural History Comes to Old Mexico." *Hispanic American Historical Review* 79 (May 1999).

Garza Toledo, Enrique de la. "The Crisis of the Maquiladora Model in Mexico." *Work and Occupations* 34 (New York, 2007).

Gill, Richard. "The Great Maya Droughts." *Harper's,* June 2003.

González de la Rocha, Mercedes, and Barbara B. Gantt. "The Urban Family and Poverty in Latin America." *Latin American Perspectives* 22 (1995).

Harner, Michael. "The Ecological Basis for Aztec Sacrifice." *American Ethnologist* 4 (February 1977).

Izquierdo, Rafael. "Protectionism in Mexico." In *Public Policy and Private Enterprise in Mexico,* ed. Raymond Vernon. Cambridge, 1964.

Lambert, L. Don. "The Role of Climate in the Economic Development of Nations." *Land Economics* 47 (1948).

McDonald, James H. "NAFTA and the Milking of Dairy Farmers in Central Mexico." *Culture and Agriculture* 51–52 (1995).

Salvucci, Richard J. "The Origins and Progress of U.S. Mexican Trade, 1825–1984: Hoc opus hic labor est." *Hispanic American Historical Review* 1973 (December 1991).

Stern, Steve J. "Feudalism and the World System in the Perspective of Latin America and the Caribbean." *American Historical Review* 93 (October 1988).

Webster, David. "The Fall of the Ancient Maya." *Harper's Magazine,* June 6, 2003.

Index

Text:	10/14 Palatino
Display:	Univers Condensed Light 47 and Bauer Bodoni
Indexer:	Marcia Carlson
Compositor:	Toppan Best-set Premedia Limited
Printer and Binder:	Maple-Vail Book Manufacturing Group